Contemporary Iran

CONTEMPORARY IRAN
Donald N. Wilber

Doug Marshall
2-24-64
Tehran, Iran —

FREDERICK A. PRAEGER
Publisher · New York

Published in the United States of America in 1963 by
Frederick A. Praeger, Inc., Publisher
64 University Place, New York 3, N.Y.

© 1963 by Frederick A. Praeger, Inc.

Library of Congress Catalog Card Number: 63-8836

Printed in the United States of America

Preface

Long independent, Iran has maintained its identity throughout periods of military strength and economic prosperity as well as in times of internal insecurity and instability. As recently as the opening months of 1921, the country was on the verge of chaos and foreign exploitation, but a timely revival of authority saved the nation. A proud heritage, respected traditions, religious conformity, and the cement of a graduated society, all served to foster continuity and preserve the country's integrity. Although subject to external pressures, semimodern Iran was never colonized by any power: The counterforces of competing interests, first Great Britain and Russia and then the United States and the Soviet Union, served to inhibit such domination.

Contemporary Iran is relatively stable. It is not more stable than it is because there is no public consensus of recognition of the enlightened goals of authority, and hence no widespread popular enthusiasm for the regime, and because of the disinclination of the Iranians to join in constructive efforts. And it is not less stable than it is because of the inability of the Iranians to unite in opposition to situations that seem to be inimical to personal or group interests. The key to the understanding of most aspects of the national scene continues to be a recognition of the marked individuality of the Persian character—as expressed in their overriding concern for the welfare of families, relatives, and friends —and of the lack of focus upon community interests.

Public consensus within Iran is a vital necessity for the orderly development of more stable and more effective political, economic, and social institutions. This work does not attempt to indicate how such a consensus may be achieved, but it does describe the social tensions that require resolution. Any consensus must be rooted in respect for, and confidence in, leadership and authority, and for this reason the themes of the continuity of the monarchy and the role of the ruler of Iran are woven throughout much of the text. The possible choices open to the Shah—whether to be a firm ruler, an advocate of progress who entrusts his program to strong prime ministers, or whether to be a symbolic figure who

v

reigns and does not rule—are presented, as are accounts of his experiments with these various roles.

In any presentation of a contemporary setting, events may overtake or nullify apparent trends. However, one current development—the distribution of the agricultural lands—forecasts a drastic transformation of traditional Iranian society. At present, the kind of new social relationships that will emerge as a result of this program cannot be defined, but it seems certain that the monarch has chosen to cast off the throne's ties to, and dependence upon, the traditional elite. In other words, the Shah of Iran has initiated a social revolution. While acting from a personal conviction, he may also intend to steal the thunder of the opposition elements by proving to be more liberal and more farsighted than these opponents of the Left and of the Right.

On the international scene, Iran is of major interest as a country allied to the West that has survived a series of Russian attempts to weaken and to dominate it. Its existing ties with the West are primarily the creation of the Shah himself, although the U.S.S.R. continues to attempt to sway the regime toward a neutral position. In this effort, the Soviet Union tries to arouse Iranian interest in a neutral policy by stressing the manner in which such neighbors of Iran as Afghanistan and India manage to enjoy the favors of both great power blocs.

DONALD N. WILBER

Tehran
November, 1962

Contents

Contemporary Iran

I.

The Land, the People,
and the Natural Resources

Iran comprises the western part of the Iranian plateau, a vast upland region bounded on the west by precipitous ranges and on the east by mountains and hills bordering the Indus Valley. During earlier periods, Iran frequently stretched toward India, taking in the territory of Afghanistan; less often, it extended to the west of its present frontier. Access to the plateau has always been difficult from every side except the east. To the north, the low-lying Caspian Sea littoral is cut off from the plateau by towering ranges; to the west, the plains of Mesopotamia end at the base of a high mountain system, and on the south, the littoral of the Persian Gulf is backed by bleak and rugged ranges. Only to the east, in the areas of Khurasan and Seistan, are there no formidable natural barriers.

The military invasions of Iran came usually from the east. This was due in part to the ease of access from that direction as compared to the presence of an imposing natural barrier on the west of the plateau; primarily, however, it can be accounted for by the constant influx of nomadic and tribal peoples from Central Asia, a movement that did not die out until the nineteenth century. Trade routes coincided with the paths of the moving nomads and of invading armies, and commercial traffic with Europe, India, and China flourished until the opening of the Suez Canal provided an easier, safer route. However, the strategic importance of Iran's location remained into modern times: it lay across the land route to India and separated Russia from the warm waters of the Persian Gulf.

The present frontiers of Iran are of fairly recent origin. Those

3

with Turkey and Iraq on the west are basically those agreed upon by Safavid and Ottoman rulers in 1639 and reaffirmed after World War I. Those with the U.S.S.R. to the north were defined in treaties between 1828 and 1881; to the east, the boundary with Afghanistan was determined in 1872 and 1891, and with Baluchistan, now part of Pakistan, in 1872. In 1867 the Bahrein Islands came under British protection because of Iran's inability to defend them. Some Iranians continue to cling to irredential goals regarding the Bahrein Islands and regions to the east and west of the Caspian Sea lost to superior Russian force.

The boundaries were so drawn that other ethnic elements whose habitats overlap these frontiers live around a central core of the Iranian Persian-speaking population. Thus, in the southwest, an area of Arab population merges with that of Iraq, and in the northwest there are Kurds, as well as in Iraq and Turkey. The inhabitants of the province of Azerbaijan are related to the people of Soviet Azerbaijan; and to the east of the Caspian Sea there are Turkomans on either side of the frontier between Iran and the U.S.S.R. Finally, in the southeast, Baluchis are found in Iran and in Pakistan. Some of these elements are naturally turbulent; in the past, they have resisted Iranian authority and in more recent years two of them have been incited by a foreign power to revolt against Iran.

Iran covers an area of 628,000 square miles and has some 20 million inhabitants. Its population density of about thirty-two persons to a square mile may be compared with that of Texas, which has thirty-six people to the square mile. Its size is roughly equivalent to the combined areas of Texas, New Mexico, Arizona, and California, states whose topography and climate are somewhat similar to Iran's. Its southern limits are on the same latitude as the southern boundary of Texas, and its northern frontier on the latitude of San Francisco, with Tehran on the latitude of Santa Fe.

The topography of Iran features a series of massive ranges and of salt deserts which extend across most of central and south-central Iran. Beginning close to Tehran and stretching for nearly 800 miles, these deserts cover one-sixth of the land area of the country. Stress is placed upon this aspect of the country's topography, since a casual glance at a map of Iran reveals areas that appear to have few towns and villages and therefore would seem to offer regions for future development and growth.

The great ranges of Iran form a huge V whose apex is in the extreme northwest of the country. One arm of the V is represented by the Elburz Range which strikes to the east, with 18,600-foot Demavend as its highest peak, and separates the plateau from the Caspian Sea. The other arm comprises the Zagros Range which parallels the frontier with Iraq and then turns east to run inland from the Persian Gulf. Both major ranges cast off minor spurs, and the entire complex creates a very broken topography over much of the country. The configuration of the major and minor ranges resulted in the formation of countless long, narrow valleys of flat profile with rims merging directly into abrupt slopes. Streams flow down these valleys and trails or roads parallel them; small villages are strewn along the higher ground above the streams.

With a stream to each valley, the streams are countless, but most are perennial rather than annual, rising in the spring and disappearing by midsummer. However, there are a number of rapid-flowing rivers that provide great opportunity for the exploitation of hydroelectric power. What is strange about the rivers is that most of them fail to find a natural outlet into a large body of water. Several rivers flow into the Caspian Sea and others empty into the Persian Gulf, but most turn toward the salt deserts and dissipate their flood tides into the scorching wastes. Dropping down from the high ranges, none are navigable, with the exception of the Karun in its passage through the plains of Khuzistan to the Persian Gulf.

Iran lies within the temperate zone and enjoys a modified continental climate with cold winters, hot summers, and fairly well-defined changes of seasons. Prevailing winds are northeasterly, but since they originate in the dry heat of Asia they bring no moisture to the plateau. Atmospheric depressions moving eastward from the Mediterranean Sea bring precipitation from November until early April. The desert regions receive less than five inches of rain a year, while the average fall is about twelve inches. Rainfall is somewhat heavier in the northwestern province of Azerbaijan and in the northeastern province of Khurasan; dry farming is practicable in these areas which are the major granaries of the country. Along the littoral of the Caspian Sea an annual rainfall of forty to sixty inches creates a tropical climate, reflected by spreading marshes and dense jungle.

Over a large part of the country the annual precipitation is in the form of snow falling on the high mountains, with many peaks covered with snow until midsummer. In spring, the melting snows feed trickling rivulets, dashing streams, and rushing rivers, with much of this run-off sinking directly into the soil at the abrupt bases of the ranges.

As much as two-thirds of the cultivated land of the country must be irrigated. Hand-dug channels and canals lead off from springs and streams to the fields and on larger rivers upstream from barrages, while extensive use is made of a unique system of irrigation known as the *kariz* or *qanat*. On the rim of a valley, in line with a village located at a lower elevation, a so-called mother well is dug until it penetrates to below the surface of the permanent water table. From that point a horizontal, slightly inclined tunnel is dug toward the village, with shafts put down at frequent intervals to provide air for the diggers and as a means of bringing the excavated material to the surface. Finally the tunnel emerges on the surface just above the village, providing a steady flow of water the year round. *Qanat* lines vary in length from several hundred yards to many miles, and their construction and upkeep is highly costly and a very specialized task. Large villages may be served by several *qanats*. A major agricultural problem in Iran arises from the fact that water rights and land ownership are often in different hands.

The present population of Iran may be greater than at any time in the past. However, the visible traces of a great network of ancient irrigation canals in the southwestern province of Khuzistan, together with historical records of its prosperity, indicate that it was once densely populated. Other areas are known to have been more populous than at present, while once-great cities such as Nishapur and Ray are now small towns, and even Isfahan is much smaller than in the seventeenth century. It is possible that from the Sasanian period until the Mongol invasions of the thirteenth century the area within the modern boundaries of Iran had a population comparable to that of the present day. By the nineteenth century, it had shrunk to an estimated 7 million people. The current rate of population growth is nearly 3 per cent annually, and public health and sanitation measures, including the eradication of malaria, have lowered the death rate sharply.

Current estimates suggest that some 70 per cent of the inhabitants are farmers living in 45,500 villages of fifteen houses or more, 20 per cent are urban dwellers in towns of more than 5,000 people, and the remaining 10 per cent are wandering and semisettled nomads. It is possible that this figure of 2 million nomads is too high.

Ninety-eight per cent of the people are Muslims, with 93 per cent of this number adherents of the Shi'a sect and the others Sunnis and Isma'ilis. Other religious communities are represented by some 75,000 Armenians, at least 50,000 Baha'is, 30,000 Nestorian Christians in northwestern Iran, and smaller colonies of Jews and Parsis (Zoroastrians).

The over-all rate of literacy is about 15 per cent. It is much higher in the towns, with 50 per cent literate at Tehran and over 30 per cent at Isfahan. Since Iran is a nation of young people, and the public school system is rapidly expanding, the rate of literacy will rise sharply in the next few years.

The inhabitants of Iran, settled and nomadic, include a number of ethnic and linguistic groups. None of these groups are ethnically pure strains and most Iranians resemble each other; they are brunets, with dark brown or black hair, dark brown eyes, and skin color ranging from fair to tawny. They are of medium height and build, averaging about five feet, five inches tall.

The majority of the people are of Iranian (Aryan) stock, much diluted by many centuries of intermarriage with other groups, and they speak Persian. Persian is taught in all the elementary schools and is the language of administration and business; therefore, it is spoken by almost three-quarters of the people of the country. There are many local dialects of Persian, some common to towns and other regions, such as Gilaki, which is spoken in the province of Gilan on the Caspian littoral. In addition, the languages of the tribal Kurds, Lurs, and Baluchis are related to Old or Middle Persian.

In the northwestern province of Azerbaijan and in a triangular area that juts southeast toward Tehran are some 2 million Azeris, so called because they speak a form of Turkish known as Azeri. Settled in this region for many centuries after their arrival from Central Asia, they have little racial affinity with the inhabitants of modern Turkey. Indeed, some of them are of Iranian stock and acquired Azeri through prolonged contact with that language. In the southwest of the country are some 2 million Arabs, speaking Arabic, who descend from people who came into that region in the early Islamic centuries. Still other ethnic groups are to be found among the nomads.

Farming villages are situated wherever soil suitable for cultivation and water for irrigation are available. The houses are closely clustered together, rather than set separately in the fields, and for many centuries were surrounded by high mud brick walls for protection against marauders. In some cases, in earlier times, all the villagers lived within a single massive fortress. The vital water supply, coming from a *qanat* line or a stream, flows along the narrow lanes of the village and then fans out in channels which cover the area of the cultivated fields. The houses are of mud brick, with a single doorway in a high wall facing the lane giving access to an open court. Nearly every courtyard has its pool of water, and the house may be built along a single side of the court or may occupy three sides of the area. The main rooms always face south in order to take maximum advantage of the warming winter sun, since cold is one of the greatest enemies of the villager. The better houses have a room set aside for the reception of guests, which is furnished with rugs, oil lamps, and colored prints on the walls. Chairs are not used; at meal times the men of the family sit or squat around a cloth placed on the floor and eat from bowls and dishes, usually with their fingers. Domestic animals and chickens live in the courtyard; bread is baked there in a brick oven; and in one corner is a privy. These villages are without electric lights, and drinking water comes from wells or nearby springs.

Every village of any size has a public bath, a series of underground rooms with hot and cold pools of water, in charge of an attendant who is supported by the landowner or by contributions of grain and food from the villagers. If water is at all abundant the village will have a mill; a water wheel turns one millstone on another and grinds the local wheat and barley.

The farmer is out in the fields at dawn, ploughing with oxen, cows, and even donkeys and camels. The iron-shod wooden plough does not penetrate deeply into the hard ground, and so he and his neighbors must break up the lumps of earth and then level off each plot in preparation for seeding and irrigation. During the growing season, water is let into each plot every few days until it stands an inch or so deep. Since it is necessary to have narrow earth embankments around the plots with channels and runlets related to the slope of the ground to bring in water, the contour of the land is unsuitable for the use of reaping and threshing machinery and tractors. Only in the areas where dry farming is possible, or in regions such as Khuzistan where wide plains exist, is the use of machinery practicable.

Wheat and barley, the staple crops, ripen in the early summer and are cut by hand sickles. The bundled grain is carried by donkeys to the threshing floor, a hard-packed area on the outskirts of the village. There oxen draw a wooden sled, weighted down with stones, around and around over the piled-up stalks of grain. Finally, it is winnowed by being tossed into the wind by pitchfork so that the chaff is carried away. Other important crops include rice, grown in limited areas where water is very abundant, and cotton, sugar beets, legumes, tobacco, vegetables, grapes; and, along the Caspian littoral, tea. Date palms thrive along the Persian Gulf and citrus fruits in the south and along the Caspian.

The area that can be cultivated by a single farmer is described in terms of a *juft*, or pair, of oxen. The size of the area relates to the fertility of the soil, since it should produce about ten *kharvar*, equivalent to 6,000 pounds, of cereals. Whatever the crop, the tenant farmer shares it with his landlord. The traditional division of the harvest is related to the five items essential to production: land, water, seed, draft animals and equipment, and human labor. Nearly always, the landlord supplies water in addition to the land itself and hence receives two-fifths of the harvest. In cases where the tenant can provide only his own toil, he must feed his family on one-fifth of the crop he has raised.

The marginal subsistence level of the farmer is somewhat eased by his access to other sources of food and income. He may have his own fruit and nut trees, his children may graze a few sheep beyond the cultivated fields, and he may collect the saps and resins of wild plants and shrubs for sale, while his wife and daughters weave cloth and make rugs. When his own supplies fail, the landlord will advance him cereals and seed grain against the next harvest.

The staple foods of the villagers are bread, baked in large round sheets; rice, in areas where it is easily available; and cheese and yoghurt, which is called *mast*. Tea is the favorite drink; and the diet is rounded out with eggs, vegetables, melons, and fruit in season. Less frequently, chicken and mutton are eaten with rice.

The farmer wears a blue cotton shirt, baggy cotton trousers, and a long blue cotton coat, and his wife has black trousers, a colored shirt, and probably a vest of heavier material. Much of the cloth for these costumes is homespun; but more and more comes from the nearest shop.

Shops are found only in the large villages, and their stocks are limited to such basic necessities as piece goods, sugar, salt, tobacco, rice, needles, thread, matches, kerosene, nails, dyes, and lamp chimneys. Primary schools, too, are to be found only in the larger villages.

Life is uneventful and monotonous in the villages, except for the occasional excitement of a local wedding or a religious festival. Most of the villages are inaccessible to motor traffic, and glimpses of the outer world come only in the infrequent trips to the nearest town, where donkey loads of straw, wood, or fruit are sold and the funds spent in shopping in the bazaars. Order is maintained in the villages by gendarmes who patrol from post to post and are not above abusing or extorting from the defenseless villagers. The gendarmes and the tax collectors have long been the only signs of the central government at Tehran, and the activities of these individuals have not been of a welcome nature.

The long winter months are a time of almost complete inactivity. Since no work can be done in the fields, the men gather to talk, sitting along a wall exposed to the sun. The houses are cold and cheerless, and at sundown the occupants resort to the *kursi*—a large quilt supported on a circular frame, over a brazier of charcoal which radiates out to cover the sleepers, with only their heads exposed.

The major tribal groups include the Kurds, Bakhtiari, Qash-qa'i, Mamasani, and Kuh Galui, ranging from north to south in that order. Estimates of the sizes of these groups are very un-reliable, particularly in the case of the Kurds, many of whom now live in villages. There may be 200,000 Lurs, 300,000 Bakh-tiari, less than 300,000 Qashqa'i, and a few thousand each of the Mamasani and Kuh Galui. The Qashqa'i speak Turkish, while the mixed Khamseh confederation, found south and east of Shi-raz, contains Turkish- and Arabic-speaking elements.

In the extreme southeast are some 300,000 Baluchis, certainly the most poverty-stricken inhabitants of Iran. In Khurasan, close to the Soviet frontier, are Kurds who were moved there a cen-tury ago to protect the area from external pressures, and ad-jacent to the Caspian Sea are numbers of Turkomans.

The Iranian tribal way of life may be described as vertical no-madism, based upon the requirements of their flocks. The Bakh-tiari and Qashqa'i tribes have followed this same pattern of life for many centuries. In the winter the Qashqa'i are in their *garm-sir*, or warm region, inland from the Persian Gulf, where their flocks graze and winter wheat is planted. In the spring they move up to the *sardsir*, or cold region, in the highest valleys of the Zagros Range, where grazing holds up through the summer, and in the fall they start back to the warm region. The Bakhtiari win-ter in the plains to the west of the lower Zagros and in the autumn move back again to its higher ranges.

These seasonal movements may cover as much as 200 miles and take place over a number of weeks. The routes are always the same, but careful organization and planning is required to keep large numbers moving at the same steady rate. Men and boys drive the flocks of sheep and goats, and the women and children follow behind, riding on donkeys and camels piled high with all their family property. Each evening the black, goats-hair tents are pitched along the trail.

At the seasonal encampments the tents of families of the same clan are grouped together and shelter all the tribal possessions. Carpets woven by the women or felt mats cover the ground, and along the sides of the tent are piled blankets, copper utensils, water jugs, bags of grain, and chests of clothing. Tribal life is almost self-sufficient; only tea, cotton piece goods, sugar, arms and ammunition, and jewelry come from the towns. The men look after the flocks and the horses—the tribesman is proudest of a fine horse and a good gun—while the women gather fuel and water for the cooking and weave rugs on demountable looms laid flat on the ground.

The flocks of sheep and goats nourish the nomads and provide cash income. They furnish milk, cheese, *mast*, and clarified butter for cooking, as well as meat, while the wool and the animals themselves are taken to the towns for sale.

Nomadism is an established feature in several lands of the present Middle East: vertical nomadism is common to Afghanistan, Iran, and northern Iraq, while in southern Iraq, eastern Syria, Jordan, and Arabia horizontal nomadism—the continuing search for pastures throughout the year in areas of similar topography —prevails. In earlier centuries, tribal groups were nomadic in search of suitable places to settle; the inexhaustible waves of nomadic peoples from Central Asia onto the Iranian plateau offer a characteristic example. Some of these tribes resisted settlement, while others found there was no place for them on cultivable lands, and they lacked the strength to drive out the occupants.

From choice or from necessity, the nomadic tribes were beyond the pale of settled society. At the same time, in Iran they were the hardiest individuals; also the best-armed and the most warlike elements of the country. During the seasonal migrations, they preyed upon the farming villages and found highway robbery a rewarding avocation. Until recent years, rulers of Iran placated the tribes in an effort to dissuade them from active revolt. Now, however, the situation has changed: the modern army with its heavy armor and planes can confine a dissident tribe within its summer or winter quarters, and its potential ability to overthrow the central government no longer exists.

The first question asked about the tribes of Iran is why they are not given an opportunity to settle on productive lands, and the immediate answer is that the tribes are reluctant to do so even were such lands available—and they are not. Reza Shah was determined to end the power of the tribes, and after 1930 made an effort to collect their arms and to move them into areas, some remote from their habitats, where housing had been provided. Before long these houses were deserted, and crumbled into ruins.

However, as more irrigated land becomes available the trend toward settlement by the nomads accelerates; and with adequate concern and initiative on the part of the central government, nomadism should become less and less common.

Considering the number of ethnic and linguistic groups, some settled in the farming villages and others leading a nomadic life, the population appears to lack homogeneity. However, none of these elements feel driven to attempt to detach themselves from Iran, and in the numerous growing towns such distinctions are replaced by an urban outlook which has no relationship with local origins.

Tehran was a sleepy village of some 15,000 people, situated on the southern flank of the Elburz Range, when Aqa Muhammad Khan, first ruler of the Qajar dynasty, chose it as his capital. By the end of the nineteenth century its population had climbed to 170,000, but it was not until the 1930's, when Reza Shah ordered the construction of broad avenues and numerous public buildings, that it began to grow rapidly. After World War II this growth accelerated as villagers streamed into the capital in search of employment, and as the agencies and offices of government and business multiplied. Today Tehran has some 1.7 million inhabitants.

Aqa Muhammad made a fortunate choice, for no other site in the country had such sources of water at hand to supply the inhabitants and to provide irrigation of an area large enough to grow food for so many people. The highly centralized government is located at Tehran, as well as the palaces of the shah, the buildings of the Majlis (i.e., the Iranian National Assembly) and the Senate, the offices of all the ministries, the foreign embassies, the University of Tehran, all the leading business firms, including the representatives of foreign concerns, the central offices of all the banks, and the finest shops and stores. It is the center for the most varied industrial development; and it serves as the place of assembly for the intellectual and social life of the country. Whatever is impressive, functional, and progressive in Iran exists at Tehran. Most of the 250,000 civil servants work at Tehran, and 90 per cent of the 100,000 taxis and private automobiles in the country crowd its streets.

The other important towns of Iran—towns rather than cities

because they still lack major amenities and the pulsating activity of a modern city—are growing much more slowly than the capital. These towns—Meshed, Resht, Tabriz, Kermanshah, Ahwaz, Isfahan, Shiraz, Qazvin, Kerman, Hamadan, Yezd, and Abadan—have populations ranging from 100,000 to 300,000 people, and, with the single exception of Abadan, have long been established at points where caravan routes intersected and water was moderately abundant.

In 1958, the total work force of the country was estimated at 1.37 million persons, of whom 68,000 were females. This force included all those gainfully and productively employed other than the farmers and nomads. Omitting the civil servants and the industrial laborers, the numerically important occupations included some 250,000 persons engaged in retail and wholesale selling, some 138,000 in service occupations, and some 45,000 men in road, rail, air, and water transport. About 200,000 people comprised the industrial labor force of the country. About 70,000 people, almost one-third of whom were females, were engaged in textile production, and some 70,000 in the oil industry—at the refinery at Abadan, in the oil fields, along the pipelines, and at the oil-loading ports.

The industrial enterprises have grown up at Tehran and in many of the larger towns. There are some 2,500 factories and mills in the country. They include spinning and weaving plants for the manufacture of cotton, wool, silk, and rayon textiles; cement plants; sugar factories; brick kilns; glass factories; ceramic plants; electric power plants using coal or oil; hydroelectric plants; ice manufacturing plants; chemical products plants; canneries; match factories; leather goods factories; cigarette factories; furniture factories; rubber goods and automobile tire plants; automobile assembly plants; machine shops; and automotive repair plants.

A recent development related to the industrial development of Iran has been the rise, since 1955, of an important number of local entrepreneurs. This group includes individuals who have raised funds by liquidating landholdings; repatriating deposits held in foreign banks; or who have taken out loans from the numerous, new private banks anxious to extend credit at reasonable rates. As a result, investments in the private sector of industry and processing have grown at a phenomenal rate.

The policy of the government is to encourage foreign investments in Iran, as reflected in a bill enacted by the Parliament in 1955 under the title "For Attracting and Protecting Foreign Capital." Since that time both American and other foreign investments in Iran have increased.

Figures representing the national income of Iran remain in the stage of estimates, but it is probable that the average per capita income is about $125, ranging from $740 in the towns to $70 in the agricultural villages. By Western standards the pay structure for civil servants, always below that of private industry, seems very low. For example, the lowest-paid instructor at the University of Tehran receives about $55 a month and the highest-paid professor about $235. Laborers make up to $2 a day.

In addition to the cultivable land itself, the natural resources of Iran include forests, hydroelectric sources, minerals, and oil. Less than 10 per cent of the land area is wooded and at least one-third of this total, or some 16 million acres, is represented by the humid jungles of the Caspian Sea littoral where deciduous trees and evergreens abound. The deforestation of Iran has been underway for centuries: erosion combined with scanty rainfall is one major cause and the other is the practice of burning timber for charcoal. Although measures to protect forest growth and to initiate reforestation are being taken, the forests are not a primary resource of the country.

In spite of the scanty rainfall that prevails over most of the country, Iran has very important water resources. In the spring the melting snows feed raging torrents; most of this run-off is soaked up in barren wastes, and by early summer the streams are dry and the rivers far below the level of their banks. The ruins of countless barrages and channels in the provinces of Fars and Khuzistan indicate that irrigation was highly developed in the Sasanian period and that these systems were well maintained through the earlier Islamic centuries. These systems were not designed to store water at levels well above the surrounding terrain, and by late summer the water level in the canals was below that of the fields; however, the climate of these regions was such that a second crop could have been grown had water been available. The *qanat* system was in use as early as the Achaemenid period, and throughout the country stone barriers thrown across narrow valleys retained some water for spot irrigation. Some dams, in contrast to barrages, were built in more recent times, notably in the Safavid period, and after 1930 several modern dams were constructed. However, it was not until 1950 that the concept of huge dams, combining hydroelectric works with irrigation facilities, caught the fancy of the officials of Iran. Several monumental structures have been constructed or are nearing completion, and others are in the planning stage.

The mineral resources of Iran are rather rich and varied, with increases in the present production of ores dependent upon the improvement of highways and the construction of access roads to the more remote deposits. Bituminous coal fields exist throughout the Elburz Range, and there are vast unexploited deposits of cokable coal near Kerman. Annual production has leveled out at some 90,000 tons.

Iron ores are found in the Elburz Range and at Shamsabad, near Arak. Most of the current annual output of some 14,000 tons is exported to Europe. The government, as a matter of national pride, is determined to create an iron and steel industry, for it feels that a modern country must have a steel mill. An Office of Steel has been authorized to negotiate loans and credits of $150 million for this purpose, repayment to come from oil revenues and the sale of government-owned factories. Discussions have been held with foreign builders of steel mills and the site for the industry located preliminarily on the Trans-Iranian Railroad near the ore deposits of Shamsabad.

Some 10,000 tons of iron oxide are exported annually from surface deposits on the island of Hormuz in the Persian Gulf. Varieties of chromite are scattered throughout the country, with annual exports amounting to some 45,000 tons. Lead ores abound, and about 25,000 tons move every year to the Soviet Union, the principal purchaser. Copper ore is mined at thirty places in the Elburz Range and in north-central Iran; the annual production of at least 20,000 tons is processed in a refinery south of Tehran. Annual exports of zinc and manganese ores average 20,000 tons each. Borates and sulphates of many minerals are exploited, as are ores of nickel, tin, cobalt, antimony, and arsenic. Marble, limestone, granite, and lime are available throughout the country. The manufacture of cement has increased tremendously; until 1954, rated daily output was 300 tons, while at present it is at least 2,700 tons.

According to Iranian law, building materials may be freely exploited by the private owners of the land on which they are found; deposits of coal and of the various ores and minerals may be exploited only after a permit has been obtained from the government; and petroleum, natural gas, and radioactive materials may be exploited only by the government.

Petroleum deposits represent the most important mineral resource of the country. Seepages of petroleum and of natural gas had been exploited in association with religious ceremonies in the Achaemenid and Sasanian periods in fire temples such as one whose ruins are still visible at Masjid-i-Sulaiman. In 1901, William D'Arcy, a British subject from Australia, secured from the Iranian Government exclusive rights for a period of sixty years to search for, develop, and sell petroleum, natural gas, and asphalt, and to construct oil pipelines to the Persian Gulf; only an arc across northern Iran was excluded from the concession area. In return, he made an initial payment in cash and shares amounting to £40,000 and Iran was to receive 16 per cent of the net profits of the company. Drilling began the following year, but it was not until 1908 that a very productive free-flowing well was brought in at Masjid-i-Sulaiman, some 125 miles to the north of the head of the Persian Gulf.

In 1909, D'Arcy's First Exploitation Company was absorbed by the new Anglo-Persian Oil Company which provided the capital for the construction of a pipeline from the new field to the site of a refinery on the island of Abadan in the Shatt al-Arab, and within three years both pipeline and refinery were in operation. The conversion of the British Navy from coal- to oil-burning ships and the approach of World War I resulted in action by the British Government to purchase 52 per cent of the voting shares and 55 per cent of the ordinary shares of the Anglo-Persian Oil Company, and to contract for the purchase of oil at privileged prices.

While the production of oil expanded rapidly after World

War I, the revenues received by Iran did not appear to rise in proportion, and frequently fluctuated sharply. Thus, in 1929 these royalties were £1,437,000; in 1930, £1,288,312; and in 1931 dropped to £306,872. Also, in 1931 Great Britain went off the gold standard and Iran's sterling balances in London were depreciated. As a result, on December 1, 1932, the government of Iran, acting on the personal orders of Reza Shah, canceled the D'Arcy concession. Protracted negotiations followed until in April, 1933, the Iranian Government concluded a new concession agreement with the Anglo-Persian [Iranian] Oil Company. Major features of the new agreement included a reduction of the concession area to 100,000 square miles from the earlier one of 400,000 square miles; a statement that the concession would run until 1993; surrender of the exclusive right to build pipelines to the Persian Gulf; and a requirement that royalties and revenues to Iran, based on both production and profits, total at least £750,000 annually. Through the 1930's, revenues to Iran rose to more than £3 million; in 1944, when Dr. Muhammad Mossadeq took his seat in the Majlis, to £4.5 million; and in 1950 to £16 million.

The network of highways in Iran follows the ancient caravan routes, although today Tehran, serving as the focal point for motor traffic, replaces Qazvin as the important center in the northern part of the country. Major caravan routes long traversed Iran from west to east. From the plains of Mesopotamia one route mounted over a series of passes, often blocked in winter by heavy snows, to reach the town of Qazvin, while another arrived at the same destination after crossing the highlands of Turkey and entering Azerbaijan by way of Tabriz. Beyond Qazvin the northern route skirted the southern flanks of the Elburz Range to Meshed and then continued on through Afghanistan to Central Asia, while another road swung south and east through Qum, Yezd, and Kerman in the direction of India. Another route started at Resht, the port for Russian shipping on the Caspian Sea, and climbed over the Elburz Range to connect with other roads at Qazvin. Other routes originating in the north of the country led south through Isfahan and Shiraz to the ports of Bushire and Bandar Abbas on the Persian Gulf. At intervals of a day's journey, some 20 miles by camel caravan, were caravanserais—rooms for travelers, and stables, grouped around an open courtyard. Many of these brick and stone structures still line the modern highways.

Near the end of the nineteenth century, the first surfaced roads for wheeled carriages were built on these alignments by British and Russian companies, which were authorized to charge highway tolls and provide transport and lodging. By 1914, a network of such roads extended to the Persian Gulf. Then, under Reza Shah, tremendous efforts were made to realign these routes and to establish roadbeds of heavy stones topped by gravel. New routes were opened up, notably the first direct road from Tehran to the head of the Persian Gulf, and many miles of secondary roads were built. None of these roads were asphalted until World War II, when British, Russian, and American service units paved the supply lines leading north from the Persian Gulf toward the Soviet Union.

There are some 10,000 miles of first-class highways in the country. At the present time, many miles of these roads are being reconstructed and asphalted; because of the scarcity of water along the way it is not considered feasible to lay concrete surfaces. In addition, there are some 15,000 miles of secondary roads, not all of which are graveled and, consequently, are very difficult of passage during the spring floods. Many new feeder roads are being built to areas of agricultural production in order to facilitate the collection and movement of cereal crops and of fruits.

The Trans-Iranian railway line was the personal project of Reza Shah, who pushed it to completion through some of the most difficult terrain in the world, and raised the total sum of more than $150 million required for its construction by means of local taxes on tea and sugar, without resorting to any foreign loans. Undertaken in 1927, by 1938 the line was complete from the head of the Persian Gulf to Tehran and from Tehran across the Elburz Range to a port on the southeastern corner of the Caspian Sea—a total distance of 865 miles. Even before the main line was finished, work was begun on other lines radiating from Tehran. Before 1960, Tehran was connected with Meshed on the east and with Tabriz on the west, while still another branch ran southeasterly as far as Kashan.

A present goal is to extend the line from Tabriz to the Turkish frontier where it will join an extension of the railway system of Turkey; this junction will provide direct rail connection from Europe to Tehran and the Persian Gulf. Plans have been made to extend the Tehran-Kashan line through Yezd and Kerman to the railhead of the Pakistan railways at Zahidan. All the Iranian lines are international standard gauge: a branch from Tabriz to the frontier between Iran and the U.S.S.R. at Julfa makes connection with the wider Soviet gauge, and freight and passengers to and from Russia must be off-loaded at that point.

Iran is one of the underdeveloped countries of the world—its ruler himself has stated that it belongs to this group. There appears to be no comprehensive definition of the term "underdeveloped country" which is both accepted and acceptable—accepted by the nations that extend aid and acceptable to the national prides of the recipients of such aid.

Iran may be considered as an underdeveloped country because of the low per capita income of its inhabitants but, fortunately, lacks the negative disabilities of many other underdeveloped countries and has positive advantages which most of them lack. Unlike Egypt, India, and Ceylon, it is not overpopulated, nor is its population growing so rapidly that agricultural production falls far behind demand. Indeed, its water and land resources could support a population between two and three times the size of the present one. Unlike neighboring Afghanistan, it does not lack a broadly based, rather highly developed industrial complex and adequate means of communication. Unlike Egypt, Afghanistan, and Ceylon, it is not dependent upon the export sales of a few raw materials for its economic survival.

On the positive side, also, Iran enjoys a very large income from its oil resources, and these revenues should increase with each passing year. Apart from material resources, it is blessed with a reasonable homogeneity of population and an absence of bitter rivalries among religious and ethnic groups. Finally, in contrast with other countries in its general region, it has no unresolved disputes of great magnitude with its immediate neighbors.

II.

Patterns from the Past

The Continuity of History

Iran is headed by a *shahanshah*, the "king of kings," and possibly no other country of the world has borne a single name as long as Iran, nor been ruled by as many monarchs bearing the same title.

To the inhabitant of Iran he is an Irani, although he might describe himself first as a Qashqa'i or an Azeri, or member of some other special group. This identification is not primarily to a flag, to a national anthem, or to a spirit of attachment to other members of a greater community. Indeed, most villagers may be very ignorant of the geography and peoples of Iran itself. It is an attachment to the glorious past of Iran reflecting the people's oral or written familiarity with their historians and poets.

This admired history relates to both legendary kings and the famed rulers of history, and is concerned with the Aryan period, beginning with the rise of the Achaemenid dynasty which established the first world empire. Prior to this time, the Aryan tribes were drifting down into the western and southwestern areas of the Iranian plateau and changing from a nomadic way of life to a settled one. The patriarchal organization of this society was already apparent in the ascending order from the family to the village or clan, to the tribe and, finally, to the country. Each level had its recognized chief.

Thus, in the inscriptions of the Achaemenid rulers there are references to their family (Vishtaspa), their clan (Achaemenid), their tribe (Parsa), and their nation (Aryan). From *Arya* derived *Iran* as an ethnic and geographical name. From *Parsa* came the Greek word *Persis*. The word also went into Arabic—lacking the letter *p*—as *fars*, to describe the southwest of the country, as *farsi* for the language; and into European languages as *Persia*.

As early as the second century B.C., princes bore the title of *shah* and in the Sasanian dynasty the local governors and kings were called *shah*, while the ruler himself was the *shahanshah*. The nation was *Iranshahr*.

The Achaemenid dynasty arose in 553 B.C., when Cyrus, a sub-king of the Parsa, defeated the ruler of the Medes and established a powerful confederation of Medes and Persians—the first enduring world empire. Cyrus led armies to the shores of the Mediterranean Sea, conquering all the intervening areas including great Babylon, and then moved as far east as the Oxus and Indus rivers to subdue Parthia, Chorasmia, and Bactria. His son, Cambyses, conquered Egypt and was succeeded by Darius, who campaigned on the Greek mainland until his defeat in the Battle of Marathon forced a withdrawal to Asia Minor. Darius' son Xerxes I embarked his forces in a great fleet against Greece, and Athens was burned, but losses in naval and land engagements ended all efforts to add the Greek mainland to the Achaemenid empire. Under Artaxerxes I, revolts broke out in distant areas of the empire, and it was not until the reign of Artaxerxes III, 359-338 B.C., that the earlier limits were briefly restored.

The Achaemenid empire consisted of some twenty provinces or satrapies, each headed by a satrap who came from a noble Median or Persian family. These posts tended to become hereditary; and the basic structure in which an absolute monarchy relied upon a royal council for advice, and was dependent upon the loyal services of semi-independent governors, endured for many centuries. The administrative structure was highly developed in the early years of the empire: excellent roads facilitated the passage of troops and the movement of mail; stable gold currency was in use throughout the satrapies; taxes were efficiently collected; and justice fairly administered. The practice of religions other than the monotheistic faith of the Aryan overlords was permitted. Tolerance of and clemency to subject peoples, together with the strength of the administrative structure, distinguished the Achaemenid empire from all earlier kingdoms and provided a well-remembered model for successive Iranian kingdoms. Historically speaking, it is unfortunate that most of our knowledge of the Achaemenid empire comes from the Greek historians who were anything but sympathetic to the "barbarians" of Asia. However, documentary material, now lost, was probably available in pre-Islamic Iran, while tradition and legend preserved an understanding and appreciation of the Achaemenid achievement.

Susa, Babylon, and Ecbatana (present-day Hamadan) were the administrative sites of the Achaemenid empire, while Persepolis was its religious center. Even in destruction, the great stone-built porticoes, audience halls, and palaces erected by Darius, Xerxes I, and Artaxerxes III at Persepolis remained for all later ages as a symbol, under the legendary name of the Throne of Jamshid, of the power and prosperity of the ancient Iranians.

Arising from the midst of the quarreling, mutually hostile Greek city-states, Alexander of Macedonia stabilized the situation on the mainland and then moved eastward in a deliberate search for the world's end. Making contact with the Achaemenid power, his army routed the armies of Darius III in major engagements at Issus and Arbela (Erbil today), and the way was clear for his entry into Babylon, Susa, and Persepolis. In 330 by accident or by design to avenge the burning of Athens by the Iranians, Persepolis was set ablaze. Pushing on as far as the Indus River, Alexander the Great established colonies of Greek settlers along his route, colonies which were to have an enduring influence upon the culture, language, and arts of these remote regions.

Exhausted from years of campaigning, Alexander returned with his armies to Susa and began to disclose his grand design for a universal state, which would give equal status to Macedonian and Iranian elements and establish a lasting union of the major areas of the ancient world. Suddenly, he was smitten with fever and soon died. The commanders of his armies quickly parceled out the vast areas among themselves: the Seleucid line included Iran in its share.

Seleucid authority was challenged by the growing strength of the Arcasids, a nomadic Saka tribe that had taken over the area of the satrapy of Parthia of the Achaemenid empire and hence became known to later historians as the Parthians. Three powerful rulers established and maintained the independence of the new kingdom between 248 and 190 B.C., and by the opening of the first century B.C., the ruler, Mithradates II, had extended his control from India to Armenia and called himself "King of Kings." Conscious heirs of the Achaemenids, the Parthians deserted Greek modes and Greek, the *lingua franca* of the region. They spoke so-called Middle Persian, written in the script called Pahlavi, and returned to faith in Mazdaism, the codification of the teachings of Zarathustra (Zoroaster). Some of the earlier atmosphere of tolerance remained, and Christianity spread throughout the Parthian-held lands. Parthian culture was highly eclectic, including the fields of art and architecture, and the architectural monuments linked the post-and-lintel construction of the Achaemenid times to the vaulted architecture of all later periods.

Long warfare with Rome along the eastern fringes of the Roman empire drained away Parthian military strength; and in the years immediately following A.D. 300, forces from Fars, led by Ardashir, revolted and took over most of the Parthian empire. The new rulers traced their lineage to the Achaemenids and had long survived as semi-independent lords of Fars. Ardashir, a grandson of Sasan, a high priest of Istakhr, near Persepolis, was succeeded by no less than twenty-nine rulers of this Sasanian dynasty. Mazdaism was the state religion, becoming more sterile as ritual was emphasized, and a privileged religious hierarchy dominated its practice. Many of the fire temples of this period have survived and display the basic structure of a square chamber crowned by a dome. Heretical sects, such as those headed by Mani and by Mazdak, gained many adherents before they were savagely suppressed. Christians were also persecuted because of their identification with the Roman Empire, although in the later years of the Sasanian dynasty the Nestorian Christians were treated with greater tolerance. The language of the Sasanian period continued to be Middle Persian written in the Pahlavi script, and numerous works of this period have survived, some only in Arabic translations.

As in distant Achaemenid times, a highly centralized administration controlled the region; each province was governed by a *shahrdar* who was a member of the Sasanian family, and a majestically remote king-of-kings wielded absolute power. Conflict with Rome was followed by wars with Byzantium, and Sasanian military strength was severely strained in the years when the prophet Muhammad was gaining control over Arabia.

Muhammad's followers, the Muslims, burst out of Arabia to destroy the Sasanian and the Byzantine armies. Their international religion was unconcerned with ethnic solidarity or geographical interests; rather, it had a democratic spirit of human equality, and therefore found fertile soil. An initial era in which Arab military commanders governed conquered territories gave place to the rise of local dynasties which acknowledged the temporal and spiritual authority of the 'Abbasid Caliphs at Baghdad. On the Iranian plateau such dynasties included the Saffarid, the Samanid—whose patronage of Persian literature re-awoke Iranian nationalism—the Ziyarid, and the Buvayid.

Then, after the middle of the tenth century, Turkish leaders, sprung from warrior-slaves, established the Ghaznavid empire. Mahmud, the seventh of the line and ruler from 999 until 1030, extended his power over most of the Iranian plateau, including present Afghanistan, and campaigned successfully in India. His court at Ghazni attracted poets, scientists, and historians who wrote in Persian; Firdausi was the brightest luminary of this large group.

In the eleventh century a group of Turkish nomads which had come from Central Asia across the Oxus River were allotted territory in Khurasan in northeastern Iran by Mahmud of Ghazni. More numerous and more powerful than similar groups which had been moving from Asia toward the Iranian plateau, they crushed the Ghaznavids. Their leader, Tughril Beg, established the capital of his Seljuq dynasty at Ray, immediately south of Tehran. The Seljuqs established far-reaching authority and fervently embraced Islam; the rulers placed Persians in the highest adminstrative posts and became patrons of art and culture. Patronage was extended to philosophers, mystics, and poets, and a universality of interests prevailed as typified by Omar Khayyám, philosopher, mathematician, astronomer, and poet. Nizam al-Mulk, an Iranian of genius, who was prime minister under two Seljuq rulers, erected a series of *nizamiyyas* (schools), introducing the concept of liberal education as opposed to religious teaching which pervaded the Muslim world. Ardent Sunnis, the Seljuq rulers persecuted the Shi'as, but met with strong resistance from the Isma'ilis, known to the West as the "assassins," from their practice of political murder as a weapon of defense and retaliation.

Other Turkish elements moving in from Central Asia struck at the fringes of the Seljuq empire, while within it the provincial governors, the *atabegs*, or father-lords, became increasingly defiant of the central authority. After the middle of the twelfth century, the Khwarazmshahs, a line which descended from a Seljuq courtier and took its name from Khwarazm, or Khiva, opposed the Seljuqs, replaced that dynasty, and in the opening years of the thirteenth century were in possession of the Iranian plateau.

Hordes of Mongol horsemen under Genghiz Khan were moving westward across the entire breadth of Asia, and in 1219 they attacked and destroyed the great Iranian cities of Bukhara, Samarqand, Balkh, Merv, and Nishapur. Successive waves of Mongols swept across the Iranian plateau, and in 1258 Hulagu, a grandson of Genghiz Khan, took Baghdad and wiped out the family of the 'Abbasid Caliph. Retiring to Maragheh in northwestern Iran, Hulagu took the title of *Il-Khan*, or khan of the tribe, and established the Il-Khanid dynasty of Iran as one of the units of the vast Mongol empire.

Grievous damage had been inflicted upon Iran by the Mongols: towns completely destroyed, irrigation systems wiped out, and countless hundreds of thousands of people slaughtered. Indeed, it is customary to say that the plateau has never recovered the prosperity it enjoyed before the Mongols came. However, Hulagu himself began to adapt to the surroundings, and Iranian culture and civilization had a strong impact upon the rude Mongols. The local administrative system was retained, Iranians were appointed to high posts, and the Mongols became Sunni Muslims; in a sense, they became "Iranianized" as had the Seljuqs before them. Architecture and culture were promoted and material prosperity enhanced in the opening years of the fourteenth century by Ghazan Khan and Oljaitu at the capitals of Tabriz and Sultaniya. Parallel in position and influence to the *vazir* Nizam al-Mulk under the Seljuqs, was Rashid ad-din, *vazir*, historian, and patron of learning. Most notable among the many literary figures of this period were the mystic Jamal ad-din Rumi and Sa'di, poet of Shiraz.

In time, the Il-Khanid dynasty reflected the pattern of earlier periods in being subject to internal conflicts and external pressures, which resulted in a diminution and disintegration of authority. Then, a new force arose in the region in the person of Timur, a member of the Berlas tribe of Turks. From Samarqand he led his forces westward, and before the end of the fourteenth century was master of the Iranian plateau and most of the area as far as the Mediterranean Sea. Timur was a Muslim and the ruler of a Turkish kingdom, but Iranian culture permeated his court at Samarqand and the courts of his sons and grandsons at Herat. Hafiz, another great poet of Shiraz, was active during the Timurid period as was Bihzad, the most renowned of all miniature painters.

The decay of the Timurid kingdom coincided with the rise of an Iranian line, the Safavid, whose members were descended from a Shi'a saint, Shaykh Safi ad-din, who lived in northwestern Iran during the Il-Khanid period. Soon at war with the Ottoman Turks, the Safavid rulers took the precaution of transferring the capital from exposed Tabriz to Qazvin, and later to Isfahan. A regular standing army was recruited to supplement the tribal forces of the Shahsevens, or Friends of the Shah, and inspired by devotion to Shi'ism successfully opposed the Sunni Turks. Shah 'Abbas, one of the greatest monarchs of Iran, made the shrine of Imam Reza at Meshed the goal of national pilgrimage, built roads throughout the country, and took other measures to enhance feelings of national identity. At Isfahan he ordered the construction of splendid mosques, palaces, bazaars, and garden pavilions, and the looms of the capital turned out magnificent carpets and rich brocades shot through with threads of silver and gold. For nearly a century after the death of Shah 'Abbas in 1629, his successors and the country itself benefited from his efforts, until an invasion of Afghan tribesmen brought the dynasty to a virtual end with the capture of Isfahan in 1722.

Once again a man arose in Iran to drive out foreign invaders. This was Nadir, an Afshar tribesman from northeastern Iran, who ascended the throne in 1736. Nadir Shah was a fabulously successful campaigner, penetrating India to take Delhi, conquering the Uzbek region, annexing the Bahrein Islands in the Persian Gulf and restoring the prestige and power of Iran in a wide area. Following his assassination in 1747, his empire fell apart; local tribes quarreled over the remains and the Qajars, a Turkish tribe of northern Iran, gained the ascendancy. Aqa Muhammad Khan, a eunuch, rose to power in 1779, although he was not crowned as first ruler of the Qajar dynasty until 1796. Under his successor, Fath 'Ali Shah, who ruled from 1797 until 1834, Iran entered into treaty and trade relations with the European powers and suffered disastrous defeats at the hands of the Russians. The reign of Muhammad Shah (1834-48) was followed by that of Nasir ad-din Shah, who was on the throne from 1848 until his assassination in 1896. Then, his son, Muzaffar ad-din, ruled until 1907. It is usual to denigrate the Qajar line, stressing their luxurious living and lack of application to their royal responsibilities. However, such a picture is overdrawn. They were not men of great talent, but, subject to continuous British and Russian pressures and demands for privileges, they did strive to maintain the independence of Iran. The inevitable results of centuries of fighting across the length and breadth of the land came to unhappy fruition in the nineteenth century and were apparent in a declining population, decreasing agricultural production, a breakdown of communications, increasing isolation of the provinces from Tehran together with growing resistance to central authority, and an empty treasury. The Qajars could not hope to arrest the total decline in the fortunes of Iran: they lacked financial resources, capable administrators, a loyal population, and moral and material support from nations capable of giving guidance and aid. Either Iran was to fall apart or to be revitalized by forces not then on the scene.

In summarizing the emergence and fall of only the major dynasties of Iran, no stress was placed upon the almost unbroken story of warfare and conflict, the constant interdynastic struggles, and the incredible savagery and cruelty to which the people were exposed. The fact that there was such continuity in the patterns of history is the more remarkable, and seems to stem from several factors. One would be the availability of areas in which traditional patterns were preserved regardless of prevailing conditions. Many towns, including Nishapur, Ray, Tabriz,

Qazvin, Isfahan, and Shiraz, were capitals of the country, serving as repositories of learning and tradition after the royal seat
moved elsewhere. In addition, many thousands of farming villages were so remote from the incidents of war that they offered
secure refuge to individuals capable of preserving or recording
history. Other factors included the strength of Islam and the persistence of Iranian culture. On several occasions, Turkish and
Mongol conquerors adopted Islam and were "Iranianized." Finally, there was the presence of a single enduring institution, the
shah of shahs.

On many occasions, the characteristics of the shah were clearly
defined. In all periods he was the defender and propagator of the
faith: in Islamic times he was the shadow of God upon the earth.
In his *Shah nama*, Firdausi stated that Allah's order is the shah's
order. Allah wanted man to obey His orders, those of the Prophet
and those of the shah, since there was no difference between
them. At the end of the eleventh century the renowned vizier
Nizam al-Mulk composed his *Siyasat nama* or *Book of Government*. On the subject of the ruler he wrote that "in all ages the
Great God chooses one from among mankind and bestows the
arts of ruling upon him. He makes him the guardian of the prosperity and peace of his people; he closes the door of corruption
and evil to him; and his might enables the people to live in his
justice." In A.D. 1082, a local ruler in the Caspian area compiled
the *Qabus nama* and described the qualities of the shah as including wisdom, avoidance of hasty action, devotion to truth
and honesty, and sternness with mercy.

In a word, the ideal shah possessed in unrivaled quantity the
most valued characteristics of this society. They were not the
qualities, however, of the ideal man, for the shah could exercise
qualities which were beyond the attainment of lesser individuals
in the society. For example, for a long, long time the individual
in Iran has desired, usually vainly, absolute justice. Expressing
this desire are the many tales extolling the just behaviors of the
shah; a Sasanian ruler was much honored as Anushirvan the Just,
and many folk stories accumulated around his name.

To the Iranians history is not a tale of the long-distant past
for the time scale is compressed. It so happened that the greatest
periods of Iranian history happened a long time ago, while re-

cent centuries have been ones of a steady decline in material prosperity and armed strength. While the Persians look back with pride to Nadir Shah and to Shah 'Abbas, their real admiration is reserved for the Sasanian and Achaemenid periods. These are regarded as the golden ages and are viewed, as it were, without the perspective of time so that they seem to have occurred just yesterday.

Families established a personal relationship to rulers by naming their sons after real or legendary kings of the ancient times. Many came from the *Shah nama,* which stressed the role of the king as hero. Naming a son after Jamshid, Anushirvan, or Firuz was assurance that he too would display manly qualities.

Local historians have long emphasized the role of the ruler in the life of the country: his battles, his deeds, a chronicle of his times. In fact, there has been almost no other kind of historical writing until modern times. Naturally, then, the emphasis has been upon the institution of the monarchy and it has been the single institution to endure over these long centuries. Even today, the ruler is regarded as *khodayi kuchek,* or the small God, in contrast to Allah the *khodayi bozorg,* or great God.

The shah was despotic and he was strong; without his strength the country could not be held together from internal and foreign threats. The kingship was entirely personal in character; the country and the people were the property of the shah. The feudal lords were loyal to the monarch who protected them, and the people were loyal in hope of receiving his bounty.

Reza Shah the Great was the last of the despotic rulers of Iran. Nowadays, circumstances are so different that no such ruler is likely to emerge in Iran. Yet, with all the current emphasis on constitutional government and the freedom of the individual, which will appear in later pages, there are not a few Iranians who feel that their country has always prospered best under a stern hand. This has been the role of the institution of the monarchy in Iran: if this role is outmoded then what of the institution?

The Continuity of Culture

The long cultural continuity of Iran found its most striking and persistent expression in the fields of religion, literary expression, and the arts. In each of these fields the Iranians displayed a great aptitude for the assimilation of ideas and forms, and for re-casting them in new ways, stamped with a special individuality. Local intellectual and intuitive expression played their roles: it was never a question of sterile copying.

All the major religions of the world had their origins in the regions to the east of the edges of the Mediterranean Sea, and Iran was the home of Zoroastrianism, of Mani, and of Mazdak, as well as of the Shi'a sect of Islam. In Iran no intellectual idea or concept is ever totally lost, and today the religious outlook of the fervent believer and even of the modern sceptic remains colored by century-old beliefs.

The prophet Zarathustra, probably contemporary with the rise of Achaemenid power, preached the eternal conflict between good and evil, with Ahura Mazda representing all that is good and Ahriman all that is evil. A parallel contrast, emphasized in the rock-cut inscriptions of the Achaemenid rulers, was the con-flict between truth and the lie. The emphasis in Zoroastrianism on the occupations of agriculture and cattle breeding and on the purity of the elements of air, water, fire, and the earth reflects conditions of life and environment on the Iranian plateau which were not to change in later centuries.

However, the conflict between good and evil continued: it was by no means certain that good had prevailed or would pre-vail, and, indeed, in later periods there was a belief that evil had gained the upper hand and that only a saviour could weight the balance in favor of eternal good.

As the continuity of history derives from the institution of the *shahanshah*, so the continuity of culture rests upon the insti-tution of Islam, which has pervaded all aspects of life and expres-sion in the community of the faithful.

The Sasanian empire had been overthrown by the Muslim armies by the middle of the seventh century and the inhabitants of the plateau embraced Islam, a new force to replace organiza-tions torn by corruption and decay. However, these plateau dwellers, called *ajami* by the Arabs, soon brought their own re-ligious traditions and culture to bear upon the form of this new theology, fostering the growth of Shi'ism in opposition to the orthodox Sunni sect.

'Ali, the son-in-law of Muhammad, had been chosen in 656 as the fourth caliph or "successor" of the prophet, but was assassinated. After his death the Shi'ites, or "partisans" of the family of 'Ali, chose his son Hasan to succeed him and then, later, another son, Husein. Husein and his faithful followers were put to death on the plain of Karbala in Iraq, and the caliphate passed to the 'Abbasid line. In identifying themselves with the Shi'ites, the Iranians claimed that Husein had married a daughter of the last ruler of the Sasanian line, and they developed such dogmas as Husein's sacrifice and atonement for the sins of mankind and the sinlessness of the family of 'Ali. The Shi'ites believed that the spiritual leadership of the community of Islam was embodied in a succession of twelve imams descending from 'Ali: each imam was considered to have divine infallibility; each could work miracles; and each could name his successor. In the ninth century the Twelfth Imam, known as the Hidden Imam, or the Master of the Age, disappeared in a cave while still a child. As the end of the world draws near, he will reappear as the Mahdi, the "guide" of the Qoran, and fill the world with equity and justice.

The official religion of Iran is the Jafarite doctrine of the Twelve Imams, so named after the sixth imam who codified the obligations and ritual of Qoranic law; an article of the constitution of the nation states that it is to operate in conformity with the principles of Islam until the appearance of the Master of the Age. Only the Master of the Age will be able to bring about the triumph of good over evil and of justice over inequity. Hence, the material world and all its creatures represent a transitory state and an attitude of anticipation.

Shi'ism was favored by such local dynasties in Iran as the Saffarids, Samanids, and Buvayids, but it was not until the Safavid period that Shah 'Ismail declared it to be the only acceptable creed and used the force of a national faith to rally the country against the Ottoman Turks, whose sultans were the caliphs of Sunnite Islam. Previous to that time the Shi'ite minority had been authorized to practice *taqiya*, the act of dissimulation and of caution in matters of religion. This authorization to deceive and not to tell the truth seemed to have come out of the area of faith and to have found a place among the patterns of accepted social behavior.

The authority of Islam pervaded all of life. A very loosely knit religious hierarchy was in touch with all the population: at the level of the masses through the mullahs and at the level of the court of the shahs through the *mujtahids* (a restricted group of canonists) and *ayatullahs* (the most respected religious figures). The *shar'ia*, or religious law, was the sole legal code. All education was conducted by the clergy, and placed heavy emphasis upon the Qoran and upon the Muslim way of life. Charity, a basic tenet of Islam, found its most formalized expression in the *vaqf*, or religious endowment: hospitals and schools were established and the income from donated land was assigned to the upkeep of such institutions and to other charitable purposes. As long as the system of the *vaqf* maintained its independence and vitality, men of wealth had a meritorious channel for good works.

Over the centuries many efforts were made to bring together the moral principles and duties of Muslims into an integrated system of *akhlaq*, or ethics, defined as practical philosophy. These works derived from the early *adab* books which dealt with moral instruction and the manifestations of noble aspects of human character in the conduct of life and social intercourse.

After the middle of the thirteenth century, Nasir ad-din Tusi, a philosopher, theologian, and scientist in the service of the Il-Khanid rulers who constructed an astronomical observatory for Hulagu, composed his *Akhlaq-i-Nasiri*, an academic treatise on ethics. In the fifteenth century several works on ethics appeared: the *Akhlaq-i-Muhsini* by Husein Va'iz Kashifi contained a catalogue of the moral and spiritual virtues, each illustrated by appropriate anecdotes. Comparable treatises abounded in later centuries, and the pattern of illustration by means of stories of ancient kings and heroes and of quotations from the renowned poets of the country was further developed.

In modern times the *Akhlaq-i-Muhtashimi*, by Hasan Esfandiari, was published at Tehran in 1935, and in 1937 the *Akhlaq-i-Ruhi*, written by 'Ataullah Ruhi, appeared. The latter work was prepared for the moral instruction of Iranian students and is of particular interest. Based on earlier models, with an abundance of illustrations from the noted poets and philosophers of Iran, it placed much emphasis upon themes not stressed in earlier centuries, such as patriotism, military service, and the role of women in society.

The important fact about the ancient and modern books of ethics is that they advocated standards of ethical and moral behavior which were too remote from the general patterns of social behavior in the society: ideals that were neither attained nor desired. The works published in the reign of Reza Shah suffered from an additional disability: newly recommended patterns of social behavior were illustrated by ancient examples which had no real applicability to the life of the period. Now, however, the problem of a suitable system of ethics for modern life is even more pressing and more embarrassing. It is obvious to student and adult alike that daily behavior is no longer influenced by the long-established system of moral instruction: the society has materialistic goals and should have a system of values related to the new age.

It is common knowledge that the established priority of Islam in the fields of law, education, and social customs was challenged in the nineteenth century by knowledge of ideas and institutions of the Western world; but it also suffered a direct challenge within Iran itself with the revelation of a new religion by the Bab in 1848, although his doctrine was later diluted and proliferated to become Baha'ism. This challenge, bitterly resented and opposed by orthodox Shi'ism, was a serious attack on the bases of the existing social-religious order.

Iran has an incredibly rich treasury of writing in the fields of philosophy, theology, science, poetry, and prose, and no present effort will be made to outline the course of its development and its many ramifications or to single out its principal practitioners.

Ibn Khaldun, an Arab and the fourteenth-century author of the remarkable *Muqaddimah*, or *Introduction to History*, pointed out that most Muslim scholars both in the religious and in the intellectual sciences had been non-Arabs, people of Fars. Whether they wrote in Arabic or in Persian, they engaged in the tasks of preserving knowledge and writing systematic scholarly works very largely based upon Greek sources.

Themes from Persian literature, especially those expressed and re-expressed by the beloved poets of the country, colored the thinking and attitudes of all classes: of the literate upper strata through reading and of the masses through memorization and recitation of these works.

Firdausi, in recording in 60,000 rhyming couplets the history of Iran from the creation of man to the end of the Sasanian empire, stressed the perennial glory of Iran and of its heroes, preserved its legendary and actual history in an easily memorized form, and preached loyalty to the throne and to Iran as opposed to the realm of Turan, inhabited by Turks. By indicating the pattern of renewal from age to age of the strength and glory of the nation, he held out the promise of renaissance to the people of later centuries when the country had fallen on bad times. It is through the *Shah nama* that even the illiterate peasant identifies himself with a national entity.

Just as there was a polarity of ethical behavior between the recommendations of the books of *akhlaq*, and the actual practice of morality—advocated by the poet Sa'adi in terms of expediency and common sense—so a polarity of Persian psychology exists in the works of many poets, both in the very familiar *ruba'yat*, or four-line verses, and in the longer poems.

On the one hand, there was ever present the mystical doctrine of Sufism. By imagery, allusion, and implication, often only vaguely understood by many, the poets provided a transcendental interpretation of the transitory phenomena of existence. According to this doctrine, mortal flesh suffers and the soul longs for union with the one reality, its creator, and for escape from this realm of conflict between good and evil to that of absolute good.

On the other hand, some poets moralized on the uncertainty of all human affairs and the futility of man's attempt to master circumstances. Rather than devoting attention to preparing for a better life to come, as the Sufis recommended, he should seek ways to enjoy his fleeting existence. The earlier Western scholars who saw, falsely, Islam pervaded by fatalism were joined by others who found fatalism in this poetry, but they failed to see that these works are permeated with concern for the fate of humanity.

Both these very different streams of thought could serve a common end. With Iran torn throughout the centuries by devastating warfare and by man's injustice to man, in such misfortune the Persian had the choice of denying the validity of the material world or of resigning himself to accepting the inevitable.

Because of the vast body of Persian literature and the existence of the Persian language for some 2,500 years, there have been countless studies made of the development of Persian, which since the advent of Islam, has been written in the Arabic alphabet and script, not well suited to the language. The Persian of Firdausi has vigor and clarity, and is so relatively free from foreign intrusions that it is easily understood today. In fact, the Persian of the year 1,000 is closer to the modern language than is Elizabethan English to that of our day. However, Arab words and constructions did flood into Persian, and many of the historians employed a turgid style with long and complicated sentence structure. By the Safavid period the age of the great poets and philosophers was ended, and the minor figures of this time and of later centuries substituted form for content. Ornate and elaborate language was used, and figures of speech were over-developed. These devices included homonyms, anagrams, palindromes, adornments, quadrilaterals, and suppression, while the rhetorical figures included hyperbole—most highly regarded—simile, ambiguity, antithesis, allusion, and enigma. Turkish words, notably military terms, invaded the language, to be followed at the end of the nineteenth century by borrowing words from Italian, French, and English for terms relating to modern means of transportation, institutions of government, and other areas in which no Persian words existed. Then, in 1935 Reza Shah himself inaugurated a campaign to purge the language of words of Arabic and other foreign origin. The new Iranian Academy was charged with the task. Older Persian words were brought back into circulation and old roots used for the construction of the terms needed in the modern world. The effort was successful, for the new words and terms took root in common speech and in writing, and even the style lost its complexity and elaborateness, so that today the written language has again its earlier clarity and precision.

Familiarity with the language makes one aware of some fascinating facets: its reliance upon polite figures of speech and honorifics; and its peculiar idioms, for example, the hundreds of expressions based on the word *sar*, or head. It is hard to escape the feeling that there must be a strong relationship between the psychology of the Iranians and their language, but this subject remains to be explored.

Although particles are not employed in Persian, and there is no distinction of gender, there is not too much ambiguity in ordinary conversation. However, in serious discussion and in writing on subjects on which the reactions of the individual to a social situation come to the fore, the language seems to be curiously inadequate, especially in containing the kinds of words that may be more used today than in earlier periods. Such English words as "frustration," "disappointment," "positive," "compromise," and "unequivocal" appear to have no precise equivalents in Persian, and it would be quite impossible to say "unfrustrated" or "maladjustment." In these cases, and many others, recourse must be had to rather unfamiliar Arabic words or to compound expressions made by combining a noun with a verb of action or by using "without" before a noun. Often the results have a negative connotation, which seems not inconsistent with the Persian's outlook on the world around him. For example, the word used for "compromise" suggests surrender or submission rather than give and take, while the term "without a side" expresses neutrality.

Throughout its long history, Iranian art has been decorative, usually based upon geometric or floral patterns, and normally nonrepresentational. A vocabulary of symbols and patterns came into being on the prehistoric pottery of the plateau, and many of these same forms carried over into much later periods. The capacity of the Iranian artists and craftsmen for assimilation and re-expression of foreign forms is readily apparent in the structures at Persepolis. Motifs and techniques from Asia Minor, Assyria, and Egypt are all present but are combined in an acceptable harmony. The bas-reliefs depicting the rulers subduing mythical beasts and the long processions of tribute bearers and royal guards display a stylized, static, repetitive character far removed from the realism, movement, and plasticity of the Grecian sculptured friezes of this same period.

At all periods, Iranian art and architecture display a steady stylistic development of forms such as is common to the arts of the Western world, but the rate of change was much slower and the impetus toward experimentation much less than in the West.

There was no real break between pre-Islamic and Islamic art: familiar decorative forms were continued, and the basic plans and methods of construction common to Sasanian palaces and fire temples reappeared in the Muslim monuments of the country.

The introduction of Islam did bring with it a prohibition against the representation of living forms, a characteristic feature of Semitic religions. Although this prohibition was not always observed in Iran, its existence did favor the natural predilection for decorative detail. Architectural monuments were decorated with carved-plaster panels, then surfaces displayed ornamental brick-bonding patterns, and finally glazed tiles were featured. By the early sixteenth century, the exterior and interior surfaces of the mosques were clad in faïence mosaic: a technique in which geometric and floral patterns were formed of myriad tiny pieces of glazed tile in many colors. Great technical skill and years of unremitting effort were required for the decoration of such monuments as those of the early seventeenth century, which still stand in all their original splendor at Isfahan. It is easy to believe that this use of bright, glowing color was in deliberate contrast to the drab character of the towns and to the general arid and colorless landscape.

In the realm of architecture most attention centered upon the construction of splendid mosques and shrines. Such monuments were built around a vast open court with its pool for ablutions before prayer. Great arched portals cast areas of deep shade. In contrast to the great structures of the Western world, such as the cathedral, which were designed to be free standing and to make their impact upon the beholders from both distant and closer points of view, the mosque was a structure turned in upon itself. Within the open court all was calm and conducive to meditation and prayer; beautifully decorated arcades rose so high that only the sky was visible, and the bustle and noise of the town seemed infinitely remote. This same sense of isolation marked domestic architecture. However, in the mosque the individual found the atmosphere appropriate for his obligations as a member of the community of believers, while in the home the patriarchal family carried on the private life of its own community. Thus, the houses were set behind high walls, entered by a right-angle corridor which shut off a view from the street and featured a similar open court with a pool, both small in scale.

All that the court offered to the mosque and the house, and much more, was to be found in the Persian garden. From ancient times the garden was equated with Paradise, first *pardes* and later *behisht*. As far as our knowledge extends into the past, the landscape of Iran was always arid, scorched, and generally barren of trees. Paradise had, however, unlimited water and vegetation, and it is exactly these two inclusions that create the Persian garden. Such a garden, and there are many of this type, may be set squarely in a desolate landscape. High walls enclose it; a spring or underground channel provides quantities of water, which dashes along channels, irrigates flowers, shrubs, and fruit trees, and settles in great dark pools. To these gardens both the Sufis and the sceptics long fled from the cares of the world, and it is not mere chance that the collected works of the poets bore such names as the Rose Garden or the Orchard Garden. The beauties of nature were praised by these poets, but never the beauty of landscape in which man was not present—only of nature controlled and enjoyed by man.

If there was a quality of timelessness and escape from the pressures of the material world in the courts of the mosques and houses and in the gardens, so this same quality pervaded the Persian miniature paintings. Incredibly delicate, detailed, and technically proficient, these scenes of hunting, warfare, life at the courts, in the open country, and in the gardens reflect a world frozen in time. Perspective drawing is not used, hence an urgent sense of reality is missing. The skies are always blue or gold, no storms sweep through the foliage, the flowers grow in eternal loveliness at the edges of sparkling streams, and the actors in each drama carry out their roles without emotion and anxiety. Violence and death may be shown, but sorrow is remote from this world of colored images. In a word, these miniatures provide the Persians with another link to Paradise.

Much this same quality of timelessness pervades the Persian carpets, an artistic expression unsurpassed by any country in the world. Rugs and carpets are everywhere—in the meanest village house and in the palaces of the shahs. As in other fields of artistic endeavor, geometric and floral patterns predominate, but there are also garden carpets and hunting carpets which, quite naturalistically, recreate these familiar scenes. Well-known symbolism is expressed in designs, motifs, and colors, and to the Persian such a carpet means far more than it ever could to a foreigner, for it may establish his own identity with the past and the present. How else could one explain the fact that a conspicuous feature of festivals and occasions of great moment is the display of Persian rugs on the facades of buildings and on triumphal arches?

As a final word, the architecture and arts of Iran were not produced by a class of artists and architects at a higher social level but by craftsmen and artisans in villages and towns who were intimately involved in the continuing stream of Iranian culture. They did what their parents and ancestors had done, not what they chose to do. Their horizon was limited, but their devotion to tradition was unlimited.

The Continuity of Social Patterns

Concurrent with the ancient Aryan structure of family, clan, tribe, and country was the ideal division of all society into the classes of priests, warriors, farmers, and traders. In spite of the similarity to divisions within the caste structure of India, castes never appeared in Iran in early periods and would, of course, have been impossible within the community of Islam. During the Sasanian empire, these groups became the religious hierarchy, the warriors, the scribes or bureaucrats, and the farmers, shepherds, and traders.

In Islamic times, with the extension of stable government and a carefully organized system of tax collecting, a capable bureaucracy grew up and men of learning were much admired. As a result, men of the pen ranked highest in the new division of society, followed by the warriors, the traders and artisans, and finally, the agriculturalists. By the seventeenth century, landowners were distinguished from the working farmers, and the civil and military authorities were attached to the court. In general, the court and the religious hierarchy were above these classes, constituting the forces that guided and controlled the community of believers.

A series of changes in the divisions of society reflected shifts in the bases of royal power. The warrior class, represented by the levies furnished by the feudal lords, lost importance after reliance was placed upon tribal forces and, finally, upon mercenaries serving a central command. As foreign invasions came to an end during the time of the Safavid rulers, and internal security was more pronounced, the importance of the large landowners increased. The class of nobles recognized in 1906 included individuals whose loyalty to the throne had previously been rewarded by titles, exemption from taxes, and grants of land; numbers of them became increasingly influential in the provinces. The guilds had been in existence since at least as early as the fourteenth century, with perpetuating organizations in all the towns; but they were not recognized as a separate group within society until the end of the nineteenth century.

Another persistent division of the Iranian community was that between the tribal nomads and the settled villagers. Both elements retained the ancient structure of family, clan, and tribe, but in the villages it tended to decay slowly as people moved to other areas and as newcomers came into the villages. More hardy and warlike, and less affluent than the farmers, the tribes had won much of their living from raiding the trade routes and the villages; and the long-nurtured feelings of mutual antagonism and distrust still linger on between these elements.

Such dynasties as the Seljuq, Afshar, and Qajar sprang directly from leaders of tribal groups, while others, such as the Safavid, came to power through tribal support. As late as 1906, tribal forces influenced the course of political development at Tehran. However, only too frequently rulers discovered that, once unleashed, the tribal forces escaped from their authority and either moved toward regional autonomy or rose in revolt against the central government.

Tribal elements and settled communities had their distinctive systems of internal authority. The authority within a tribe or confederacy of related tribes resides in the *khan*, and, below him, in the *kalantars* who head each sub-tribe. These chiefs come, generation after generation, from the same tribal families, and power emanates from these families rather than from authority delegated by the tribespeople to individuals. The *khan* must be strong and conciliatory, blunt and devious, for he uses coercion to enforce discipline and must be successful in promoting the economic well-being of the tribe. He is unfailingly hospitable, accessible to everyone, and is the sole repository of intertribal justice, which does not depend upon the shar'ia but upon long-established tribal custom. He is the point of contact between the tribe and the civil and military authorities; the former interested in the collection of taxes and the latter in conscription and the maintenance of order. The requirement of contact with central authority led these leaders to establish elegant residences in the nearest provincial capitals and then, more recently, to rent or buy houses at Tehran, where they spend a part of each year. At these centers their wealth and prestige permitted them to move in the upper circles of society. After 1906 these *khans* entered the Majlis as deputies, welcomed by the government, which saw this channel as a means of bringing tribal activity into conformity with national interests.

After Reza Shah came to power his immediate concern was to establish security throughout the country. A strong central army was his arm in this successful operation; and the army was used to attempt to break the military power of the tribes by disarming the tribesmen, by conscripting the youth into the armed services, and by settling tribal groups on areas in other parts of the country. Naturally enough, both the *khans* and the tribesmen resisted these efforts, and as recently as 1946 tribal uprisings occurred. However, the martial strength of the tribes has been largely destroyed: some *khans* are in exile and others have been removed from office; and military commanders exercise authority throughout the tribal regions.

Within the villages, local authority is vested in the *kadkhuda*, literally "the god of labor." Among the tribes the *kadkhuda* is the respected head of the extended family or clan, and his presence in the village may be a distant reflection of the same patriarchal system of society.

In early Islamic times, the *kadkuhda* seems to have been elected, while later he was appointed by the government but was nearly always a local inhabitant. More recently, he came to be the personally named representative of the landlord who owned the villages, its houses, and its fields. This role was recognized by law in 1935, and in 1937 a bill passed by the Majlis stated that a *kadkhuda* was to be appointed by the local governor from among the inhabitants of the village, upon the recommendation of its owner.

In more distant times the villages were self-sufficient, self-governing units, paying taxes to the court through the medium of the *kadkhuda*, but at present the village comes directly under civil and military authority, the latter represented by the gendarmerie. Other common village functionaries include the *dashtban*, or watchmen of the fields, the *mirab*, who regulates the flow of water to the fields, and, less frequently, the bathkeeper. In addition, the *rish safid*, or village elders, contribute their experience to resolve minor intervillage quarrels and rivalries.

The large towns were long administered by officials selected by the inhabitants themselves. They were physically divided into separate quarters or wards, with each such unit supervised by a *kadkhuda* who was responsible to the *kalantar* of the town. The civil authority of the *kalantar* was supplemented by the religious authority of the *muhtasib*, who was concerned with the enforcement of the shar'ia and the related preservation of public morality. By the end of the nineteenth century, the *kalantar* and the *muhtasib* were being replaced by the *darugha*, who had police powers in civil and religious fields.

Extensive covered bazaars distinguished the towns from the villages, and separate sections of the bazaars were occupied by the combined workshops and retail sales outlets of the *asnaf*, or craft guilds. The guilds stressed the hereditary aspect of the crafts by controlling the privilege to carry on business in the bazaar, assured high standards of workmanship, and provided for mutual cooperation and assistance among its members. Gradually losing their importance in modern times, they had a revival of influence in broader organizations, called the *anjuman-i-asnaf*, which favored the Constitutional Movement and, later, supported the rise of Reza Khan to the throne.

Other municipal associations include those of the *lutis*, the *dashha*, and the *zur khaneh*. The first two of these were guild organizations devoted to the preservation of public morality and security and to the aid of those in distress: in fact, *dash* appears to be a shortened form descriptive of a person who comes to the help of another. Unfortunately, by the opening of this century these groups had tended to become gangs of strong-arm men and knife wielders who preyed on the populace, while their present importance lies in the ability of their leaders to round up gangs of toughs to terrorize political opposition in city and town.

The *zur khaneh*, or house of strength, is an ancient institution of Iran which continues to flourish with the active encouragement of the state. Essentially, it is a physical culture society with its members drawn from all social levels. It is believed to have originated in a period when Iran was under foreign occupation, and the young men were trained in secret against the day they would be able to drive out the invaders. A series of exercises are performed to the accompaniment of drumbeats and the chanting of verses from the *Shah nama,* and the military origin of the *zur khaneh* is attested by the manipulation of heavy wooden shields and bows of iron with links of chain.

Although the villages and towns have a certain sense of corporate feeling and local solidarity against the outside world, their inhabitants have lacked the kind of pride in their birthplace which would be expressed in efforts to enhance its amenities and to construct public facilities. In the opening years of the twentieth century many of these towns had been long stagnant and there was an air of steady decline. Reza Shah was personally responsible for a considerable revival by giving orders for the building of wide new avenues through the crowded quarters, the construction of public buildings, and the installation of electric plants to light the towns and provide power for new industries. However, even today Shiraz may be the only town in Iran where a sense of civic pride and a devotion to development are readily apparent.

Factional strife and community isolation remained as factors inimical to communal solidarity and national unity. In the villages and towns, the Haidari and Ni'mati factions—one taking its name from Sultan Haidar and the other from Shah Ni'matullah, whose shrine is at Mahan, near Kerman—had long engaged in bitter rivalry and in conflicts which resulted in serious loss of life. In addition, violent outbursts of enmity occurred and still occur between neighboring villages.

Above all, few Iranians have a good word for people in other parts of the country. The villagers who have seen little of the country beyond their immediate horizon view the townspeople with distrust and have them neatly categorized with epithets which are often uncomplimentary. Thus, the people of Kashan are regarded as cowardly and complaining, those of Isfahan as shrewd and grasping, those of Shiraz as more enlightened than most because of its good climate, those of Meshed as tricky and untruthful, those of Semnan as frugal, and those of Tabriz as aggressive and brave. Also by common repute, the people from Kerman and Tabriz are the most enterprising businessmen and politicians, and individuals and families from these towns who have settled in Tehran are said to be successful in these fields out of proportion to their relative numbers.

The peasant, *ra'iyat* or *dehgan*, normally cultivates fields belonging to others and lives in a house that he does not own. The lands owned by others than the cultivators fall into three categories: *vaqf* land, or endowed land; *khaliseh* land, owned by the state; and, *arbabi* or *amlak* lands, under private ownership. Formerly, it was not customary for the ruler to hold land in his own name, but Reza Shah acquired vast tracts throughout the country, which were registered in his name: it is these holdings which have been distributed to the peasants by his son. In addition, land which is owned jointly by several proprietors or by the people of the farming community themselves is called *khurdeh malik*, literally "owner of a small piece."

Certain shrines continue to hold and operate or lease extensive tracts of land; this is particularly the case for the shrine of the Imam Reza at Meshed, which owns a goodly part of the province of Khurasan. The *khaliseh* lands are operated or leased by agencies of the state; in recent years there has been much talk of turning over these lands to small proprietors, but comparatively little progress has been made in that direction. Much of this land is believed to be unirrigated.

Most of the irrigated land of the country falls into the *arbabi* category, and its owners may hold the peasants in comparative serfdom. *Rab*, the word for lord, master, or possessor, appears in its plural as *arbab*, which may be translated as lord of lords: the parallel to the use of the term shah of shahs is not without interest and significance.

Useful statistics on the ownership of *arbabi* land are not available: that is, how many individuals control how many villages.

Some such holdings are known to be enormous, and it has been stated, without evidence, that twenty-seven families own 20,000 villages. One landlord, Mehdi Batmangelich, has boasted that his holdings were as large as all Switzerland. Making a random selection of some important landowning families to indicate areas of the country where large holdings occur, one can cite the Ardalan family of Sanandaj, the Afshar in Azerbaijan, the Alam in Birjand, the Amini family in Gilan, the Bayat and Beyklik families in Arak, the Khalatbari in Mazanderan, the Qavam al-Mulk in Fars and the Qaraqozlu at Hamadan and elsewhere.

These landlords should not be identified with a stable landed aristocracy which has transmitted its holdings unbroken from generation to generation. On the one hand, the Islamic law of inheritance makes the division of property almost obligatory, and on the other, years of insecurity and warfare worked to separate proprietors from their land. A few vast holdings have been in the same family for nearly two hundred years, perhaps even longer, but the adoption of family names under Reza Shah makes it somewhat difficult to establish the relationship between present and earlier owners known only by titles. In general, most of the large holdings seem to have been formed in the nineteenth century, while in this century many of them were acquired by Reza Shah or sold to a newly prosperous class of merchants and contractors. In many regions, landowning families are bitter rivals for seats in the Majlis, since a deputy is able to protect and foster the interests of his extended family. The more recent proprietors have acquired land less for its economic value in the way of annual revenues, than for the social prestige attached to the ownership of land and to membership in the Majlis, to which land ownership could lead.

It is customary for the Persians themselves to say that their country is ruled by 1,000 families and to identify these families with the major landowners. Preliminary research seems to indicate that there may be some 150 families who possess great influence and prestige in Iran, with approximately half this number on a somewhat higher level than the others. As could be expected, members of these families and their relatives constitute more than a third of the members of the Majlis and the Senate and two-thirds of the total membership of successive cabinets.

The headquarters of the families are at Tehran rather than in the provincial towns nearest their major holdings. They are the frequently abused absentee landlords whose holdings are in the hands of *kadkhudas* and *mubashirs*, or agents. Settled at Tehran, these families have become engaged in a pattern of very diversified activities and interests. This pattern is well illustrated by the careers of the several Amini brothers, descendants only two generations removed of the Qajar ruler of the country. One of the brothers went into government service as a specialist in finance and in 1961 became prime minister; another has been a member of the Majlis; another is a leading businessman and the representative for foreign firms in a number of fields; another rose to the rank of major general in the armed forces; another, trained as an engineer, managed government factories; and still another managed the family estates.

These families intermarry to an extraordinary degree and engage in interlocking commercial enterprises. More and more of the higher level of the ruling families dispose of their land and invest in business. Their number is slowly increased by members of the newly rich whose energy and acumen have brought them into business relations with the ruling families and whose position is recognized by marriage into the social elite. It is largely these newcomers whose recently acquired habits of conspicuous consumption attract the unfavorable attention of foreign observers who are unaware of the fact that they are not the true elite.

While usually stated that the 1,000 families are basically reactionary and opposed to political, economic, and social reform, this cliché is wide of the mark. These families had the means to provide higher education, usually abroad, for sons and relatives, and it is these "doctors," that is, doctors of philosophy, who play an ever more important role in the conduct of economic planning and of the government in general. Not only is this current generation of these families largely opposed to the preservation of the *status quo*, but a considerable number of its members are counted among the leaders of the National Front, the opposition to the government.

Below the so-called ruling families appears the newly emerging urban middle class, growing at Tehran by leaps and bounds. So new is this class that it falls outside the field of established

social patterns and will be examined in connection with the contemporary political scene.

Despite the changes in the order and importance of the social
classes and groups over the centuries, the relative positions of the
shah, the religious leaders, the tribal chiefs, the landowners, the
artisans, peasants, and all others on the social ladder of Iran were
known to everyone. In the Safavid period, a manual of administration took cognizance of the existence of this social ladder by
listing the titles awarded to every occupation or position in the
state from that of the shoemaker up through the entourage of
the shah. Many of the present family names of the social elite
have derived from the resounding honorary titles conferred by
the shahs on their immediate ancestors, such as the "Upholder of
the Realm," the "Intelligence of the Empire," and the "Splendor
of the Country." In the interests of erasing class distinctions, and
distinctions between nomadic and settled peoples, Reza Shah in
1935 abolished all such titles, all honorifics, and all such terms as
mirza, khan, beik, and *amir.* However, even a royal decree was
not adequate to erase century-old customs and titles, and honorifics are still employed in the press and in polite conversation.

The use of honorifics has continued because they are directly
related to the place of an individual upon the social ladder. When
Reza Shah decreed that family names must be chosen, there was
to be only one such new name in each town, but there was a certain amount of confusion and, at present, families bearing the
same name may be both numerous and unrelated. As a result,
each time a young man meets a member of the established elite
and gives his name he is queried as to his family connections.
Whether or not a person comes from a "good family" is still a
matter of real importance in his relations with his superiors.

Related to the use of honorifics is the general practice, so developed in Iran, of *ta'arof,* an Arabic word with the meaning
of ceremonial courtesies. The practice of *ta'arof* is an important
ingredient in the cement of the social order, since formulae of
address and manner of behavior relate to positions on the social
ladder and must be observed when people come into direct contact. The many forms of polite address constitute a formal ritual
of great variety with many subtle nuances of expression. Thus,
one may say, "I submit to the service of your excellency

that . . ."; begin a remark with the words, "This slave believes that . . ."; while the phrase "you and I" may be rendered as "this slave and your honor." When a person enters a room, his equals or inferiors on the social ladder will rise, bow, sit down after he is seated, and then half-rise again in a final submissive greeting. In the presence of a superior, an individual will stand erect with arms folded across his chest, alert for "commands." Many of the educated members of the present generation scoff at these practices, but the same phrases continue to appear in their conversation, and the same mannerisms are practiced. In fact, at the height of the strength of the Tudeh Party its members deliberately set out to mock at and disregard every form of politeness between individuals in an effort to promote intergroup hostility.

Individual character should be reflected in a number of positive qualities. *Sha'n* denotes the relative rank and dignity of the individual: his "face" within the system of *ta'arof*. *Gheyrat*, or honor, concerns a person's self-respect, his obligation to do his "sacred duty" under appropriate circumstances, while *shaksiyat*, or personality, relates to the personal integrity of an individual. In an effective, recognizable combination these positive qualities serve to give a man a "good name" and to imply that he behaves correctly, gets on well with others, and is hospitable and generous.

Personal relations should be, as much as possible, devoid of friction, and the good person should be able to adapt to different situations. The ability to assimilate—so characteristic of Iranian culture—is equally an aspect of their personality: educated Iranians will blend harmoniously into any background—in France they are as French as the natives and in the United States almost indistinguishable in behavior from the Americans.

The primary importance of the family, the basic unit of the old tribal society, continues into modern times. In sociological terms, the family is described as being extended, patrilineal, patrilocal, patriarchal, endogamous, and occasionally polygamous. The patriarch shares with the other males the responsibility for the welfare of the family, and the primary concern of the individual in Iranian society is his family. The background of long years of national decline and of conditions approaching internal anarchy, lasting until well into the present century, has given rise to feelings of basic insecurity which still linger on.

To protect themselves and foster family security, individuals in the upper levels of society united to form combinations in the overlapping fields of business and politics; and such combinations are continually being augmented, altered, dissolved, and re-established. Many of the young men look for patrons among the elite, whom they serve as legmen and sycophants, expecting in return their backing in order to move to higher posts or memberships in successful combinations.

The relationship of the individual to the state and to the ethos of his society remains tenuous and unsatisfactory. As would be expected from the material here presented, the Iranian is not a joiner and does not readily subscribe to group efforts in which membership cuts across social lines and restricted interests. In fact, the terms symptomatic of an organized society as we know it, such as *sazman*, organization, *bonyad*, foundation, and *bongah*, institute, are all new Persian words created not much more than a score of years ago.

As an individual, the Iranian is reluctant to give wholehearted and enduring allegiance to a national leader or to other leaders. Leaders possessed of charismatic appeal rarely emerge from this society; and when such a one as Dr. Mossadeq did come on the scene the first wave of enthusiasm gave place to declining interest as personal rewards and advantages failed to follow from allegiance given to him. The same attitude carries over into the arena of politics, where most political parties amount to no more than shifting alliances and combinations—interest groups rather than parties of principle. Dr. Mossadeq himself showed his awareness of this attitude when he said, "In our Parliament each deputy has his own personal opinion and this is why bills, even the simplest, cannot be passed rapidly by this body."

It has long been believed by the despotic rulers of the country that the individual must be brought under severe controls that will insure his service and loyalty to the state, and stern authoritarianism has the sanction of long-traditional acceptance. Force alone was considered to be the means by which the people of Iran could be made to do their work, remain obedient, and be loyal to the ruler. Thus, authority emphasized coercion and punishment rather than inspirational leadership and suitable rewards for proper behavior. Potential personal or group opposition to authority was prevented by a combination of threats, criticism, close supervision, constant pressures, sudden revenge, and severe physical punishment, all of which served to increase the individual's feeling of insecurity and increased his unwillingness to risk playing a larger role in society.

In the nineteenth century and during the first decades of the twentieth, members of the elite sought refuge from severe and often capricious internal authority by seeking to serve the interests of the British and the Russians, thereby receiving the protection of those powers.

On all levels of society above that of the peasants, a contradiction long existed between admired values and virtues and the willingness to display these virtues in public life. While greatly respecting in principle such qualities as courage, sincerity, honesty, self-sacrifice, and the ready expression of deeply felt emotions, in practice those individuals who wished to move up the social ladder or who continued to cling to privileged positions behaved with caution, adapted themselves to dishonest conduct, and were careful and reserved in their actions and in the expression of their true convictions. Although the display of these theoretical virtues on the part of rare individuals was admired, there was usually a lingering suspicion that apparent virtue must be a mask for more normal behavior. Two factors, possibly more, lay behind this practical retreat from conspicuous ideal behavior: the ingrained habit of dissimulation; and the advisability of not attracting the attention of authority.

Probably it was the helplessness of the individual in the face of authority which fostered the negativism that seems to pervade Iranian character. As individuals, as editors of newspapers, and as writers, the Persians appear to delight in destructive criticism; criticism of each other, of groups, and of the government. The deputies of the Majlis have displayed this same attitude, and it may be assumed that this spirit of negativism will persist until some drastic events or developments result in the rise of a national purpose.

III.

Challenges to Patterns of Continuity

The challenges to the persistence of past patterns have all had
their origins in the impact of the Western world upon Iran.
However, Iran has never fitted into the so-called classical pattern of a colony of a foreign power—exploitation as a source
of raw materials and as a market for processed items, with insuf-
ficient preparation given for eventual independence. Iran never
lost its independence, nor was it completely overrun by foreign
powers. Influenced and at times dominated by the rival Russian
and British empires, the rulers of Iran and their more capable
vazirs, or ministers, played off these rivals against each other and
resorted to such tactics as procrastination, promises made but not
fulfilled, and offers made and then withdrawn. The British and
the Russians were in a hurry to achieve specific objectives, while
the Persians hoped that time was on their side.

Contacts with Europe had begun as early as the Safavid period, but in the early seventeenth century the magnificence of the
court of Shah 'Abbas and of Isfahan, his capital, was equal to that
of any court and town in Europe. Indeed, London was then
less populous than Isfahan. Shah 'Abbas and his successors desired only one thing from England and the continent: the knowledge of how to make cannons. After the Safavid dynasty came
to a disastrous, disgraceful end, the military strength and economic prosperity of Iran steadily declined. Except for the visible
evidence of deserted agricultural villages, the Iranians saw few
apparent signs of this decline. However, defeats by the Russians
in northwestern Iran finally brought home the sorry plight of
the country.

Early hostilities between Iran and Russia ended in 1813 with
the Treaty of Gulistan, which ceded Georgia to the Russians,

while in 1828, the Treaty of Turkoman Chai gave the provinces of Nakhichevan and Erivan to Russia.

Later in the nineteenth century, the British and Russian empires successfully sought concessions in Iran, recruited ministers and other members of the elite, and granted loans, which were dissipated on costly tours of the Qajar rulers throughout Europe. Nasir ad-din visited the continent and England in 1873, 1878, and 1889, and dictated to secretaries descriptions of the high points as well as all the minutiae of his experiences there. Quickly published at Tehran, these memoirs disclosed the Western world to the literate Iranians, made them fully aware of how far their country had fallen behind these powers, and brought home the belief of this shah that Iran must copy the West.

Other foreign influences were at work to stimulate the Persians to emulate the West. Foreign mission societies operated hospitals, elementary schools, and finally, colleges. In 1852, the government opened the Dar ol-Fonun, or House of Learning, at Tehran, and not long thereafter this school offered instruction in the liberal arts. Toward the close of the century, an increasing number of the sons of the elite drifted toward Europe for higher education, combining studies with a good time.

The chronology of the impact of the Western world upon Iran, notably the maneuvers of the British and Russian empires, has been described and detailed at length in many publications; here the concern is primarily with the continuing psychological impact—and reaction to the impact—within the country. Increasing awareness of the superior military strength, economic power, material prosperity, democratic institutions, and the well-organized systems of law, education, and administration of the West aroused feelings of frustration, jealousy, resentment, envy, and even hatred. Some of the intellectual leaders advocated copying all aspects of Western materialism and institutions, others sought refuge in the spiritual superiority of the ancient traditions and religion, while still others anticipated internal social and political reforms that would spark successful competition with these relative upstarts on the stage of history.

To deal with these reactions in brief compass, it is necessary to compress the account, relating selected spokesmen of the nineteenth century with those of recent decades. Jamal ad-din

Afghani was born near Hamadan in Iran in 1838, but his years of residence in Afghanistan were reflected in his adopted name. Traveling and living in Turkey, Egypt, London, Paris, and St. Petersburg, he founded journals in the Arabic language at London and Paris, which inspired Muslim intellectuals in several lands. In 1878 appeared his only long work, written in Persian and translated into Arabic, entitled *The Refutation of the Materialists*, which included a description of the functions and duties of a modern government. Jamal ad-din has been called the originator of Pan-Islamism; according to his belief, all Europe was hostile to the Muslim world, which could advance only through unity and devotion to its faith. He pointed out that the Europeans exalted patriotism, national pride, and national honor at home, but when these sentiments appeared in the Muslim countries they were labeled by these same Europeans as fanaticism, chauvinism, and xenophobia. Although he had attacked the despotic rule of the Shah, Nasir ad-din called him to Iran and appointed him to the royal council: he became a focal point for activity against the Shah and was expelled from the country in 1890.

Jamal ad-din Afghani opened the door of nationalism to the Muslim world, but he failed to outline a positive system for progress under Islam. Others came forward to present more concrete proposals.

These individuals were active in Egypt, Turkey, India, and Iran, and it would be wrong to consider Iran as an entity isolated from the rest of the Muslim world. In the writings of journalists, poets, and philosophers, terms common to Arabic, Persian, and Turkish were given new meanings. *Watani*, the place of birth, became "patriotism"; *mellat*, the religious community, became "nation"; *hurriyyat*, the condition of free men, became "liberty"; and *mashrutiyyat*, from the root meaning "conditional" or "limited," became "constitutional." In addition, the three primary virtues of a nation, described by Jamal ad-din Afghani as honor, loyalty, and truth, were emphasized by these writers.

In local Iranian writings, and from newspapers published abroad in Persian, fresh themes appeared. After nearly a thousand years the theme of patriotism so stressed by Firdausi reappeared. Poets exalted love of the homeland, recollection of the past glories of Iran, the urgent need for a national resurrection; and bitterly condemned Russia and England as forces opposed to a national rebirth. The poet Ashraf began with these lines: /"Alas. Our homeland is plunged into grief and affliction. Alas, O homeland, alas."/Bahar identified the causes of Iran's misfortunes when he wrote: /"Russia and England are the tyrants over us. We are attacked on all sides by disasters and grief."/ 'Arif wrote: /"With the bones of our sacred ancestors this soil has been mingled, And so it is holier than anything else."/

As moving and as influential as such verse was in Iran, it was primarily a protest against the *status quo* rather than a program for the future. However, few poets have been political scientists, even in the Western world.

In India, Muhammad Iqbal began to express new sentiments and convictions in Persian. Iqbal was convinced that nationalism resulted in warfare and international conflicts, and issued his *Warning to the West* on this theme. He followed it with the *Message of the East*, which gave priority to love over intellectual striving. He was vehemently opposed to giving in to the West or to a sterile copying of its material achievements, and advocated a renaissance of Islam in terms similar to those of Western humanism. Finally, in 1934, after he had outlived most of the reformers of his era, he published in English *The Reconstruction of Religious Thought in Islam*, which stressed the basic principle of movement in Islam, a principle that can be identified with religious reform as the answer to the impact of the West.

Obviously, the Iranians and the intellectuals and literates in other Muslim lands had a rich variety of fare available for them to make their own choices as to ways of responding to the challenges of the West. Less emotional and more scholarly studies followed in due course. For the Iranians there was the book by 'Ali Akbar Siassi published in Paris in 1931 and entitled *La Perse au contact de l'Occident*, and as recently as 1948 Fakhr ad-din Shadman published at Tehran a work whose title may be translated as *The Mastering of European Civilization*. Siassi had presented a chronological account of Western influence on Iran, while Shadman pointed out to the Iranians the deficiencies of Iran and of themselves in any competition with the Western world.

The writings mentioned, and many others, have carried over from the late nineteenth century through the Constitutional Movement, the period of Reza Shah, and into the present era. Any real understanding of the political developments of this period, discussed in later chapters, depends upon an awareness of the persistent, interwoven strands of thought and speculation. These diverse thoughts persist; they have not found their culmination in a single, acceptable philosophy of national aims.

The least popular of the methods of reaction to the West were those recommending a return to traditional Iran with pan-Islamic overtones or a reformation of Islam to bring it into tune with the times. Such goals seemed too visionary to the newly pragmatic Iranians in search of immediate, practical solutions. Since it was the inadequacy of the patterns of the past that had brought Iran to its sorry state, these patterns should be discarded.

In attempting to establish basic motivations of societies, some sociologists and anthropologists have put forward the theory that behavior in one type of society is determined by the urge for expiation of guilt, while in another type the emphasis is on feelings of shame as the motive for individual conformity to its customs. Without laboring the point, it may be suggested that there was a shift in Iranian psychology from the guilt reaction to that of shame: shame, not yet shared, for inadequacy in the face of new challenges. For example, among the intellectuals there was shame at their own lack of patriotism.

As the twentieth century wore on, a new generation began to repudiate the formalism and authoritarianism of Iranian society. Its members questioned the validity of allegiance to the monarchy, to Islam, to traditional ethics, and to the structure of society. However, their revolt against the family structure, long the microcosm of the social structure as a whole, and their disorientation from the family preceded their disorientation from established social patterns.

In searching for new allegiances and fresh standards, they found nothing that would help, and many of them still remain suspended between two alien worlds—that of older Iran and that of an unknown future. Some, notably those educated in the West, turned to a vague humanism. More, however, placed their faith in materialism.

Materialism is, of course, far from a new force in Iran: it has long been a primary objective of the extended family to achieve material security. What is new is the intensity and single-mindedness with which wealth is sought by members of the privileged elite, by the intellectuals, and by the upper and lower levels of the middle class. This shift in emphasis was inspired by the example of material progress displayed in the more comfortable position of the individual in the West, by increasing opportunities for making money in Iran, and by the desire to find security in a society in which insecurity was so rampant.

However, financial security was not to be won by persistent application to a single business or endeavor over an extended period. Rather, it was to come from speculation: speculation in commodities, on luxury items of import, and in land and housing at Tehran. Initial success brought in capital which could be loaned to other speculators for short terms at very high rates of interest. Even moderate financial success brought with it an urge to show signs of material prosperity. Individuals competed in the acquisition of houses, expensively and garishly furnished, automobiles, expensive clothes for the women of the family, and television sets. Tehran has been blessed with a television station for some years, but several years before construction on the station began, scores of wealthy Tehranis had television sets on display in their homes, just as the less affluent had an electric refrigerator in a corner of the living room.

Along with the continuing emphasis upon conspicuous consumption, social intercourse became oriented toward expensive entertainment of friends and acquaintances, of attendance at gala benefits, and of gambling, while leisure was taken at local resorts, or, if at all possible, in Europe and the United States.

Those Iranians who have been most prosperous tend to withdraw from the cultural interests common to previous generations of the privileged elite: a pride in familiarity with the poets and philosophers of Iran, an interest in Sufism, and pleasure in conversation on the meaning of life. Lacking concern for deeper meanings and spiritual values, these individuals seem to feel no obligations to society. As one result, few wealthy individuals continue the tradition of establishing charitable foundations.

However, the lack of interest on the part of the wealthy elite in culture is not at all typical of the attitude of the urban population. Tehran is the scene of a remarkable growth of intellectual interest, of a voracious appetite for information. The ratio between the number of books published annually in the United States and the population of the country shows the figure of one new book to every 18,000 people. In Iran the ratio is one book to every 20,000 people, in spite of the fact that less than 20 per cent of the population is literate. In the United States the output of books has mounted steadily over a half century and more, while in Iran it has grown enormously within the last decade. In both countries more books appear on religion than on any other single subject, but there the similarity of subject matter ends.

Book production includes original writing in Persian, scholarly editions of old manuscripts, technical publications, and translations from foreign languages. In the first quarter of this century, translations of such authors as Balzac, Zola, Rousseau, Verne, Hugo, and Walter Scott appeared, and then interest shifted to Gorki, Gide, Maurois, London, Steinbeck, and Dale Carnegie. Currently, *avant-garde* writing from Europe and the United States has a receptive audience. There is no present intent to trace the impact of foreign novelists, poets, and biographies upon modern Persian writing in the same fields. Of more interest as relating to the changing patterns of social consciousness is the flood of nonfiction in translation. This includes renowned works in the fields of ancient and modern history, economics, philosophy, science, world cultures, sociology, and biographies of intellectual and political figures. The demand for such works seems almost amazing; edition follows edition.

The comprehensive knowledge of the intellectual, social, and political life of the entire world thus made available to the Iranians is brought into current focus by the flood of material emanating from radio broadcasts, newspapers, and local and foreign periodicals. Certainly, many Iranian intellectuals are drawing upon all these materials in their speculations about Iran itself: some are seeking ways by which traditional Iran and traditional Islam may be integrated into progressive movements, while others are constructing systems in which tradition plays no role. These materials serve to keep alive the spirit of intellectual enquiry in a period in which outlets for expression are very limited. Under Reza Shah, criticism and critical evaluation of the government and of the actions of authority and of society were not permitted. After his abdication in 1941 an era of "new freedom" produced a rash of critical commentaries among which the hostile Marxist evaluations of the Iranian political and social orders were the most knowledgeable and severe. In addition, socialists, conservatives, and religious figures took part in the literary debate, as did literally hundreds of ephemeral newspapers at Tehran. In line with the Iranian predilection for negativism, the consistent emphasis was upon what was wrong in Iran. After 1953 the period of the new freedom came to an end, and again the government refused to permit destructive criticism of authority and of the country's institutions. However, such criticism continues and even waxes in intensity and bitterness. It comes from Iranian students abroad and from Iranian historians and scholars resident in foreign countries, and their publications do find their way into Iran. The relation of these challenges to established patterns of authority and society are properly considered in a following section.

IV.

The Turbulent Present

1. THREE CHALLENGES TO THE HISTORICAL PAST

Incipient Nationalism: The Constitutional Movement

In the nineteenth century Iran, at its lowest ebb in military strength, administrative competence, and economic prosperity in many centuries, had the misfortune to be the object of the rival ambitions of the expanding British and Russian empires, and, to a lesser extent, of the similar aims of France and Germany.

Ruling the country was the Qajar dynasty, whose members no longer exercised absolute power. The spiritual authority of the throne had been acquired by the religious leaders, the provinces were milked by tax collectors who paid the throne for their privileges, and in the southwestern region local feudal lords were in open defiance of the central government.

Throughout the second half of the century, Nasir ad-din Shah ruled the country, and during these years not only did foreign powers strive to establish their hegemony over Iran, but Western political, social, and economic theories and institutions had a strong impact upon the educated Iranians.

The schools operated by foreign missionaries were primary channels for Western ideas, and served also as a stimulus for the creation of government schools oriented away from the traditional religious education, in offering courses somewhat comparable to those of European schools. Printing presses were established in the country and translations of French books appeared. Newspapers published abroad in Persian came into the country, and foreign trade and the founding of European firms in Iran in the fields of banking and communications all represented additional channels of influence.

Such influences stimulated an intellectual ferment, which was initially apparent in the field of religious speculation and reforms. One of several important religious philosophers of the period, Mirza 'Ali Muhammad, began to advocate the reform of Shi'ism and then announced that he was the Bab, or Door, which provided access from the world of flesh to that of the spirit. He attracted an ardent following and wrote a series of treatises expounding his revelations. Accompanying the somewhat obscure theology of these works was material pertinent to the local scene, such as severe attacks on officials of the government, letters admonishing the ruler, and declarations abrogating the laws and regulations of the Qoran on prayer, marriage, divorce, and inheritance. Regarded as a threat to both spiritual and temporal authority, in 1850 the Bab was executed as a heretic. His new revelation was altered and transformed to appear as Baha'ism, and in material published outside of Iran, some of which found its way into the country, it espoused public freedoms, an end of class distinctions, universal education, and the equality of the sexes. It found later reflection in local writing.

The direct penetration of foreign influences into the country began with the clauses of the Turkoman Chai Treaty of 1828, concluded after the defeat of Iran in the Caucasus, which granted capitulatory rights, including consular courts, to Russia. In the second half of the nineteenth century identical rights were acquired by Great Britain, France, the United States, and some thirteen other countries: the citizens of these countries were free to operate as they chose in Iran without regard for local law and authority. In addition, both Great Britain and Russia gained special privileges in the field of commerce and trade.

Nasir ad-din Shah believed that Iran should institute Western institutions, industries, and methods of communication, but efforts along these lines were more rewarding to foreigners than to the Iranians. Great Britain and Russia obtained concessions to construct and operate toll roads, railways, street-car lines, and telegraph lines; to establish banks; and to exploit the forests, mineral deposits, the fisheries of the Caspian Sea, and the oil resources of the country. On the one hand, the Iranian Government was not strong enough to resist pressures brought by these empires on behalf of its citizens desiring concessions, and, on the other, the Qajar rulers, including Muzaffar ad-din, the successor of Nasir ad-din, were only too ready to grant concessions in cases where a sizable down payment was offered, or as a return for loans granted to their regimes. The European tours of these shahs were vastly expensive and could not be financed from the meager revenues of the country. The conditions attached to loans granted by Russia contained guarantees for repayment related to the customs revenues of the country and provided for lower tariffs on goods imported from that country.

Both Great Britain and Russia sought the raw materials of Iran and worked to develop it as a market for manufactured goods, following the customary pattern of imperialist exploitation of colonies, or according to more recent Soviet terminology, of semicolonies. The degree of their success was not due principally to the incapacity of the much maligned Qajar rulers but to a prevailing atmosphere of lethargy and defeatism.

However, there were many Iranians who believed in a regeneration of their nation that must begin with internal changes capable of uniting the country against the designs of foreign powers. In spite of the heavy hand of the state, many patriots spoke up in poems and other writings, which were circulated throughout the country. For example, Aqa Khan Kermani wrote verses deploring the sorry state of the nation and attacking Nasir ad-din Shah, who had impoverished the country by his trips abroad and who had shirked his duties and responsibilities. In 1904, the poet Farrukhi recited a work which attacked the autocracy of the government and concluded with the line, "Never was [Iran] so trampled upon as now by British and Russian oppression." As an apt punishment, his lips were sewed together.

A resurgence of patriotism in the new form of nationalism was in the air. It had appeared as early as 1890 when a British concern had been granted a monopoly on the sale of tobacco products within Iran: the religious leaders of the country forbade the use of tobacco, and the monopoly was soon canceled. Local hostility toward Russia was heartened by the defeat of Russia by Japan in 1905 and the concurrent Russian revolution; these events suggested that it was time to stand up to the forces that had exploited the country as well as to the dynasty that had permitted this exploitation.

Both within and without the country, satirical and politically oriented periodicals and papers increased in number, with the latter introducing new terms for reforms, principles of administration, and law and justice which passed into current usage in Iran and supplied the vocabulary of the revolution. Several books offered unfavorable comparisons between the political conditions existing in Iran and those in other countries. Between 1886 and 1890, Jamal ad-din Afghani was in Tehran, and his influence was felt in the outburst against the tobacco monopoly and in the assassination of Nasir ad-din Shah (1896) by one of Afghani's disciples.

Despite the Iranians' long-time revulsion to foreign interference in their country and to the stifling authority of the Qajar rulers, the Persian revolution erupted almost without a plan and developed by chance. At the end of 1905, the grand *vazir* had a number of merchants and religious leaders bastinadoed. In protest, the Tehran bazaar closed down, and hundreds of clerics, merchants, and students sought sanctuary at a shrine to the south of the capital. After negotiations with Muzaffar ad-din, the new ruler, and his officials, they returned to Tehran upon receiving assurances that the grand *vazir* would be dismissed, that the Shah would establish a House of Justice, and that reforms would be instituted. Tehran resounded with cries of "Long live the Nation of Iran," and nationalism had come into its own.

When the promised reforms were not implemented, religious leaders preached against tyranny and misgovernment and in July, 1906, these leaders, accompanied by crowds of merchants and students, traveled south to Qum to take sanctuary in the shrine. About the same time, hundreds of residents of Tehran took sanctuary in the extensive grounds of the British Legation at Tehran until their number reached some 13,000. With such important elements of its population taking *bast*, or sanctuary, the commercial, religious, and social life of the capital ground to a halt, and the regime was powerless to cope with this massive movement of passive resistance.

Early in August, the Shah gave in and granted a constitution and a Parliament. The occasion was widely celebrated as the National Victory, and on subsequent anniversaries as the National Festival. Before the end of the year, the first Majlis had been elected, and the Fundamental Laws of the Constitution promulgated; and at Tehran newspapers supporting the Constitutional Movement had appeared.

Early in January, 1907, Muzaffar ad-din died and was succeeded by his son Muhammad 'Ali. After the first flush of almost unexpected victory, the nationalists soon began to realize that the road ahead was not an easy one: they found that their own interests were in conflict, that the new ruler was still powerful and implacably opposed to the liberal trend, and that neither Great Britain nor Russia had had a sudden change of heart with respect to their interests in Iran.

The first electoral law of 1906 had grouped the voters into six classes: princes and members of the Qajar family, religious figures, nobles and notables, merchants, artisans, and landowners and peasants. The first three of these classes had risen against the regime because they expected to have positions of priority in the new kind of government, while the merchants and artisans were motivated both by patriotism and by the desire to escape from heavy taxes and other stringent controls over their activities. The landlords and peasants played a negligible role. The first to be disillusioned were the clergy who soon found that liberal, Western ideas and institutions served to undermine, rather than strengthen, their authority. Not described as a social class were the younger Persian liberals who expected to direct the future of the nation and whose motives were nationalistic and patriotic; they hoped for the regeneration of Iran and for vengeance against Russia, the prime enemy of progress within the country.

The British had supported the Constitutional Movement—called by the Iranians the Constitutional Revolution—primarily because it promised to do away with Russian influence close to the throne, and secondarily, because it was logical to support a movement directed toward the type of constitutional monarchy common to their own country. However, larger considerations were now involved, including the necessity to solidify British hegemony in the Persian Gulf and to insure that an aggressive Germany found no foothold in the area. Great Britain took the initiative in negotiations that concluded August 31, 1907, in a treaty with Russia, which defined their mutual interests in Iran, Afghanistan, and Tibet.

According to the terms of this treaty, both parties agreed to respect the integrity and independence of Iran. Then, in order to take into account their special interests in maintaining peace and order in certain provinces of the country, the clauses of the agreement divided Iran into three zones. That to the north, in which Russian influence was to predominate, included Tehran and was by far the largest. In the south, the British zone paralleled the Persian Gulf and came into contact with the Indian empire on the east. The neutral zone, across the center of the country, was tacitly recognized as being open to British interests. In addition, both parties agreed to take measures, as necessary, to insure that outstanding debts to either party were repaid.

Although a British memorandum to the Iranian Government reiterated that the agreement was not aimed against the integrity of the country, there was a wave of hostile reaction in Tehran, voiced in the press and in a number of poems which spread from mouth to mouth. Iraj wrote, in part:

> They say that England with Russia
> Has concluded a new treaty this year
> . . . .
> As a result of peace between the cat and the mouse
> The grocer's shop was ruined.

Most of the published material was much more bitter in tone, and Great Britain lost the popularity gained by its initial support of the Constitutional Movement.

Although the final articles of the Constitution were ratified during 1907, several deeds of violence by reactionary elements gave notice that the Shah was determined to destroy the constitutional regime. In June, 1908, the Persian Cossack Brigade, directed by Russian officers, bombarded the Majlis building, nationalist leaders were arrested, and the constitution was suspended. Tehran was ominously calm under a Russian military governor, and Russia began moving troops into the country to support the reactionary coup. These forces occupied Tabriz and put down the nationalists, but elsewhere in the provinces volunteers flocked to oppose the ruler and the Russians. An armed force moved from the Caspian littoral to join with Bakhtiari tribesmen coming from Isfahan, and in July they gained possession of the capital after heavy fighting. Muhammad 'Ali took refuge in the Russian Legation, an action tantamount to abdication, and he was succeeded by his son, Ahmad Shah, then eleven years old.

The Second Majlis assembled in November, 1908, and began to display political activity. The leading parties, nearly of equal strength, were the Popular Democrats and the Moderate Socialists, while the Alliance and Progress Party had fewer members among the deputies. The Popular Democrats were led by individuals most familiar with Western political institutions, while the Moderate Socialists represented the opinions of the religious leaders. According to the terms of the constitution, five religious figures were to have special powers to review pending legislation and to eliminate any bills or articles contradicting the principles of Islam. The Socialists seemed to feel that the Democrats were not sufficiently devoted to the defense of the faith in pressing for reforms inspired by the non-Islamic world. Although these parties had supporters outside the Majlis, and had their own newspapers, they did not manage to bring into being active and permanent political organizations.

The inability of nationalist sentiment to coalesce behind a single party and to agree upon a constructive program marked the pattern of political development of the following decade. However, the climate was not propitious for orderly developments of any kind. Without continuing with a recital of the events of these years, it may be said that Russia continued its direct interference through such actions as the support of an attempt by Muhammad 'Ali to regain the throne, the occupation of Tabriz in 1911 followed by the murder of many nationalists, and the ultimatums of 1911, which resulted in the dismissal of W. Morgan Shuster, the able American financial adviser. Then, too, although Iran declared its neutrality in World War I, it soon became a battleground, with Russian and British forces opposing those of Turkey.

During the earlier years of the war, Russian forces strengthened their hold over the northern provinces of Iran, and there was reason to believe that these regions would be absorbed within the Russian empire. Suddenly, the Bolshevik Revolution burst forth, and the disintegrating Russian units disbanded or made their way back to home soil. At the end of the war, a Persian delegation appeared at the Versailles Peace Conference, but it was not received. Its demands had included abrogation of the 1907 Anglo-Russian Agreement, the end of capitulatory rights in Iran, the restoration of the boundaries of the country to those of the early nineteenth century, and reparations for damages suffered through the presence of foreign troops during the war.

In 1919, the governments of Great Britain and Iran concluded an agreement that provided for British advisers to the Iranian Government, for British officers, arms, and equipment to train and supply a uniform Persian Army, for steps toward the construction of a railway and other means of transport, for the revision of customs' tariffs, and for a substantial British loan, which would be guaranteed by the revenues from Persian customs and other sources. The fact that the agreement would have given Great Britain effective control over the administration, finances, armed forces, and transportation system of the country clearly reflected the disappearance of Russia from the Iranian scene. Since the agreement included a provision for a foreign loan, it could not become effective without the approval of the Majlis. Within Iran there was violent reaction to the agreement: revolts broke out in several parts of the country, and there were numerous anti-British and anti-government demonstrations. The cabinet that had concluded the agreement fell, and throughout 1920 a new one resisted strong British pressure to summon a Majlis and present the agreement for ratification.

The hostility toward the agreement had gained momentum as the result of a declaration made by the Soviet Government in 1919, which denounced the former Russian imperialistic aims against Iran. In addition, it included the abandonment of Russian-held concessions in the country, and the canceling of debts to the Czarist regime. However, at the same time the Bolsheviks were encouraging the peoples of the East to rise against their rulers, and in May, 1920, Soviet troops landed at the Caspian Sea port of Enzeli (later renamed Pahlavi) to support an armed rebellion against the Iranian Government, and aided in the establishment of a Persian-Soviet Socialist Republic in the province of Gilan.

As 1920 drew to a close, Iran seemed even weaker than at any time in the nineteenth century. It had so suffered during the war years that famine was rampant in many parts of the country, the government had lost control over many areas, the treasury was empty, and the future appeared very bleak. The incipient nationalism of the period of the Constitutional Revolution had failed to achieve its objectives, largely through circumstances beyond any control. These objectives had been rather limited. There had been no strong desire to get rid of the Qajar dynasty but only to control its despotism by adopting the Western form of constitutional monarchy. However, the functioning of a constitutional regime, with its political parties, was a concept completely foreign to Iran and could only have become viable in a tranquil atmosphere and under more prosperous economic conditions. The nationalists were also determined to put an end to the pattern of balancing off the interests and pressures of the British and Russian empires by granting a concession to one, and another to the other, and to resist all foreign influences and interference in the country. With respect to this latter objective, time was on their side since the aftermath of World War I had created an atmosphere more favorable for an attempt to establish national integrity and independence. Finally, waiting in the wings were the actors of a new golden age who believed in deeds rather than words, even the fiery words of the nationalist poets.

The Ardent Nationalism of Reza Shah

Reza Shah was born in 1878 into a local family of landowners and military men at Alasht, a small village high on the northern slopes of the Elburz Range in the province of Mazanderan. His father, while in Tehran the year preceding, had met and married a young woman from a family of immigrants who had left the town of Erivan in the Caucasus some generations earlier, after the region had been taken from Iran by Russia. The father died before his son was a year old, and the young mother, having no ties in the village, returned to Tehran with the baby. Relatives and friends belonging to similar Caucasian families helped the boy, saw that he learned to read and write, and enrolled him as a private in the Cossack Brigade when he was sixteen.

This brigade, later a division, had been established some years earlier following a request from the then shah of Iran to the Russian Czar for help in establishing a force modeled upon the Russian Cossacks. Staffed in part by Russian officers, it was the best-trained force in the country.

Over a period of many years, Reza Khan advanced from rank to rank and became a man of impressive stature, great reserve, and renowned for his bravery and initiative in engagements throughout the country. A man with few close friends and no confidants, he burned with a consuming zeal to rescue Iran from "the villainy of foreigners and the treachery of mean Iranians," and "from foreign oppression and the incapacity of our statesmen." It was his belief that the armed forces had been disgraced by the governments of Iran and that it was up to the army to rejuvenate the country. He was convinced that all foreign advisers in the service of Iran were motivated by evil designs, and he was determined to put an end to British and Russian influences in the country. His military service had made him bitter against Russia, for he noted that the Russian Cossack officers were primarily concerned with advancing the interests of their mother country.

By 1921, he had risen to the rank of general in the Cossack Division. Having just tasted defeat at the hands of Soviet-organized forces in Gilan, he was retraining his ill-equipped men at Qazvin, some 60 miles to the west of Tehran. The command center of the British forces then in Iran was located in this same town. Suddenly, chance plunged him into the political arena, but it seems most probable that in time he would have made his own move to rise to power.

At Tehran, Sayyid Zia ad-din Tabatabai, a crusading journalist, was preparing for a *coup d'état* which was to overthrow an ineffectual cabinet and install a government which would wage a determined struggle against Communist forces, resist foreign influences, and institute reforms based on Western models. He needed a military force to occupy Tehran, and when the first ranking officer whom he approached declined the honor, he sent emissaries to Reza Khan. On February 21, 1921, Reza Khan led a band of the Cossacks into Tehran. There was almost no resistance, and a few days later Ahmad Shah, the Qajar ruler, named

Tabatabai as prime minister. Reza Khan became commander of the armed forces and began with great vigor to bring about a consolidation of the Cossacks, the regular army units, and the gendarmerie, to see that the armed forces received regular pay and adequate equipment, to wipe out the Communist forces in Gilan, and gradually to restore security in the provinces where a state of near-anarchy prevailed.

Confronted by the opposition of entrenched social forces, some supported by the British and some by the Russians, Tabatabai was unable to carry out his program of reforms. He left the country that May, and Ahmad Qavam, a member of one of the extremely powerful families, took over the post of prime minister.

Having consolidated his hold over the armed forces by naming former military associates to key command posts, Reza Khan moved into the realm of politics, aided by the conviction that was growing in the capital that he was the only person capable of maintaining internal security. In his own statements to the armed forces on their role in preserving Iran, he helped to create the image of himself as the sole indispensable man in Iran.

In October, 1923, Ahmad Shah named Reza Khan as prime minister and a few days later left for Europe for "reasons of health"—he was never to return. Reza Khan, who also retained the post of minister of war, soon announced that Iran had fallen into decline because of continued domestic insecurity and chaos of thought and morals. Now that security had been established, he proposed to foster self-reliance and put an end to dependence upon foreigners. He informed the Iranians that it was a thousand times better to starve in poverty than to prostrate themselves humbly before foreigners, and he stated that all subservience to and dependence upon foreign authorities must cease at once and forever. While this proclamation may have had little immediate impact in Moscow and London, it constituted a precise statement of one aspect of his ardent nationalism.

Within a year from the time he took office as head of state, some of Reza Khan's advisers were advocating the establishment of a republic, pointing to the successful example of Turkey and trying to convince him that more rapid progress could be made under that form of government. He seems to have financed the country-wide campaign in favor of a republic: the papers published scores of articles denouncing the Qajar dynasty, and provincial groups flooded the capital with wires calling for a republic. Suddenly, the campaign collapsed. The Majlis had been reluctant to embark on the necessary legislation, and religious leaders rallied thousands of opponents to the plan in the square in front of the Majlis building. Shortly thereafter, Reza Khan traveled to Qum, some 80 miles south of Tehran, to confer with the spiritual leaders of the Shi'a sect. In his own statement after the meeting, he declared that it had been agreed it would be best for the welfare of the country if efforts to promote a republic were halted, and he added that the nation should direct its efforts toward reforms, the strengthening of the fundamentals of religion, and the preservation of the independence of the country.

The enemies of Reza Khan among the powerful families felt that the collapse of the republican movement was a personal defeat for him and still believed that he could be replaced by a more pliable individual. They were heartened by a wire from Ahmad Shah in which the ruler expressed his lack of confidence in the prime minister. Reza Khan resigned and went to a village some miles from Tehran. A special committee appointed by the Majlis called on him and urged him to resume his post. In reply he said that he could not work singlehanded; he must have the kind of wholehearted cooperation that would make Iran a prosperous country and show its enemies that the nation was united. Given the necessary assurances by the Majlis, he returned to Tehran and to the task of governing the country.

In May, 1924, the Marquess of Curzon addressed the British Parliament on the reasons for the decline of British prestige in Iran and the wave of Persian hostility against Great Britain. He pointed out that they resulted from a spirit of exaggerated nationalism, which was not specifically directed against the British, but was a reaction to the former attitude of instinctive deference to Westerners and Western ideas and opinions. Curzon went on to say that the British would have to learn to meet this insurgent spirit of nationalism and to adapt to it: his remarks were most prophetic.

In his continuing effort to establish the administrative authority of the central government throughout the country, Reza Shah came into conflict with Shaykh Khaz'al, the semi-independent head of the province of Arabistan, in the oil-rich region of Iran at the head of the Persian Gulf. Relying upon his close relations with the British and their repeated promises to defend his interests, Khaz'al refused to pay taxes to Tehran and attempted to stir up feeling against Reza Khan at the capital. Against urgent warnings from the British Legation, in November, 1924, Reza Khan left for the south, after ordering four army groups to converge upon Arabistan. Khaz'al submitted without a struggle, and the British failed to react. Iranian units occupied the area, administrators from Tehran took over and restored the ancient name of Khuzistan to the province, and gradually the Arab coloring of the region became Persianized.

In 1925, Reza Khan initiated the first of a long series of actions designed to promote national unity. Actually, they established conformity rather than unity—which is not responsive to decrees. In May he eliminated the use of honorary military titles and led the way in the adoption of family names by taking that of Pahlavi.

The events of the fall of 1925 and the spring of 1926, which changed his role from that of prime minister to shah and founder of the Pahlavi dynasty, were important to him primarily because they entrenched his absolute authority. He did not reign; he ruled.

In May, 1927, following his instructions, the Majlis passed a law providing for the founding of a National Bank (Bank-i-Melli), and at a later date this institution took over the right of issuing bank notes from the Imperial Bank of Iran, a long-established, British-owned bank. In that same month, again on direct orders from the ruler, the minister of justice informed the representatives of seventeen foreign countries which maintained relations with Iran that all capitulary rights would be abolished in one year's time. Other steps pointed up the fact that special privileges enjoyed by foreigners in the country were at an end. Military guards were withdrawn from the foreign legations and the ministers of these missions informed that they could display the flags of their countries only on their own national holidays, and then only on the facade of the structure, never on a vertical pole. A bill passed by the Majlis prohibited foreigners from owning agricultural land, and members of the foreign service of the country were forbidden to marry foreigners without express permission. Restrictions were placed upon foreign-owned shops and businesses and the press urged that aliens should be driven out of business. Officials of the government were told not to attend functions at the legations and to avoid social and other contacts with foreigners. Communications from foreign governments and diplomatic missions addressed to the Foreign Office had to be in the Persian language, and Reza Shah decreed that all other countries must call the country "Iran" rather than "Persia." Mail addressed to Persia was returned to the sender. At Tehran, the Tehran Club, a British stronghold, was forced to admit local Iranians. Finally, the ruler himself wore uniforms of homespun and insisted that officials must follow his example and not wear clothes made of imported textiles.

In an interview with a visiting journalist, Reza Shah said that Iran must learn to do without foreigners and that after a very few years foreign specialists and advisers would be no longer required. He added that for too long his people had relied upon others and their characters must be hardened, so that they could become independent in thought and action.

In July, 1927, Dr. Arthur C. Millspaugh, head of an American financial mission employed by the Iranian Government, resigned when the Majlis refused to renew his special powers. Active in Iran since the end of 1922, the mission had labored diligently to put through fiscal reforms and had enjoyed the support of Reza Khan. However, the presence of the mission had failed to attract American capital investments and to attract the United States itself to play the role of counterforce to British and Russian pressures. Moreover, in time Reza Shah could no longer put down his latent mistrust of all foreign advisers. Near the end, in talking about Dr. Millspaugh, he is said to have remarked, "There can't be two shahs in this country, and I am going to be the shah."

When Reza Shah broke ground for the construction of the Transiranian railroad, he was determined that it would be built without recourse to foreign loans, and it was financed exclusively by special taxes levied upon tea and sugar. Later in his reign he was to summarize his objection to borrowing money abroad in these words, "There are strings attached to all foreign loans, and [in accepting them] we would be bound to come under the influence of those countries."

Throughout these same years, Reza Shah was on the alert to react sharply to any real or fancied insults to the country. A staff of translators scanned the foreign press for derogatory material, and upon occasion relations were suddenly broken off with such nations as the United States and France. In addition, selected periodicals or even all published material coming in from the offending country was destroyed at the Tehran post office. Steps were taken against the foreign mission schools, which had been active for so long and which had introduced modern education into Iran. Initially, they were instructed to cease giving instruction in Christianity to Muslim students, then to use only the Persian language in teaching subjects other than foreign languages; finally, in 1939, all were closed down.

Reza Shah's personal pride in Iran was certainly more intense than that of anyone else in the country. He was extremely proud of the record of the culture and civilization of the pre-Islamic periods of Iran's history. He was convinced that the country had the most beautiful scenery in the world and that it possessed boundless natural resources. While he instructed students sent abroad and his officials to learn from the West, he frequently reminded them that they were in no way inferior to Europeans and that in time Iran would surpass the achievements of the Western world.

His efforts continued at building national unity by imposing conformity. First, the men of the country were made to wear the Pahlavi hat, a visored headgear very similar to that of a French army officer. Then, in 1928 the Majlis passed a "uniform dress" law, which made the wearing of Western clothes compulsory throughout the country. In his own words, he explained, "I am determined to have all Iranians wearing the same clothes, since when Shirazis and Tabrizis and all others no longer wear different costumes there will be no reason for differences among them." In 1934, after his trip to Turkey and his long talks with Ataturk, the Pahlavi hat gave way to the European felt hat, solely on the grounds that the Westerners had seemed superior to others who did not wear that kind of headgear.

Reza Shah was disturbed at the natural rift which existed between the more than 2 million nomads of the country and the settled population. It was his belief that all Iranians should lead the same kind of life; and then, too, he had an interest in curbing the predatory and warlike habits of some of the nomadic tribes by restraining their ability to move about.

Throughout his reign, the ruler was concerned with education, believing that in universal education lay the key to national strength and unity. Schools all over the land taught Persian rather than the local tongues of some of the regions, and the textbooks and readers were designed to instill the same habits and patterns of behavior in all areas. In addition, he was the initiator of the reform of the Persian language.

For the first time in history, women were considered to be a worthy element in the social structure. Not only did the ruler tear off their veils and introduce them to Western clothing and the facilities for education, but he insisted that they had both rights in and responsibilities to society. He said, "Up to this time one half of the population was not taken into account and there were no statistics of the female population; it seemed as though women were some other type of individuals who did not form a part of the population of Iran. Now that you have entered society, it is your duty to work, [and] you are to be the educators of the next generation."

Another step toward uniformity was the abolition of all honorific titles, as well as the use of special titles to mark the status of tribal chiefs, important landowners, and relatives of the earlier ruling dynasties. Only terms corresponding to *mister, madame,* and *miss* were to be used in conversation and writing. Obviously, the intention of Reza Shah was to convey equal social status upon all citizens of the country and hence enhance their feeling of belonging to a single community.

Other specific actions taken to promote uniformity, such as the establishment of a single system of civil courts, the opening of notary offices for the recording of vital statistics, contracts, and land ownership, and the introduction of the metric system in place of widely differing regional weights and measures, were not specially related to the larger cause of nationalism.

Reza Shah failed to establish an effective channel through which his nationalist goals could be explained to the people and which would serve to draw them into active participation to achieve these objectives. He was not indifferent to the need for some such channel or organization, and at several times took up the subject and made specific plans. In 1927 four political parties —Iran-i-No, Iran-i-Javan, Taraqqi, and Tajaddod—were active, with some of the high officials of the government engaged in their promotion and direction. The motto of the Iran-i-No Party was "Loyalty to the Shah, and Devotion to Progress," and word got around that the ruler planned to follow the Turkish model and build it up as the majority political party to support the programs of the government within and outside of the Majlis. The Iran-i-No Party criticized the Millspaugh mission and expressed other anti-foreign sentiments. However, all these parties faded from the scene within a few months.

In October, 1932, the ruler raised the subject again in addressing a group of deputies. He informed them that the existence of the Majlis without political parties was a defect, that the organization of patriotic parties would be advantageous, and that a political party should be created which would take effective steps toward the realization of further reforms. However, nothing came of this proposal. Although it is not at all clear why Reza Shah failed to follow through with his intentions, it seems quite probable that his concept of a patriotic party was one which would praise the efforts of the government and not engage in criticism. For example, in meeting with a group of the deputies in the Tenth Majlis just before the end of its sessions, he praised them for having enacted necessary legislation and, in particular, because they had "succeeded in avoiding useless rhetoric and disputes, as well as the tactics and speeches of obstruction which may be observed in certain other countries."

In January, 1939, the Society to Guide Public Opinion (Sazman Parvaresh-i-Afkar) was founded upon instructions from the ruler. Following the models of the Nazi and Fascist propaganda machines, the society was to divert public opinion along specific lines, to inform the public about the plans of the government and to solicit its support, and to promote national pride. Numerous committees and commissions were active throughout the country until the Allied occupation of Iran in 1941. Some of the material put out stressed that individuals should subordinate their personal interests to the higher ones of the state and that the intellectual elite of the country must give its enlightened service to the nation. Certainly this kind of organization was much closer to the comprehension of Reza Shah in that it represented a more constructive force for promoting uniformity of opinion and reaction than had been presented by the political parties. Before he had come to power he had been able to observe the parties of the earlier periods and had received the impression that they lacked cohesive force and programs and had been apt to go off on undesirable tangents. However, near the end of his reign he speculated whether his efforts would be maintained, since he had not had time to establish the necessary institutions. And, on many occasions, he had deplored the quality of the human material at his disposal: in a word, he lacked confidence in the ability of the people to assume responsibility.

Other than a mention of the Transiranian railroad, little has been said here concerning the efforts of Reza Shah to modernize and industrialize the country. This program was quite stupendous in scale considering the limited financial resources of the country. An extensive network of graveled roads was built, sugar refineries, cement plants, cotton, silk, and woolen textile mills erected, the growing of tea promoted, and a number of state monopolies covering major items of export and import established to maintain a generally favorable balance of trade. Tehran itself lost its quiet air: new quarters sprang up, and wide avenues were lined with impressive public buildings tending to display ornamental motifs from earlier periods of Iran's architectural history.

No extended discussion of the details of the modernization program will be attempted within the scope of these pages, although this program directly reflected the ruler's spirit of ardent nationalism. His basic thesis was that Iran must increase its exports of raw materials in order to obtain the foreign exchange required for the construction of those enterprises and industries that would enable the country rapidly to become self-sufficient in the staple items of food, wearing materials, and the materials of construction. Before World War II broke out the foundations for a steel mill were in and the equipment on order in Germany. Unfortunately, it never arrived.

Few foreign institutions survived the implacable hostility of Reza Shah toward what he regarded as channels for foreign influences and pressures. Among those left intact were the Imperial Bank of Iran, founded in the nineteenth century and operating under a sixty-year concession, the Soviet-owned Russian Bank, the joint Irano-Soviet fisheries company, which had a concession monopoly on the foreign sale of fish and caviar from the southern shores of the Caspian Sea, a few insurance companies, and the Anglo-Iranian Oil Company.

The two banks had their usefulness in foreign trade and in the financing of local enterprises, although with the growth of the National Bank they lost their early priority in the banking field. Although Iran was not happy with its share of the profits of the Russian-managed Caspian fisheries, the government was not disposed to incite a sharp Soviet reaction by moving to alter the terms of the concession or to cancel the agreement.

The Anglo-Iranian Oil Company (earlier called Anglo-Persian Oil Company) remained as the prime target of xenophobic hostility. With a good deal of reason, the Iranian Government believed that its British management was primarily concerned with returning large profits—up to 25 per cent per annum—to the stockholders, while resorting to planned efforts to pay a bare minimum to Iran under the terms of the concession agreement. In addition, the company was reluctant to provide adequate housing and other facilities to its thousands of Iranian employees and deliberately kept these employees in subordinate jobs, while providing British clubs and other amenities for its foreign employees. No one was more aware of this general situation than Reza Shah himself, but he was prepared to maintain a balance between the country's interests and its need for the revenues from the operations of the company.

In 1928, when he was at Ahwaz in Khuzistan, he saw lights on the southern horizon where the refinery was burning off excess gases and asked what the flames meant. Informed, he said, "Curse the British oil company." During his reign, concession agreements were concluded with the Amer-Iranian Oil Company and the Standard Oil Company in an effort to bring in American interests that would operate under more generous terms. Neither agreement was carried out to the stage of the actual discovery of oil reserves outside of the concession area of the British company, and in spite of his willingness to invite these companies, he remained motivated by a distaste for opening Iran to new companies owned and controlled abroad.

Acting under his instructions, Iranian officials began negotiations with the Anglo-Iranian Oil Company, looking forward to a redress of the grievances of Iran, but after an extended period of time no concrete results had been obtained. When the Iranian cabinet announced the cancellation of the D'Arcy concession, under which the Anglo-Iranian Oil Company had been operated, the Majlis gave its unanimous support to this decision.

Quickly, the British Government intervened and submitted the legal aspects of the dispute to the League of Nations. In February, 1933, Dr. Eduard Benes, acting as mediator on behalf of the League of Nations, announced that the parties to the dispute had agreed to initiate direct negotiations relative to drafting a new concession agreement. Reza Shah was determined that the dispute should be resolved on terms favorable to Iran.

Representatives of the British oil company came to Tehran, but little progress was made in the discussions until Reza Shah intervened. Informed by the British representatives that the talks had been broken off, he stated that he would not accept this situation. In April, 1933, he insisted that a settlement must be reached. Later, one of the British officials said, "The Shah, and only the Shah, made the agreement possible." In regard to the new agreement, at a much later date Iranian officials who took part in the negotiations leading up to the new contract stated that Reza Shah had been strongly opposed to extending the British oil concession and then suddenly had given orders that a settlement must be reached. These officials have not hesitated to imply that Reza Shah was paid off by the British: Not one of them made such a statement while the Shah was still alive.

The new concession agreement was ratified by the Majlis, although eight members abstained from voting, and there was a strong undercurrent of resentment against permitting the British company to remain. Those who criticized Reza Shah for concluding the new agreement at the time of its signing, and again, after his abdication, with more strident voices, lacked any real understanding of his motives. He had balanced the merits and disadvantages of concluding a new agreement and was swayed by the need of Iran for increased revenues to finance industrial projects. Who, familiar with his entire career, could question his intent to do away with the British oil company at such time as the Iranians themselves were trained and able to take over its operations and have a guaranteed access to world oil markets? Reza Shah, unlike so many of his fellow Iranians, was not dominated primarily by emotions. A man of reason and logic, he made decisions based upon the greater good of the country and upon the realities of the international situation. Always in haste to carry through constructive enterprises, he had a reservoir of patience and was prepared to wait, in this instance until conditions were ripe for Iran to nationalize the oil industry.

In July, 1940, the minister of finance of Iran complained to the Anglo-Iranian Oil Company about the drop in oil royalties, stated that sums due must be paid either in gold or in dollars at a more favorable rate of exchange, and suggested in his note that failure of the company to meet the demands of Iran could result in a cancellation of the concession. Within a few weeks the oil company agreed to make payments for the period 1938 through 1941 at the high rate of £3.4 million attained in 1937, and to make an additional payment covering the difference between the gold and the paper values of the pound sterling. Also, it was settled that a new agreement covering the amount of oil royalties would be negotiated in 1941. Engaged in a desperate struggle for survival, the British Government had been compelled to yield to Iran's demands, but the timing of the action aroused enmity toward Reza Shah that contributed directly to his downfall. Following the Anglo-Soviet occupation of Iran in August, 1941, the British radio stations launched bitter attacks on Reza Shah, calling him a tyrant and stating that he had forced the poverty-stricken peasants of the country to sweat and toil to fill his pockets with gold. Abdicating in favor of his son, he had no regrets for any of his actions over the years, but felt that in the end the foreign powers had, through the use of force, managed to dominate Iran once more. He said, "What will happen to all the things which I created for Iran; the railways, roads and factories? They will all be used to serve the ends of others."

Reza Shah did not fit the traditional stereotype of the head of state who plays off conflicting interests against each other, shows favoritism to powerful elements, and seeks security through inaction. In spite of his conspicuous faults—his acquisition of great wealth, his abuse of power, and his persecution and destruction of individuals—he had clear insight into the nature of his people and realized the nature of the ingredient most essential for the progress of Iran. This ingredient was work: he was consumed by his determination to put an end to the prevailing climate of lethargy, to make the people work hard, and to channel their efforts into constructive enterprises. He himself had no hobbies and took no vacations, and was happy only when his unrelenting efforts brought such concrete results as new roads, factories, and schools and hospitals. In the course of a cabinet meeting he asked the ministers present to tell him what they regarded as his most important contribution to the national welfare and progress. One minister said the railroad, another the system of compulsory education, and still another, the industrial development of the country. He replied that they were all wrong; his greatest contribution had been to make the people aware that in work lay the salvation of Iran and its brightest hope for the future. He said, "I have made the Iranians realize that when they get up in the morning they must go to work and work hard all day long."

Reza Shah's concept of work as the salvation of the nation now appears very prophetic. In the world of today many so-called underdeveloped countries are struggling for national survival. Facing overwhelming problems, which include overpopulation and inadequate natural resources, they must manage to step up the tempo of the national effort. Only two channels are open: either to operate under a totalitarian type of government, which compels the individual to work hard in the service of the state, or, under a more responsive kind of government, to attempt to persuade the citizens that hard work will benefit both themselves and their country.

However, upon the abdication of Reza Shah, much of the Iranian nation breathed a collective sigh of relief and settled back into the traditional posture of self-interest and lack of cohesiveness.

The Negative Nationalism of Dr. Muhammad Mossadeq

Muhammad Mossadeq was born in or near Tehran in 1879 into a family of landowners. His father, Mirza Hedayat, was a moderately important government official and his mother a princess of the Qajar family. After early studies at Tehran, in 1896 he entered the Ministry of Finance for a brief period before taking courses in a new school for government officials. Then, he was assigned to a series of provincial posts in the service of the ministry.

About 1906 he went to Paris and studied political science, majoring in finance. Taken seriously ill, he came back to Tehran to recuperate, and then went to Switzerland to study, receiving his doctorate in law just prior to World War I. Upon his return to Iran he was known as Dr. Mossadeq, or by the honorific title of Mossadeq as-Saltaneh.

With his family background and his training in finance and law, he was a logical candidate for the Majlis and in 1915 was elected to the Third Majlis. There he served on a committee concerned with the reorganization of the Ministry of Finance. In 1917, at the end of that session of the Majlis, he took a high post in the Ministry of Finance and after a few months transferred to the Ministry of Justice. From the middle of 1918 until July, 1920, he was in Europe, and then returned to the Ministry of Finance and served at Shiraz and Tabriz in the period just before and after 1921. In October, 1921, he became minister of finance in the cabinet of Ahmad Qavam and was given plenary powers to execute fiscal reforms. When that cabinet resigned in January, 1922, he became governor-general of Azerbaijan and was minister of justice from June, 1923, until October of that year.

He was elected as a deputy from Tehran to the Fifth Majlis, which opened its term in January, 1924. In November, 1925, the Majlis was engaged in debate upon a single-article bill, which provided for the deposition of the Qajar dynasty and the entrusting of the affairs of state to Reza Pahlavi pending the calling of a constituent assembly. In this debate he made a very lengthy speech in which he stated that the fundamental laws of the country must be preserved. He insisted that they would be destroyed if the Qajars were removed and Reza Khan put in their place, adding that Reza Khan had been an effective prime minister, but that as shah he might become a dictator. Disregarding frequent interruptions, he completed his speech and then left the hall. In these remarks he had shown himself to be a man of most unyielding character who was absolutely sure that he was always in the right, invoking Islam, patriotism, and love of freedom in support of his views.

By this time, his reputation as a member of the new intellectual elite and an interpreter of institutions of the West had been established by the publication of several works in Persian. These included *Capitalism and Iran; Stock Companies in Europe; Parliamentary Law in Iran and Europe;* and *Financial Laws and Regulations in European Countries and in Iran.* He was re-elected to the Sixth Majlis, but Reza Shah saw to it that he was not elected to the Seventh Majlis.

About 1930, upon the order of Reza Shah, he was told to take up residence at Ahmadabad, an agricultural village owned by his family, situated some 100 kilometers from Tehran. In 1936 he spent a month in Berlin for medical treatment—he has suffered from poor health all his long life—and then came back to the village. In 1940 he was briefly jailed at Tehran and then sent off in his car, together with his own chauffeur, his cook, and a police escort, to enforced residence at Birjand, a small town in eastern Iran. The account of this trip is colored with reflections of his implacable obstinacy in the face of authority: he was illegally detained and he never let anyone forget it for a minute.

One of his sons, Dr. Gholam Husein Mossadeq, managed to plead his father's cause with Crown Prince Shapur Muhammad, and near the end of 1940 a telegram went to Birjand stating that on orders of the heir to the throne Dr. Mossadeq was to be returned to Ahmadabad. In September, 1941, upon the direct orders of Muhammad Reza Shah, he was informed that he was free to live wherever he pleased.

Although allegedly reluctant to return to public life, in 1944 he was elected as a deputy from Tehran to the Fourteenth Majlis, where he was an attractive symbol of a man of principle who had endured the enmity of Reza Shah and survived. Then sixty-four, he had spent nearly ten years in Europe and a total of less than twelve in the administration and the Majlis. Out of touch with the course of events for more than a decade, at times he seemed unaware of all that had happened in Iran and appeared to be concerned with turning back the clock and seeking revenge for old grudges. Critical of all the material progress inspired by Reza Shah, he was even less prepared to admit that the former ruler had himself been a fervent nationalist.

On October 29 and October 30 of 1944 he made a very lengthy speech to the Majlis, which, although it attracted little attention within the country and none at all abroad, was a significant indicator of future events. Dr. Mossadeq stated that the Iranians should pursue the same policy as that of their ancestors and went on to say that "the Iranian nation wants a political equilibrium which will be in the interests of the country, and that will be a negative equilibrium." In reviewing the speeches and remarks of Dr. Mossadeq on a number of occasions, one should not expect to find that reason and logic were prevailing characteristics. These "ancestors" had followed a policy of positive equilibrium by skillfully balancing the demands and pressures of the British and Russian empires, while his new policy of negative equilibrium stressed the point that Iran should grant no concessions and no favors to any foreign powers.

Most of this long speech was directed against the Anglo-Iranian Oil Company and included a detailed review of its operations with special emphasis upon how unrewarding these had been to Iran, its host. A decade earlier Reza Shah had said, "Curse the British oil company," but Dr. Mossadeq implied that the late ruler had favored the company. Dr. Mossadeq cited facts and figures regarding concession agreements, oil production, and revenue received by Iran, which may well have come from publications of the Iran Party.

In contrast to his extreme antipathy to the British oil company and to the British Government, the major shareholder in the company, Dr. Mossadeq had some good words for the U.S.S.R. He said, "We have always rendered homage to the generosity of that state," and went on to read several articles of the Iran-Soviet Treaty of 1921, adding that "one could not find better articles than [these] to advance the happiness of humanity." After more words of praise for the attitude of the U.S.S.R., he went on to suggest that the oil resources of northern Iran should be exploited by an international company and sold to the Soviet Union.

Finally, he came back to the subject of equilibrium as it was related to internal affairs and stated that "a political equilibrium will be established when the elections are free. Once the true representatives of the people will be in Parliament, political equilibrium will be automatically established, and, once this is established, all uneasiness will be dispelled for the neighboring states."

Throughout this speech there were reflections of the almost psychopathic concern for the so-called "hidden hand" of the British in Iran. According to this prevailing belief, the government of the United Kingdom tried to undermine the authority of the central government of Iran by supporting divisive elements and used a variety of means to attempt to misrepresent the goals of the U.S.S.R. and the United States in Iran in order to maintain its own position of predominant influence. Other and more specific views, such as the feeling that the British had deliberately brought Reza Khan to power and supported him throughout his reign, were reflected by Dr. Mossadeq.

In early November, 1944, when Prime Minister Muhammad Sa'ed-Maraghai resigned, a number of deputies approached Dr. Mossadeq offering him their support for the post. He is reported to have said that he would accept on the condition that he retained his seat in the Majlis. Since this condition was in direct violation of an article of the constitution, the matter was dropped. On December 2, 1944, he introduced a bill which he described as being in the interests of negative equilibrium. Its terms prohibited any member of the government from negotiating or concluding agreements relating to oil concessions. Contrary to earlier proposals of this nature, its terms were not related only to the period of the war in which foreign troops were in Iran. No term was named and the prohibition was to be absolute: The bill was quickly passed against the opposition of the Tudeh Party.

Early in January, 1945, Dr. Mossadeq and his followers and the deputies representing the Tudah Party joined with the majority of the Majlis in voting for the repeal of the special powers of Dr. Arthur C. Millspaugh, head of the American financial mission. Throughout that year and in 1946 the attention of the government and of the Majlis was centered on difficulties with the Soviet Union concerning its support of the autonomous regimes in Azerbaijan and to its demands for an oil concession in northern Iran. However, Dr. Mossadeq continued to reassert some of his basic beliefs: in March and May of 1945 he rose on the floor of the Majlis to castigate that body as a den of thieves and stated that he would offer proof of his assertion.

The Fifteenth Majlis was convened in July, 1947, and in October Prime Minister Ahmad Qavam presented a report on the agreement reached in April, 1946, concerning the establishment of a joint Irano-Soviet oil company. The Majlis reacted forcefully with near unanimity and quickly passed a law that voided the agreement as being in violation of the law of December, 1944. Included in the clauses of the law were statements to the effect that if oil was found in northern Iran it might be sold to the U.S.S.R., that no oil concessions were to be granted to foreigners or to companies in which there were foreign interests, and that the government was to study the terms of the southern oil concession with the aim of obtaining increased revenues to Iran from its operations. Repudiated by the Majlis, Qavam resigned early in December.

By 1947, some twenty-five deputies, including most of those elected from Tehran, had clustered around Dr. Mossadeq. In December of that year when a successor to Qavam was to be named, he received fifty-three votes in the Majlis as against fifty-four in favor of Ebrahimi Hakimi who then became prime minister. Why would so many of those individuals whom Mossadeq had labeled as thieves want him as prime minister? In addition to the votes of the members of the National Front he received those of the Tudeh Party, and also of moderate elements who were thoroughly disgusted with the lethargy and lack of responsibility of the Majlis.

The National Front came into being in October, 1949, when a number of like-minded individuals gathered at the home of Dr. Mossadeq to consider how they could exert influence and pressures for free elections for the Sixteenth Majlis. Drawing up a petition addressed to the Shah, which called his attention to the prevailing mismanagement of the elections and the public dissatisfaction with this situation, on October 14 a group headed by

Dr. Mossadeq walked from his house to the royal court. They presented the petition and indicated that they would take *bast*, or asylum, within the palace grounds until they had received a reply satisfactory to them. Led by Mossadeq, some twenty men entered the grounds, where they were sheltered and fed. After four days of fruitless discussions with the Minister of the Court, the group withdrew. It issued declarations attacking the attitude of the government and even of the Shah and condemning in the ruling circles the prevailing spirit of hypocrisy, dissimulation, injustice, and despotism.

When the elections for the Sixteenth Majlis were held, a number of supporters of the National Front were chosen and formed a faction which called itself Vatan, or Homeland, and was the forerunner of the formal establishment of the National Front within and without the Majlis. Before this Majlis, Muhammad Mossadeq brought up several of his favorite subjects: the need for a liberal revision of the press law, the necessity of ending martial law and of providing freedom of speech and assembly, and the need for the amendment of the election law. In June, 1950, he presented a bill to annul the decisions of the Constituent Assembly of May, 1949, which had amended the constitution to enable the ruler to dissolve the Parliament. In his speeches he also insisted that the Majlis should demand its privilege of giving a vote of inclination to a candidate for the premiership prior to any such appointment by the shah. However, the bill failed of passage, and the government failed to take action on his other objectives.

By June, 1950, the attention of the Majlis and of the country as a whole had become concentrated upon the oil issue, a situation which was to prevail until 1954. The story of the negotiations of the government with the Anglo-Iranian Oil Company relative to an agreement that would have nearly doubled its royalty payments to Iran, the rejection of this proposed agreement, the nationalization of the oil industry and its consequences has been told in such detail in several published works that present attention will be centered on those highlights relating only to the actions and policies of Dr. Mossadeq.

In June, 1950, Dr. Mossadeq read to the Majlis a statement from Sayyid Abol Qasem Kashani opposing the agreement with the Anglo-Iranian Oil Company and added his own belief that the Iranian nation would never accept such a bill and that the proposal must be amended for the sake of the welfare of the nation and of international peace. However, he made no concrete suggestions as to such amendment. Finally, in October, 1950, the government submitted the Supplementary Agreement, which had been signed the previous July by its representatives and those of the Anglo-Iranian Oil Company, to the Majlis. It was at once referred to that body's Special Oil Committee. Dr. Mossadeq was the chairman of this eighteen-member committee, which included four other members of the National Front. In December the committee reported that the agreement did not give adequate protection to the rights and interests of Iran.

On February 19, 1951, Dr. Mossadeq presented his Special Oil Committee with a proposal for the nationalization of the oil industry, and the National Front conducted demonstrations in favor of the proposal. Advisers consulted by the government reported that nationalization was not practical at the time and that such procedure would be of doubtful legality. On March 3, 1951, Prime Minister 'Ali Razmara presented this report to the Special Oil Committee of the Majlis and also made it public.

Dr. Muhammad Mossadeq had been implacably opposed to Razmara since he had taken office the previous July. He had attacked the "coup d'état-like" nature of his government and stated that the National Front would "not accept a government brought to power by the instigation of foreigners and through dishonest plots. The members of the National Front will be honored if they sacrifice their lives in order to preserve national and religious traditions, the Constitution, and democracy."

Razmara appeared before the Special Oil Committee to stress his agreement with the report, and on this occasion Dr. Mossadeq is reported to have burst into tears. Word of these events and distorted rumors quickly reached the emotionally charged supporters of Dr. Mossadeq, and on March 7, Prime Minister Razmara was assassinated by a member of the Feda'iyan-i-Islam, attached to the National Front through the person of Sayyid Kashani.

Few individuals in public life were now prepared to risk the serious displeasure of the fanatical supporters of the National

Front, but on March 11 Husein Ala accepted the post of prime minister. He was confirmed by both the Senate and the Majlis, although the members of the National Front walked out when he appeared before the Majlis. A single-article bill providing for the nationalization of the oil industry was passed by the Majlis on March 15 and by the Senate on March 20. By May 1, both bodies had passed a more detailed bill, which spelled out the details relating to nationalization, including terms for the sale of Iranian oil to former purchasers.

On April 29, following the unanimous vote of approval of this bill in the Majlis, Dr. Mossadeq became prime minister. Within a matter of days he had established a pattern of personal behavior that seemed to people outside of Iran to be both theatrical and irrational—he conducted affairs of state clad in pajamas, lying on an iron bedstead, weeping copiously upon occasion. Indeed, in May he entered the Majlis to seek refuge from possible opponents, donned his pajamas, and retired to bed. In thus behaving, Mossadeq was, perhaps very consciously, presenting the antithesis of the stern, authoritarian figure common to traditional Iran. Instead, he substituted the figure of tragedy, the man of sorrow who took upon himself burdens and obligations to be resolved by self-sacrifice. Although never so expressed in words, it is possible that the Iranians saw in him the image of the martyred Husein, the son of 'Ali. According to patterns of traditional behavior in Iran, a man should stand up to adversity and not give way to emotional displays reflective of weakness, but a figure whose saintly qualities were recognized was not expected to conform to these standards. Only some such interpretation of the impact of Mossadeq upon Iranian society can explain his present worship by important segments of the population of the country.

In addition, there were other ways in which Muhammad Mossadeq was to represent the antithesis of traditional behavior. As has been noted, there has long been a contradiction in Iranian society between admired values and the interpretation of these values in private and public life. As noted earlier, such qualities as courage, honesty, sincerity, self-sacrifice, and the expression of deeply felt emotions were admired in principle, but in practice individuals who advanced in society or who retained privileged positions did so because they behaved with caution, and were re-

served in the expression of their opinions. Although the rare individuals who displayed these theoretical virtues were admired,
there was nearly always the lingering suspicion that apparent
virtue must be a mask for more conventional behavior. However, Mossadeq drew his major support from a younger generation than his own which, influenced by the mores of other countries, really believed in such virtues. It was inevitable that he
should become the saint of this cult, for he had displayed these
qualities throughout a long life with such consistency that it was
generally conceded that this image did not conceal a more conventional one. At the same time, he was not an unknown: he
came from a family of wealth and status. He could afford to be
virtuous.

On assuming the premiership Dr. Muhammad Mossadeq stated
that the program of his government would be based upon two
major goals: the nationalization, not the expropriation, of the
oil industry, and upon electoral reforms. Once he had taken office
he was supported by a vitalized National Front, which was never
a political party but a tentative alliance of groups and individuals
opposed to the *status quo* and desirous of political change. Best
organized of these groups and, in the beginning of his premiership, the most influential, was the Iran Party. This party had
been founded in 1944 with the slogan of "work, justice, and freedom." Its founding members were individuals of good families
who were well educated, and a number of them were active as
engineers or in related technical fields. The party published a
series of pamphlets and books which elucidated its principles and
program and explained its position on internal issues and on the
foreign policy of the country. In the early years of its activity
the party did not seek for mass following. Instead, its leaders
cultivated officials within the government and persuaded many
of them to subscribe to the principles of the party. Convinced
that the party had the answers for Iran, it believed that in due
time a sufficient number of converts would be made so that a
gradual and bloodless revolution would effectively displace the
more reactionary elements and place its supporters in all the key
positions of the government.

In spite of his early studies and publications, Dr. Mossadeq
was never inclined to dispassionate research and analysis, and

the publications of the Iran Party supplied the sound basis for his emotional reactions. These publications attacked foreign influences within Iran, such as the (British) Imperial Bank of Iran and the Anglo-Iranian Oil Company. For example, in 1949 the party published a book entitled *Proceedings of the Discussions Relating to Oil in the XVth Majlis, and the Speech of [Husein] Makki* and a book by Engineer Kazem Hasibi entitled *Concerning the Oil of the South*. The latter publication provided Dr. Mossadeq with the ammunition required for his continuing attacks on the governments that were trying to conclude a new agreement with the Anglo-Iranian Oil Company.

It seems fair to say that the Iran Party provided the brains of the National Front, while other elements furnished the volatile emotions and the unreasoning excesses which, in time, escaped from his control. However, the Iran Party had, in 1944, entered into a temporary alliance with the Tudeh Party, and this record of collaboration with Soviet-directed political efforts had tarnished its reputation.

Most influential among the supporters of Dr. Mossadeq was the late Sayyid Abol Qasem Kashani, a member of the religious hierarchy who claimed that he was hostile to any foreign forces that threatened the interests and independence of Iran. Actually, he was motivated by a boundless hatred of the British, by a somewhat less intense feeling against the Pahlavi dynasty, and by personal political ambitions.

He was born at Tehran in 1885—or perhaps earlier—and as a child accompanied his father, a Muslim divine, to the holy towns of the Shi'a sect in Iraq. The family settled there and the boy engaged in religious studies under some of the leading spiritual authorities. At the outbreak of World War I, his father and some of these leaders declared a holy war against the British forces who were moving into Iraq from the head of the Persian Gulf. While engaged in this struggle, the father was killed and at the end of the war Kashani was compelled to return to Tehran, where he lived in the family house and concerned himself with a growing family of his own which was to total thirty children by several wives.

During the reign of Reza Shah he was careful to refrain from any political activity, but he did stress the vital interests of Islam and was most distressed by the series of actions taken by the ruler to undermine the authority of the Muslim clergy, to unveil women, and to secularize education.

In 1942, a few months after the Allied occupation of Iran, the British arrested Kashani as an alleged collaborator with the German fifth column in the country, and he was detained until 1945. When Ahmad Qavam became prime minister early in 1946 he was again arrested and forced to reside in the town of Qazvin until almost the end of 1947. In 1948 he delivered a speech before a large audience in a mosque at Tehran, calling for volunteers to oppose "Jewish terrorists in Palestine." Volunteers flocked to his house, and although they never got to Palestine they did form the nucleus of the Devotees of Islam (Feda'iyan-i-Islam). One associate of Kashani headed that group, while another edited the Tehran paper *Parcham-i-Islam* (*Standard of Islam*). Thus, in February, 1949, the would-be assassin of the Shah carried a press card issued by this paper. Since he was killed on the spot, there was no opportunity to trace possible connections between the Tudeh Party and the Devotees of Islam. However, Kashani was arrested once more and sent into exile in Lebanon.

Kashani's position among the spiritual leaders of the country was unique. He was not quite on the uppermost level of these leaders, he was more politically minded than any of the others, and no one could be sure what turn his fanatical convictions might take. Successive governments feared his influence with the masses and with other fanatics but were unable to keep him isolated for any length of time. In the Majlis, Deputies Husein Makki and Ha'erizadeh attacked the government for illegally exiling him, and in June, 1950, Kashani was allowed to return to Tehran and take his seat in the Majlis to which he had been elected while in Beirut. As previously, his house was open to visitors, who streamed in and out during the day. To his admirers he was honest, friendly, and unpretentious, while to his enemies he was sly, devious, revengeful, and dangerous. Perhaps his detractors were more nearly in the right, and certainly it was the murder of Prime Minister Razmara by an illiterate Devotee of Islam, incited by Kashani's bitter attacks against him, that hastened Dr. Mossadeq's inevitable rise to power. Particularly revealing were the brutal cartoons, photographs, and articles reviling Razmara, which appeared immediately after his death in organs controlled or influenced by Kashani, and the threat of the Devotees of Islam to kill the Shah if the murderer of Razmara was not released within three days.

Dr. Muzaffar Baghai brought to the National Front his own political following, the Hezbeh Zahmatkeshan-i-Mellat-i-Iran, or Toilers' Party of the Iranian Nation. Founded in 1951 to appeal to the industrial workers of the country in liberal, non-Communist terms, and alleged to have attracted 5,000 members, this group was headed by a powerful orator, a man who combined openly expressed defiance of reactionary authority with an inclination for making opportunistic deals. Born in Kerman, he had been an employee of the Ministry of Education there prior to his election to the Majlis, first from that town and later from Tehran.

Khalil Maliki joined the National Front along with a handful of intellectuals who were members of his Niruyi Sevum, or Third Force. Earlier an important leader within the Tudeh Party, he had broken from it about 1947 to form a socialist, anti-Communist group which, as its name implied, was to establish relations with groups in other countries not aligned either with the West or with the Communist bloc. In time Maliki was to become the secretary of the National Front, but he never had a powerful voice in its inner circles.

Lunatic fringe groups rushed to ally themselves with the National Front in an effort to advance their own theories and goals. One of these was the Pan-Iran Party which had irredential aims, agitating for the recovery of territory lost by Iran to Russia and to Afghanistan in the nineteenth century. Another was the Sumka Party, a national-socialist organization which copied the uniforms and the pro-Aryan aims of the Nazi Party.

Most notable among the individuals who attached themselves to the National Front were Husein Makki and Dr. Husein Fatemi. Makki, then about forty years old, came from a family of merchants at Yezd and appears to have had little formal schooling. Early in World War II, he joined the administration of the Iranian State Railways, moved up to become deputy mayor of Tehran, and was then elected to the Majlis from Arak. A good speaker and possessed of considerable political acumen, Makki had made a reputation as a writer. He was the author of numerous lengthy volumes on the history of Iran in the nineteenth and twentieth centuries, works which contained valuable source materials but which displayed a definite bias against all earlier regimes. In July, 1950, he spoke in the Majlis over a period of four days in opposition to the agreement that the government had negotiated with the Anglo-Iranian Oil Company. Dr. Fatemi came from a very large and influential family. He had marked talents in the field of journalism and was a master of invective; he became the spokesman for the National Front as well as a power second only to Dr. Mossadeq himself.

Finally, the several fronts organized by the Tudeh Party gave qualified support to the National Front, or, rather, attempted to push it along a more extreme course. Typical of these fronts was the National Association for the Struggle against Imperialism, headed by an individual who years later was to attack the government of Iran as a speaker on the radio stations of the satellites of the U.S.S.R.

Clearly, the National Front was never a political party but a tentative association of heterogeneous elements and individuals who had little in common except feelings of xenophobia. The right wing of the National Front was represented by the Iran Party and the middle wing by Dr. Mossadeq himself. All the other elements took more extreme positions on the oil issue and continually urged their leader toward stands from which there was no possibility of compromise. Of course, the Tudeh Party took the most extreme view. Within a week from the time Dr. Mossadeq became prime minister, its Central Committee called for the complete liquidation of the Anglo-Iranian Oil Company, the nationalization of the country's oil resources, the expulsion of all foreign advisers from the country, and the restoration of the sovereignty of Iran over the Bahrein Islands. While consistently criticizing the national bourgeois attitude of the National Front, the Tudeh Party was able to influence it in the direction of its own goals. As a result of pressures from the more extreme elements, the National Front regime raked up old disputes with Iraq and Afghanistan and, at one point, issued a call for an expeditionary force to seize the Bahrein Islands.

Once Dr. Mossadeq had taken office he was immediately concerned with obtaining the daily income of £300,000, which he had promised would come to Iran upon the nationalization of the oil industry. Following the closing down of the Abadan refinery in July, 1951, a variety of suggestions for settling the oil crisis were put forward. The Anglo-Iranian Oil Company accepted the principle of nationalization and made a series of proposals, President Truman sent W. Averell Harriman to Tehran where he was greeted by a hostile demonstration staged by the Tudeh Party, and the United Kingdom submitted the dispute to the Security Council of the United Nations. Dr. Mossadeq came to New York City to appear before the Security Council and then went on to Washington to request a loan of $120 million. Although the loan was not forthcoming, Dr. Mossadeq continued to stress at home that his government enjoyed the good will and backing of the United States.

Elections for the Seventeenth Majlis were held early in 1952, somewhat ahead of the required time, since Dr. Mossadeq wanted to eliminate those deputies who were attacking his government. However, the elections were suspended after only 81 of the 136 seats in the Majlis had been filled, and this in spite of the fact that Dr. Mossadeq announced that 80 per cent of those newly elected represented the will of the people. Friction now appeared within the National Front itself: In February, a youthful member of the Devotees of Islam shot and seriously wounded Dr. Fatemi. In the early months of the year efforts of the International Bank for Reconstruction and Development to play an active role in the settlement of the oil dispute met with failure.

On July 5, 1952, Dr. Mossadeq took the mandatory step of resigning just before the opening session of the Seventeenth Majlis. Renamed to the post, he stated that he would accept only if granted the power to govern by decree for six months and be permitted to take over the post of minister of defense. The Shah rejected the latter condition and on July 17, Ahmad Qavam was selected to fill the post. On July 19 and 20, Tehran was the scene of riotous demonstrations in which sympathizers of the Tudeh Party took a leading part. On July 22, Dr. Mossadeq returned to office with his conditions met.

Additional proposals by the Iranian Government and from

abroad concerning the oil issue were unproductive of results, and on October 16, Dr. Mossadeq informed the Iranian nation that relations with the United Kingdom were being severed and that the budget of the country would be balanced upon the basis of present revenues. By this time only a thin trickle of oil was moving out of the country to Italy and Japan, and Dr. Mossadeq rationalized his failure to produce the promised income from oil by stating that Iran would keep its oil in the ground and thereby advance the greater cause of negative equilibrium.

Before the end of 1952, the two major goals of Dr. Mossadeq —the nationalization of oil for the benefit of the Iranian nation and the implementation of public, democratic freedoms—seemed to have lost their priority. To the Soviet observers his behavior had become typical of the "bourgeois of oppressed countries which, although it supports national movements, manages to find common cause with the imperialist bourgeois and together with it fights against all revolutionary movements and revolutionary classes." To those who had studied the Iranian scene over the years a different interpretation seemed plausible. Here was a man who had risen to power because of his long defiance of the prevailing exercise of illegal and unconstitutional authority by the ruling elements of the country and who was now employing the same measures, which he had so often denounced, to cling to his own position. It is not suggested that Dr. Mossadeq had evil designs against his own country. Instead, he had become the victim of the lack of constructive goals within the framework of negative nationalism, and as his more moderate supporters fell away he took advice from those who felt that the traditional social order must be swept away before real changes could be accomplished. Besides, he may have believed that the time was not ripe for those freedoms he had long advocated: he may have thought, as did others, that chaotic conditions would have resulted.

Dr. Mossadeq entrenched his personal authority through a number of restrictive actions. In 1952, he made changes in the higher military command and in the assignment of army units in an effort to insure that the army would be directly responsible to him as minister of defense rather than to the Shah as its commander-in-chief. In November, the Majlis passed a bill providing for the dissolution of the newly inaugurated Second Senate, a body that was conservative in character, also, bills authorizing the confiscation of the property of Ahmad Qavam and calling for his prosecution as being responsible for the riots of July 19 and 20; and a bill pardoning and freeing the assassin of General Razmara on the grounds that the murdered man had been guilty of treason. This last-named law defies adequate condemnation, and yet it would not have been passed without the consent of Dr. Mossadeq.

Early in 1953, Dr. Mossadeq won an extension for an additional year of his plenary powers, after a bitter debate in the Majlis in which both Dr. Baghai and Sayyid Kashani criticized his exercise of dictatorial and unconstitutional powers. Soon thereafter, he put into effect a stringent press law, banned strikes by government employees and workers in public utilities, and had General Fazlullah Zahedi, a former member of his cabinet, arrested. On February 28, the first overt public opposition to Dr. Mossadeq broke out when supporters of the ruler, hearing that he had been asked by the prime minister to leave the country for some weeks, stormed his residence: Wearing gaily-striped pajamas, Mossadeq escaped up a ladder set against the back wall of his garden and went on, still in pajamas, to recount his experience to the Majlis.

By the end of June, 1953, Dr. Mossadeq had alienated most of the groups and more influential individuals who had flocked to join the National Front: Some merely withdrew from politics, while others became vocal opponents of his regime. Some were motivated by disappointment over lack of recognition of their services and of political rewards, others disapproved of the absence of a constructive program, while still others objected to the measures taken by Dr. Mossadeq to concentrate all authority in his hands. These elements included Sayyid Kashani; the Devotees of Islam, which had turned against Kashani and Mossadeq in the spring of 1951; Husein Makki; Dr. Baghai and his Toilers' Party; and the Sumka and Pan-Iran parties. Other restrictions and actions had included the prolongation of martial law, the arrest of newspaper editors and of opponents of the regime, the banning of papers, the dismissal of the Supreme Court, the forced retirement of government officials and military commanders thought to be unsympathetic to the regime, and the requirement that citizens and foreigners traveling in the oil-producing areas obtain special passes and permits.

On June 18, Kashani, then president of the Majlis, accused the government of acting in defiance of the constitution and of staging demonstrations in order to terrorize those opposed to the regime. As a result, on July 1, a more pliable supporter of Dr. Mossadeq was chosen in Kashani's place.

In these months, Dr. Mossadeq continued to assert that the Iranian nation was not left alone to face a hostile world, since his government enjoyed the support of the United States. On the other hand, in a message addressed to the American Government he indicated that the country might fall to the Communists unless massive financial aid was supplied by the United States. By this time the financial situation of Iran was extremely critical, but in June, President Eisenhower informed Dr. Mossadeq that the United States was not prepared to extend additional aid or to purchase Iranian oil until some agreement had been achieved.

What proved to be the final stage of the regime began with the decision of Dr. Mossadeq to do away with the Majlis. That body still contained a few individuals who were outspokenly critical of his policies and actions and who still enjoyed immunity from the stringent measures of control already described. Between July 14 and 16, the thirty-one deputies of the National Front resigned from the Majlis, allegedly because of the "vicious atmosphere" prevailing in that body. Their resignation meant that the Majlis could no longer conduct business, since it could not muster a quorum. Although this action left Dr. Mossadeq free to govern by decree, he was not satisfied. Following a huge demonstration, stage-managed by the Tudeh Party, commemorating the riots of the previous July 20 and the fall of Qavam, on July 27 he addressed the nation by radio, charging that the presence in the Majlis of deputies opposed to him made it the center of anti-government subversion and appealing to the people to vote for its dissolution. His speech followed a decree of July 25, which provided for a referendum on the question of whether or not the Majlis should be dissolved. Kashani attacked this decree on the grounds that it was unconstitutional, which it certainly was, and placed a religious boycott on the referendum. The voting, carried out between August 3 and 10, was alleged to have resulted in 99.93 per cent of the ballots in favor of dissolution. Considering the variety and extent of the opposition to Dr. Mossadeq, it may be questioned whether the voting was any freer than in the elections that he had so long condemned: as an innovation, separate booths were provided for those casting affirmative and negative ballots.

However, the political situation had so evolved that no clear pattern of future events was discernible. Did Mossadeq expect to continue to govern by decree? Would he ask the Shah, who alone had such authority, to call for new elections, and, if so, would the Ruler who alone had the constitutional authority to dissolve the Majlis and the Senate, respond? Some of his associates, and notably Dr. Fatemi, by this time minister of foreign affairs, spread the word that a second referendum would be held on the question of whether or not the monarchy should give way to a republic—a republic with Dr. Mossadeq as its president. Then, to complicate the situation, the prime minister had not as yet issued his decree dissolving the Majlis, so that, although repudiated, it still had legal existence.

On August 13, the Shah, then resident at Ramsar on the Caspian coast, issued two imperial decrees: one dismissed Dr. Mossadeq and the other named General Fazlullah Zahedi, then in hiding, as prime minister. On the night of August 15 and in the early hours of the next day, an officer of the Imperial Guard, subsequently arrested, presented the decree of dismissal at the house of Dr. Mossadeq and obtained his own receipt of its delivery, while several members of the government and of the National Front were briefly detained by detachments of the Imperial Guard. On the morning of August 16, Radio Tehran broadcast a brief item about the collapse of an attempted military *coup d'état*, while Mossadeq, meeting with his cabinet to discuss counteraction and to issue a decree dissolving the Majlis, said nothing about his dismissal. That afternoon, the news that the Shah and his queen had gone by air to Baghdad was announced at a mass meeting of National Front supporters by Dr. Fatemi. Crowds assembled by the Tudeh Party shouted for the death of the Shah and the end of the dynasty and streamed through the streets smashing windows in order to seize and tear up pictures of the ruler.

On August 17, Dr. Fatemi employed his paper, *Bakhtar Emruz*, to pour out a flood of abuse against the ruler. Mobs pulled down statues of the two Pahlavi rulers, and the Tudeh Party called for the establishment of a democratic people's republic. The following day the cabinet met to discuss the appointment of a regency council and to plan for the republic-to-be, and the government used force to break up Tudeh Party demonstrations that threatened to get out of hand. By afternoon, copies of opposition papers containing reproductions of the imperial decrees and the text of a statement from Zahedi that he was prime minister were circulating from hand to hand, and the first demonstrators in favor of the monarchy appeared on the streets.

As August 19 dawned, bands of people began to move from the poorer, southern quarters of Tehran toward the center of the capital shouting "Long live the Shah." Instead of opposing their movement, the police and soldiers joined with the ever-increasing throngs, which ransacked all the newspaper offices and other headquarters associated with the National Front. Supporters of the ruler turned on the headlights of cars and trucks, and a column of these vehicles drove to the north of the town to take over the station of Radio Tehran. By early afternoon the station came on the air with news of the overthrow of the illegal government, and somewhat later General Zahedi was heard. A heavily armed unit loyal to Dr. Mossadeq put up strong resistance at his house, and once again he fled over the garden wall. On August 22, the Shah flew from Rome to Tehran and received an overwhelming public welcome.

In November, 1953, Dr. Mossadeq was brought before a military court and charged with rebellion against the constitution by abusing his plenary powers to abrogate constitutional processes and basic laws and by his refusal to accede to the imperial decree dismissing him from office. Dr. Mossadeq was in fine fettle at the trial, displaying no feelings of guilt or remorse, and alternately challenging the competence of the court and displaying a total lack of interest in the proceedings. Prior to the verdict of the court—the prosecutor had asked for a sentence of death—

the ruler issued a statement recognizing the prisoner's earlier services to the country, and in the end he was sentenced to three years' imprisonment. Since 1956, he has been living quietly on one of his own estates.

Explanations for the failure and dismissal of Mossadeq have come from a variety of sources. Soviet authors have written that Dr. Mossadeq feared his own people and had recourse to police measures in order to suppress the masses that had risen in the struggle for the complete liberation of their country. According to the Soviet view, the oil issue itself was not of major importance. What was of real meaning was the movement toward a realignment of the foreign policy of the country away from the imperialist powers in the direction of the democratic countries and the democratic transformation of the country. The Tudeh Party agitated for these goals and in the last days of Mossadeq's power called for a united front to destroy all the nests of conspirators following the flight of the Shah, the number-one agent of imperialism. Regardless of this Soviet reconstruction, acting upon its own, or in response to Soviet direction, on August 16 and 17 the Tudeh Party both overestimated its strength and misjudged the temper of the populace. In overturning the statues of the ruler and his father, in instigating riots against the monarchy, and in insisting upon the immediate proclamation of a republic, it brought on a counterreaction. Had it bided its time and had Mossadeq been willing or able to keep Dr. Fatemi under control, the people and the members of the armed forces might not have been forced to make a choice between the monarchy and some uncertain future.

To the faithful adherents of the National Front, Dr. Mossadeq is still the legal prime minister of Iran. Not vocal on the question of what he would have done had he remained in office, they condemn his dismissal as an illegal military *coup d'état*. Drawing upon material published in the United States in magazine articles and a book, they claim that his overthrow was inspired and planned by the United States Government. Muhammad Reza Shah has given his own answer to these charges in his autobiography, which describes in detail the hectic August days, alludes to charges that Americans and British made payments to opponents of Mossadeq, and musters the evidence in support of a popular uprising against the negative policies of Mossadeq, and in favor of the institution of the monarchy.

Yet another explanation may be drawn not from rumors and speculation but from the current of events within Iran itself. In other countries of the Middle East where so-called nationalist governments have come recently to power, they have been able to whip up popular emotions against foreign intervention and influence over a fairly long period of time as they have directed attention to a series of targets. However, as we have seen, in Iran the nationalist revolution took place years earlier under Reza Shah, and the only surviving target, the Anglo-Iranian Oil Company, would have come under his attack in due time. Thus, Dr. Mossadeq was very limited in his opportunities for driving out the foreigners. Once rid of the oil company, what remained? He was not prepared to sever all ties with the West and to move toward the Communist bloc. All his life he had been opposed to the *status quo*, but the habit of opposition was so ingrained that he seemed unable to consider moving toward a positive position in which he would try to meet the criticism of his own opposition. To Dr. Mossadeq, the innovations inspired by the West—railroads, highways, and industry—and executed by Reza Shah had been disastrous to Iran. Living in the past, he continued to dream of the golden ages of ancient Iran when the country had nothing that foreign powers coveted and was so safe from exploitation.

2. INSTITUTIONS OF AUTHORITY

Muhammad Reza Shah: Advocate of Positive Nationalism

Muhammad Reza Shah has been the ruler of Iran for more than twenty years and yet he has never held his coronation ceremony. In these years he has gained in stature, risen slowly to a commanding role, and his personal views and actions continue to shape the future of the country. As the ruler he is confident and commanding; as a man he is beset by doubts, worries, and indecision. Exhilarated and despondent by turn, he shakes off his personal concerns and thinks first of all of the needs of Iran. It is difficult to believe that the country has ever had a ruler more sympathetic to the aspirations and desires of its people. Nowadays, it is customary to criticize individuals in high office: Muhammad Reza is so criticized by many of his compatriots, and yet without him on the throne the stability and integrity of Iran would certainly be in instant danger.

In reviewing his life and years on the throne, and in making an effort to trace his development, judge his actions, and describe his personality, a variety of sources are available. His own autobiography, *Mission for My Country*, is less valuable for this effort than would be supposed, since he chose to write the story of the country rather than his own. That account can, however, be supplemented with material contained in his speeches to the Parliament, his remarks at press conferences, the record of his actions in critical situations, his forthright statements to individuals, and his support of legislation related to economic development and social reform.

Born on October 26, 1919, he was the first son of Reza Khan and named Shapur Muhammad. He was six and a half years old when his father was crowned as Reza Shah Pahlavi. At this ceremony the solemn little boy, clad in a simple khaki uniform, entered the great hall of the Gulistan Palace ahead of all the dignitaries and took his stand beside the throne. From that day his father trained him with patient care and unceasing affection to become his successor. As he grew up this role did not come easily to him, for it entailed a conflict between the authoritarian attitude of his much admired father and the outlook toward life resulting from the schooling arranged by his father. His own personality seemed to complement that of Ashraf, his twin sister: Ashraf appeared to display the aggressiveness of Reza Shah, while Shapur Muhammad was of a more cautious and speculative frame of mind.

Soon after the coronation the Crown Prince began to attend an elementary military school, established for the purpose of educating him in company with some of his brothers and a few other boys. Fluency in French was acquired from his governess. In these years he was quite frail, beset not only by the common diseases of childhood, but also by critical attacks of typhoid fever and then of malaria. On the occasion of one of these serious illnesses he experienced the first of several mystical experiences:

dreams in which Muslim saints appeared to him. As he grew stronger he became very much interested in sports: at first in wrestling, boxing, and riding, and later on in tennis and in piloting planes.

In 1931 he was sent to Switzerland to school. Several months earlier Reza Shah had received a group of older students who were being sent to Europe by the government for technical education. He had informed them that they would receive the kind of moral education available in the West but not to be found in Iran and that he had decided to send his son abroad for the same reason.

Shapur Muhammad set off, accompanied by a brother and a few boys of his own age, a guardian-physician, and a Persian teacher. Four years were spent abroad, three of them at Le Rosey, a boarding school situated between Lausanne and Geneva. At the school he was very active in soccer, tennis, and track, and from his own account was an excellent student. However, school life was not always too pleasant. His classmates, as friendly to him as he was to them, were not impressed by having in their midst the crown prince of an unheard-of dynasty in some remote part of the world. While his studies were not too demanding, he was held in close check by his guardian and obliged to spend a large part of what should have been free time in lessons in the language and the literature of Persia. In addition, he sent weekly letters to his father who kept in close touch and brought up many questions that required answers. According to his own story, in these years the crown prince began to speculate as to how he would act as shah: foremost in his thoughts were possible ways of improving the condition of the peasants and of insuring social justice.

In April, 1936, he completed his studies at Le Rosey and started home on a circuitous route through Russia on orders from his father, who had been informed that there was a plot afoot to assassinate his son in Europe and so strike at the ruler himself. Reza Shah met him at the Caspian seaport of Pahlavi: the ruler, nearly always dignified and very reserved, shed tears of joy at seeing his son again.

That fall they set off together on a month-long inspection tour throughout western and central Iran. This first trip set the model for a number of others. Reza Shah explained his plans and projects in detail and asked for his son's opinions and advice, and when they were in the company of local officials quite frequently called his attention to certain characteristics, not always the most admirable ones, of Iranian behavior. From this time on, only his son could intervene with the ruler in favor of individuals in disgrace, and only he spoke to Reza Shah with complete frankness.

That same year, in accordance with his father's wish, Shapur Muhammad entered the Military College at Tehran. Two years later he was graduated first in his class with the rank of second lieutenant. However, during these same years there was opportunity for tours of inspection with the ruler, and he was with his father every day at lunch and at teatime for at least a half hour of private conversation. By this time numerous brothers and sisters were on the scene; the offspring of Reza Shah's second, third, and fourth marriages. His first wife, divorced many years earlier, had produced a daughter who was not at the court. Taj Malek, the queen mother who resided at the Gulistan Palace, was the mother of a daughter, Shams, of the twins Shapur Muhammad and Ashraf, and of 'Ali Reza. Turan, also divorced, had produced Gholam Reza, while Esmat, who lived in the magnificent Marble Palace built in Tehran by Reza Shah, had borne Abdur Reza, Ahmad Reza, Mahmud Reza, Hamid Reza, and a daughter, Fatima. According to Muslim law and custom, Reza Shah could have had as many as four wives at the same time, but he never achieved this maximum.

Prior to Reza Shah's coronation, the constitution of the country had been amended to bar from sucession to the throne any members of the former Qajar dynasty. Since both Turan and Esmat came from distinguished Qajar families, and because only males could succeed, only Shapur Muhammad and 'Ali Reza (killed in 1954 in a plane crash) were in line to the throne.

Groups of sycophants swarmed around this younger generation, urging them to indulge in sophisticated pleasures and dissolute practices, but Shapur Muhammad kept clear of these activities. It is fair to say that habits formed when these boys were in their teens were not easily discarded in later life. With the exception of Adbur Reza, who was later to be graduated from Har-

vard, none of the brothers of the crown prince displayed particular attention to princely duties and responsibilities. However,
they never had a chance to compete for the attention of the
ruler: the crown prince enjoyed a unique position and his seri-
ousness and sense of responsibility perfectly satisfied Reza Shah.

In May, 1938, the engagement of Fawzia, one of the daughters of King Fuad of Egypt, to Shapur Muhammad was announced. The match was arranged by Reza Shah, and it was
believed that he had some difficulty in winning the consent of
the ruler of Egypt to the alliance. The following March, the
crown prince went to Egypt to meet the prospective bride and
her parents, and in April, 1939, the couple came to Tehran, to a
capital gaily decorated with triumphal arches. With the length-
ening shadows of tension in Europe the spirit in Tehran had been
somber, and the sudden atmosphere of festivity was most welcome. In 1940, the only issue of the couple, a daughter, Shahnaz,
was born.

On the outbreak of World War II, Iran had declared its
neutrality but was beset by pressures from the major parties to
the conflict, and the war itself caused the economic situation of
the country to deteriorate. Soon, the British and Soviet governments were insisting that all Germans and other Axis nationals
be expelled from Iran. By August, 1941, at a time when diplomatic notes on the subject were still being exchanged, the Allies
had determined upon the occupation of Iran in order to deny
the area to advancing German armies and to provide a protected
supply route to the Soviet Union. At the end of the month they
struck, the Russians from the north and the British from the west
and south, and the army of which Reza Shah was so proud
quickly succumbed.

As these forces approached Tehran, radio stations under their
control put out bitter attacks on the person of Reza Shah. Although he would have suffered anything to remain in Iran, the
ruler realized that the Allies would be unwilling to make any
accommodation with him and that he must act promptly in order to preserve the succession for his son. On September 16 he
left Tehran for Isfahan, sending back a letter of abdication,
which entreated the nation to recognize his heir and legal successor and to follow him for the improvement of the country's

affairs. On the following day, September 17, 1941, Shapur Muhammad took the oath of office as Muhammad Reza in the presence of the Majlis.

In the following days there were a number of speeches and statements from the throne, all prepared or recommended by elder statesman Muhammad 'Ali Foroughi, which were designed to assure the public that they were in no peril and that food supplies were ample, to display the Shah's personal concern for the country, and to indicate that a new era of political and public freedoms had begun. Muhammad Reza declared that the properties inherited from his father would be devoted to the welfare of the nation, and he issued a decree of amnesty to all political prisoners. As an officer suddenly promoted to the post of commander-in-chief of the country's armed forces, he continued to rely upon the generals who had served his father, but he established personal contacts with countless officers, defended the interests of the army against the Majlis, and labored to increase his familiarity with modern armaments and his knowledge of strategy and tactics.

The years of World War II were very difficult ones for Iran. Bread, meat, and other staples were in short supply, largely on account of the requirements of the British, Russian, and American service units which had streamed into the country to operate the supply route from the Persian Gulf to the Soviet Union. The removal of the stern authority of Reza Shah had predictable results: a resurgence of the influence of the religious leaders who advocated a return of women to the veil; an outbreak of highway robbery and a series of tribal uprisings; and a general weakening of effective administration and legislation by the government itself.

The cabinets of the war years and those immediately following were made up of the same men who had held these posts under Reza Shah. Most of them were competent administrators, skilled at compromise and the reconciliation of conflicting interests and little given to initiative. The Thirteenth Majlis was composed of individuals whose elections had been approved by Reza Shah; they demonstrated their own new freedom by endeavoring to establish control over the cabinets. Consistently, the Majlis put forward its choices for the office of prime minister and then failed to support any of them for extended periods. This Majlis and its successors failed to display any sense of urgency with respect to pending legislation; its members formed blocs in support of mutual interests, and the sudden appearance of a number of political parties enhanced its general lack of cohesiveness.

In 1942, the Iranian Government concluded a Tripartite Treaty of Alliance with Great Britain and the Soviet Union, urged to this action by the occupying powers and hoping by compliance to obtain future benefits. Clauses of the treaty included respect for the territorial integrity and political independence of Iran, an offer to ease the economic dislocations caused by the impact of the war, and a statement that the forces in occupation would be withdrawn within six months after the end of the war. At the end of November, 1943, Roosevelt, Churchill, and Stalin arrived to attend the Tehran Conference: the twenty-four-year-old ruler met privately with each of these heads of state and was not hesitant in pressing for the interests of his country. The resulting Tehran Declaration again reaffirmed the political integrity of Iran and stated that the three powers would give consideration to the economic problems of the country after the termination of hostilities.

Through his experience gained at the time of the Tehran Conference, the young ruler was plunged directly into the field of diplomatic relations. According to the constitution, the foreign relations of the country were the responsibility of the cabinet and the minister of foreign affairs, but since the heads of the Allied nations had made direct contact with Muhammad Reza they set a precedent which was to be followed in the later years of his reign. In joining the Tripartite Treaty and in subsequent declarations of war on Germany and Japan, Iran had swung sharply away from its traditional policy of neutrality. Obviously, the earlier policy had failed to avert the occupation of the country by foreign troops in both the world wars, and the ruler himself felt that the future integrity of Iran depended upon the conclusion of positive alliances.

Up until the time of World War II, the American presence in Iran had been apparent only in the welcome activity of mission schools and hospitals and in the official activities of a very small legation. Now Muhammad Reza and members of the government began to look for ways to attract the active attention and concern of the United States, to make friends with this third great power which could serve as a counterbalance to the traditional rivalry of the British and Russians in Iran. Even before the end of the war, the Shah was aware that the Soviet designs against Iran would threaten its very existence and believed that only close ties with other powers would enable his country to stand up to this aggressor.

During the war years his actions were those of a constitutional monarch: he continued to reassert his faith in democracy and traveled throughout the country, meeting people of all classes of society. In this faith he found little encouragement and support from his associates. Ranking military officers, long associated with his father, urged him to intervene against the dilatory Majlis and the ineffectual cabinets. He realized, however, that such steps would serve to alarm the occupying powers and possibly draw stronger interference in internal affairs.

His family and the entourage of the court gave him little constructive support. Queen Fawzia appeared bored at public functions, found the limited pleasures of a wartime capital disappointing, and was not an ideal companion. The numerous families of his brothers and sisters had attracted a large and very mixed circle of hangers-on whose members attempted to solidify their positions and to win appropriate rewards by activities that were anything but constructive. If Muhammad Reza had it in him to become a royal playboy, the change would have occurred at this time.

However, driven by the sense of personal responsibility so strongly inculcated by his father, he kept at his duties and built up a clearer understanding of the merits and the faults of his people. His opinions have been rather sketchily given in some of the writings and speeches: his limited description of the people's demerits may be compared with the account of the Iranian character given in an earlier chapter. Muhammad Reza became aware that the Iranians were not given to self-appraisal, to planning to overcome recognizable obstacles, and to forceful action as an antidote to lethargy. He realized that the traditional system of obtaining results through fear of punishment rather than by promises of rewards was so deeply ingrained that it could be altered only slowly. He stated openly that the matter of personal honesty was one of the country's most formidable problems and that a powerful minority were only too willing to enrich themselves at the expense of their compatriots. He was aware of the negative attitudes of politicians and civilians alike and castigated the propensity of some elements for spreading malicious and false rumors.

As his personal power and prestige slowly increased, he was to institute actions and programs aimed at changing these destructive attitudes. Events offered him increased opportunities to emerge from the shadow of his father. The first of these events came in December, 1946.

In 1945, during their occupation of northern Iran, the Soviets had brought into being two puppet states: the Kurdish Republic of Mahabad, and the regime in Azerbaijan directed by its Democratic Party. Soviet authorities then refused to allow units of the Iranian Army to enter the areas that were in open revolt against the central government. Then, in March, 1946, the U.S.S.R. failed to withdraw its forces from Iran by that agreed-upon date, although all British and American units had departed earlier. Iran brought the issue to the Security Council of the United Nations, and in May the Soviet troops were withdrawn. In retrospect, it seems apparent that the Soviet leaders were certain that their two autonomous states had so consolidated their holds that they could resist normal pressures from the central government, while through diplomatic channels the U.S.S.R. could keep the Iranian Government from sending troops to these areas.

However, early in December the Shah himself surveyed the insurgent defense positions from the air and then ordered regular forces to move on Tabriz. In response to an urgent request, he granted an audience to the Soviet ambassador who demanded that these forces be recalled: The suddenly embarrassed caller was informed that all resistance had ended and that scores of Soviet-trained agents and Communists were in full flight toward the Russian frontier.

The recovery of Azerbaijan was warmly celebrated throughout the country with public recognition of the ruler's role in the action; and the success of his bold decision seems to have encouraged him to undertake a broader interpretation of his constitutional powers.

During a period of time, he initiated a series of actions relating to the privileges and functioning of the Majlis, including measures designed to end its monopoly over legislation and to cut down its control over the cabinet. He also sought to exercise a measure of influence over the legislation enacted and to gain permission to dissolve the Majlis for stated reasons. Muhammad Reza was well aware that his father had selected the deputies to be elected and that the government still disposed of the means, through the Ministry of the Interior and the military commanders in the provinces, to influence the results of any elections. It seems reasonable to believe that he lacked confidence in the caliber of the deputies and felt that the body required supervision and direction and that completely free elections would not improve the quality and effectiveness of the chamber.

One of his actions concerned the manner in which prime ministers were selected. Reza Shah had chosen his prime ministers who, along with their cabinets, were then confirmed by the Majlis. After his abdication the Majlis reverted to the method in effect prior to 1926, a system in which the deputies discussed the merits of various candidates, then voted on the candidates and sent the name of the individual who had received the most votes to the Shah for his royal appointment. Before long, Muhammad Reza began to indicate to groups of deputies the person whom he favored for the post, and in 1950 he acted independently in naming General Razmara to the post. Since the removal of Dr. Mossadeq he has continued to select prime ministers, who then present themselves to the Senate and the Majlis for a vote of confidence. In so acting, he has not violated the constitution, which is more than a little vague on this subject, stating only that the cabinet ministers are named and dismissed by royal decree.

Another of his measures was the convening of the Senate. This chamber had been provided for in the constitution, with legislative powers similar to those of the Majlis, but it had never been formed. In 1949, the Senate was established, and its initial session was opened in 1950. Half of its sixty-man body comprises appointees of the shah, the rest are chosen by elections in two stages. In general, elderly conservative men who are personally loyal to the ruler make up the bulk of its membership, while its right of veto over bills enacted by the Majlis serves to protect the country from legislation inappropriate for Iran. The term "inappropriate" is taken to include laws that would be contrary to the principles of Islam, or that had been inspired by the enemies of Iran, the Communists.

As recently as 1957, an amendment to the constitution provided for an increase in the number of deputies in the Majlis from 136 to 200 and extended the term of each Majlis from two to four years. It also gave the ruler power to withhold his assent to bills passed by both houses; however, these bills could come into effect if three-quarters of the membership of both chambers voted in favor of the legislation. And, most important, the amendment gave Muhammad Reza the power to dissolve both the Majlis and the Senate. In his own words he commented: "I must state my reasons for doing so, may not give the same reason twice, and I must immediately call for fresh elections so that the new chamber or chambers may convene within a space of three months." These words are not without significance, since the provisions mentioned were violated in 1961.

In presenting this brief outline of the Shah's actions concerning the Parliament, the chronology of events has been neglected. In February, 1949, a would-be assassin, conveniently equipped with a press card, fired five revolver shots at the ruler at point-blank range. One inflicted a very slight wound on his face; the others tore through his uniform. Escaping certain death, Muhammad Reza felt that his preservation represented the second in a series of miracles, the first of which had been the recovery of the province of Azerbaijan, and he became convinced that he was under divine protection to accomplish a mission for his country. The immediate aftermath of the assassination attempt was the banning of the Tudeh Party of Iran, an action which did much to restore internal tranquility and security.

Near the end of 1949, the Shah made his first state visit to the United States, alone, because Fawzia, who had gone to Egypt and had not returned, had been divorced in 1948. As on the occasion of subsequent visits, Muhammad Reza pressed for economic and military aid and stressed the need for modern planes and tanks. In this first effort he was unsuccessful and left in a very discouraged mood; in later representations he emphasized the point that Iran received much less favorable treatment from the United States than was extended to its neighbor, Turkey.

In 1950, he inaugurated the Sixteenth Majlis and the First Senate. He spoke to these bodies about corruption within the government and demanded that it be eliminated. That June, he named General 'Ali Razmara as prime minister. An able military administrator who had been chief of staff of the armed forces, this "tactician"—the meaning of his name—was out of his depth in the arena of politics and was unable to come up with a strategy capable of slowing the rising tide of nationalism. Within a year he was assassinated by a fanatic.

In the early months of Razmara's tenure of office the Shah had ordered the establishment of the Imperial Anti-Corruption Commission, and before long it compiled a report which included a rather lengthy list of corrupt government officials. Soon the names on this list became known, and the influential individuals concerned raised such an outcry that the report was quickly tabled. Before long, some of these same individuals were back in high posts within the government, and the ruler sought more effective ways of achieving his objective.

As 1951 opened, the ruler made known his intention of distributing the agricultural properties inherited from his father, and in February he married Soraya Esfandiari, daughter of an important leader of the Bakhtiari tribe and of a German mother.

During the period from April 29, 1951, until August 19, 1953, Dr. Muhammad Mossadeq was prime minister and along with his other activities, waged a steady campaign against the monarchy and against the ruler who had befriended him some years earlier. Certainly his eventual goal was to establish a republic of Iran, and he moved toward that goal by undermining the royal powers and encouraging public disrespect of the Shah. The initial move against the imperial prerogatives occurred in July, 1952, when Dr. Mossadeq took over the post of minister of national defense. Previously, the Shah himself had always selected this minister, naming individuals who were personally loyal to him and who reported directly to him on all matters concerning the armed forces. Now Mossadeq was able to insure that reports came directly to him rather than to the ruler, and he removed numerous ranking officers from their posts and replaced them with men who he believed would be loyal to him rather than to the monarch. Efforts were made to undermine the loyalty of the soldiers themselves to the monarch; for example, the traditional ceremony of swearing allegiance to the shah was abolished.

In February, 1953, Dr. Mossadeq suggested to the ruler that it would help ease internal tensions if the latter would leave the country for some time. Possibly he felt that events would so develop as to militate against the ruler's return, but he had misjudged public sentiment. As soon as word of the impending trip leaked out, numbers of royalists attacked the prime minister's residence, forcing him to flee over the back wall of his garden. Not content to let matters develop more slowly, he suggested that a committee of the Majlis be appointed to investigate rumors of dissension between the court and the prime minister. It seems probable that Dr. Mossadeq expected the committee to produce a report that would castigate royal interference in the conduct of government. Instead, the report was moderate in tone, making the point that the shah was nonaccountable, and that the ministers of the government had the sole responsibility for making and executing decisions concerning affairs of state; the Majlis declined to debate the report.

Then, in April, 1953, Dr. Mossadeq forced the resignation of the minister of court, a highly experienced and respected elder statesman, and put in his place one of his own followers who was personally unwelcome to Muhammad Reza. Soon thereafter, Mossadeq halted the distribution of the Shah's estates. On July 25 came the referendum in which numbers of people voted for the dissolution of the Seventeenth Majlis, and reports circulated throughout Tehran that a second referendum would be held in the near future on the question of whether or not the monarchy should be replaced by a republic.

Finally, on August 13, Muhammad Reza issued imperial decrees dismissing Mossadeq and naming General Fazlullah Zahedi as prime minister. Why had the ruler waited so long to react to the prime minister's campaign against the monarchy and to the rapidly deteriorating political and economic situations? According to the autobiography of the ruler, he had wanted to give Dr.

Mossadeq every opportunity to secure national aims, and he had acted only when it was apparent that the prime minister was unable to formulate constructive policies and programs. However, facets of the Shah's personality may have been involved in the long delay in reaching this decision. Earlier he had acted promptly and boldly within his legal powers when confronted with clear-cut issues, such as the occasion when he sent troops to recover Azerbaijan. However, when issues and problems were less sharply defined he had been inclined to vacillate. On the one hand, he listened to many advisers and associates who advocated conflicting courses of action: confronted with multiple choices it seemed easier to resort to inaction. On the other, he may have felt that a direct showdown would plunge the country into warring camps and that there would be no real winner. His moods in this time of crisis shifted from confidence in popular support to discouragement and doubt, and the decision to dismiss Mossadeq came only after he could see no other alternative.

On August 22, Muhammad Reza and Soraya returned to Tehran to an exuberant public welcome. Deeply moved by the popular uprising in support of the monarchy and by this reception, the Shah was convinced that he had been granted a national mandate to take personal charge of the country's destiny, to supervise the actions of the cabinet and, finally, to rule rather than reign. In the months that followed he placed stress on this new role, personally outlining programs of economic development and social reform. Taking pride in being the only monarch in the world to hold press conferences, he met journalists once a month and answered any and all questions. The prime ministers became responsible to him; so much so that one of them informed the Majlis that he was the servant of His Majesty. In the field of foreign relations he assumed full responsibility and deliberately aligned Iran with the Western powers.

His actions and statements were related to an over-all program which he began to describe, about 1957, as positive nationalism. Certainly this term came to his mind as the antithesis of the negative equilibrium of Dr. Mossadeq. Muhammad Reza has defined positive nationalism as maximum political and economic independence consistent with national interests. In the field of foreign relations, it does not imply passive neutrality; rather, enlightened self-interest. It includes all public freedoms, with the exception of liberty for traitors, subversives, and demagogues to attempt to destroy the nation, and it places emphasis upon social justice and planned economic progress. In his writing and his public remarks the Shah has illustrated the practical application of positive nationalism to internal goals and to relations with other countries, but it seems fair to say that the term has not caught the public imagination. As political theory it does not identify itself with such familiar "isms" as capitalism or socialism. Emphasizing the need for constructive effort, it lacks emotional appeal, and the sceptical Iranians fail to identify themselves with specific aspects of the rather generalized program. The program requires a rational response and a willingness to believe that progress is being made toward its goals. The opponents of the regime are unwilling to view it in any of the above terms and insist that its promises and guarantees are violated in the conduct of government.

In 1957, the ruler took action in several fields related to his program. He favored the creation of the National Iranian Security Organization. Disregarding the position of the United States and the United Kingdom that Iran should not conclude arrangements for the exploitation of the oil resources of the country on a scale other than that embodied in the consortium agreement, he advocated the conclusion of agreements with joint companies representing Iranian and foreign interests that would agree to return 75 per cent of their profits to the Iranian Government.

He sponsored the formation of two new political parties, the Melliyun, or Nationalist, Party, and the Mardum, or People's, Party. The first of these was headed by the then prime minister, Dr. Manuchehr Eqbal, and the second by Asadullah Alam, a large landowner and long-time associate of the ruler. Muhammad Reza stated that the government must be supported by a majority party in the Majlis, which was the Melliyun Party, while the Mardum Party was to fulfill the functions of a loyal opposition, free to criticize the internal policies of the government but not the conduct of foreign affairs. The ruler realized the problems inherent in creating parties of principles by fiat but insisted that a start had to be made and that in time each group would attract an active following and gradually assume the role of a truly democratic and responsible party. However, the experiment did not develop as he had hoped, possibly because parties of principle evolve from parties of interest and the personal interests of the members of these fledgling parties were not deeply involved in their success or failure.

The closing months of 1957 and the early ones of 1958 were a very trying period for the Shah. Soraya had proven to be a very sympathetic, charming companion and a tower of strength in the last months of the Mossadeq period, including the days when the couple were out of the country in August, 1953, but she had not produced children. In March, 1958, the subject of the marriage was finally discussed by high officials and elder statesmen in the presence of the ruler, and it was agreed that the future of the hereditary monarchy depended upon the designation of a crown prince who was a direct descendant of Muhammad Reza. This sentiment was conveyed to Soraya, then in Europe, who immediately agreed to a divorce.

In April, 1958, the ruler established the Bonyad-i-Pahlavi, or the Pahlavi Foundation, as a philanthropic organization. Resources of the crown, other than agricultural lands, were turned over to the foundation, and the income was to be expended for public health, education, and social services. These resources included a number of hotels, and shares in the ownership of local industrial enterprises, the National Insurance Company, and the growing tanker fleet of the country.

In the fall of the year, Muhammad Reza set up the Imperial Investigation Organization to receive and review complaints from any member of the public against civil and military officials, the courts, local administrations, and any other branches of the government. Within a period of nine months this organization had received some 39,000 complaints. In cases considered justified, requests for corrective action were sent to the agencies involved and were followed up to see that they were not neglected.

In the same months, the ruler spoke again and again of the need for more effective action against corruption and in favor of land reform. Later, he was to say that the Iraq revolution was mostly due to the failure of the former Iraqi regimes to introduce land reforms.

His insistence that corruption must be curbed resulted in the drafting of two bills passed by the Parliament. In January, 1959, the first of them became law: it was entitled "A Law Prohibiting Cabinet Ministers, Members of the Parliament, and Officials of the Government from Taking Part in Transactions with the Government." Such transactions were defined in detail, and the law covered not only the officials and deputies themselves, but their fathers, mothers, brothers, sisters, wives, fiancees, and direct descendants. As an immediate reaction, some members of the Parliament and the administration resigned. In March, the Parliament passed the bill entitled "A Law Regarding the Possessions of Officials," which soon became known as the "Where did you get it?" law. According to its terms, all officials were required to complete forms listing all their properties and possessions, and in each successive year they were required to report any changes in their holdings and those of their wives and children. It was believed that such detailed records would constitute a file of material to support legal action against individuals abusing their posts. Certainly a monumental stack of paper resulted, but within a year some 2,595 officials had been brought before the courts and then dismissed from government service.

In December, 1959, the Shah married twenty-one-year-old Farah Diba, and the following months were ones of eager anticipation. On October 31, 1960, the Empress Farah gave birth to Crown Prince Reza. Muhammad Shah was overjoyed and in high spirits for months after the event. The entire country expressed enthusiasm; only the U.S.S.R. seemed displeased, and Soviet radio stations spread malicious rumors about the circumstances of the royal birth.

By 1960, the ruler's domination of the government was so all-embracing that one of his prime ministers announced to the Majlis that he could not take a position on an issue because he had not received imperial instructions. In moving to this position, the Shah had not negated any of the clauses of the constitution, and he could say that the officials of the government were not required to carry out his expressed wishes. However, his leadership was not broadly welcomed and supported by large segments of the public. Unlike the man from Missouri who believes in only what he can see with his own eyes, the Iranians did not believe their eyes when enterprises of many types came into being around them, and they continued to lack faith in the good will of the government and in its concern with public aspirations. Since the ruler had made it clear that he was directing the course of affairs, resentment was directed against his person. As long as Muhammad Reza had reigned, he had retained his position of nonaccountability. When he began to rule he lost this nonaccountability, and it became easy to blame the ruler himself, as distinct from the institution of the monarchy, for real or fancied shortcomings of the government. What does this mean in specific terms? Dr. Mossadeq was overthrown because the public chose to support the institution of the monarchy rather than to embark upon a course in which this ancient institution was to be discarded. The public rallied to the support of the institution and only incidentally to the man on the throne. However, at the present time a new crisis would force public choice between the person of the ruler, rather than the institution of the monarchy, and another alternative. The longer the Shah rules, the more he bears the brunt of dissatisfaction with the shortcomings of the government and it becomes less certain that he would again receive popular support in a time of decision.

A turning point in the affairs of the country came with the elections of 1960, which were cancelled and then repeated early in 1961, when it became apparent that the Melliyun and Mardum parties were not truly representative of important elements of the population and that the customary pattern of arranged elections had prevailed. Not only were there rather widespread protests against the results of these elections, but the ruler himself decided that a new approach was required.

In May, 1961, the Shah named Dr. 'Ali Amini, a person who had vehemently expressed his opposition to the conduct of the elections, as prime minister. This action was not a routine appointment in the pattern of the preceding years, but, rather, represented a distinct departure. Dr. Amini insisted, and the

Shah agreed, that his government was to execute the policies advocated by the ruler, but it was also to make its own decisions and be directly accountable for its success or failure. The implications were that the Shah would retire to a position of reigning, but at the same time the Amini Government would be on trial and would be replaced if it failed to make good. Immediately, this government devoted major attention to two of the Shah's primary concerns: land reform and the elimination of corruption.

Although the Shah had moved toward a position of non-accountability, he remained subject to criticism. In dissolving the Parliament in May, 1961, he neither gave his reason for the action nor issued the mandatory decrees for elections to bring new houses into being within three months. The question of these postponed elections remained a major source of discussion and dissension on the Iranian scene.

Private criticism of the ruler extended to his personal participation and that of his brothers and sisters in commercial and industrial enterprises, allegedly because such activities were not proper ones for a royal family and because they were said to involve pressures and influences originating in the court. Partly in response to this feeling and partly because of his own convictions, in October, 1961, Muhammad Reza severed all personal connection with the Pahlavi Foundation and named an independent board of directors to administer the assets, valued at some $130 million, of the foundation.

In the field of education he took the initiative in the creation of the Pahlavi University, established in 1961 under an independent board of trustees. Situated in Shiraz, the growing institution is to stress American-style education as opposed to the French model of Tehran University. Its charter and manual of organization were drawn up by an advisory commission from an American university. The ruler hopes that the university will develop as the intellectual center of the nation in an atmosphere free from public and private pressures and political agitation.

In April, 1962, Muhammad Reza and Farah made a state visit to the United States. In public he was frank in presenting his country's problems, in stressing its identification with the free world, and enthusiastic about its future: He received an excellent press. In private he took part in meetings with President Kennedy and high civil and military officials: It was reported that he was pleased with assurances that the United States Government had not modified its policy toward Iran, and that there was agreement on a joint program to streamline the armed forces of Iran and to reduce the costs of maintenance.

Then, very suddenly, Prime Minister Amini resigned, and in selecting Asadullah Alam to fill the post the ruler indicated that, for the time being at least, he was reassuming personal responsibility for the direction of the government.

By 1963, Muhammad Reza could honestly feel that he had made significant advances toward his announced goals. He had divested himself of all the properties inherited from his father; no longer a monarch of great wealth, he had become largely dependent for income upon the amounts allotted to the imperial court in the annual budgets of the government. He had managed to concentrate the attention of the government and the public upon the problems of corruption and land reform. He continued to assert his faith in the people of Iran, describing them as members of a pure, worthy race, people who are intelligent, good, deserving of liberty, and almost 100 per cent patriotic.

In spite of all his good intentions, his deeds and his words have failed to capture the enthusiasm of such important segments of society as the ardent nationalists, the urban middle class, and the rising generation of the well educated. He remains subject to vicious personal attacks by Soviet radio stations, and these attacks have had some impact upon his people who are so attached to destructive rumor. His statements and his program are rationally conceived and presented, perhaps on too high a plane for the audience to whom he appeals to work hard in the interests of the nation. Although a man of pronounced personality, he has not so acted and behaved as to give rise to the colorful stories and legends associated with his father. He has moved away from the traditional image of the *shahanshah*—the awesome figure who exercises harsh discipline and grants few favors—and the milder, more benevolent image he has tried to create may or may not become increasingly understood by his countrymen.

*The Agencies of Authority: The Cabinet, the Bureaucracy, the
Parliament and Political Parties, Savak, and the Armed Forces*

Nearly all well-educated Iranians, and some who are not, are
potential politicians, and nearly all the active politicians look
forward to the time when their abilities shall be so widely recognized that they become prime ministers of Iran. This ambition
represents the ultimate goal of the personally motivated Iranian.
Since the turnover of prime ministers is very high, many individuals have achieved their ambition. However, considering the
vocal abuse they suffer while in office, the ever-present possibility of assassination, and the fact that few ex-prime ministers
are regarded as national heroes, an outsider does not find it easy
to understand why the post is so ardently desired.

Potential candidates for the office naturally emphasize their
special qualifications. Ahmad Qavam cultivated the image of
the shrewd manipulator, able to balance off a variety of competing forces; General 'Ali Razmara appeared as the expert in
administration who could get things done in a hurry; Dr. Manuchehr Eqbal posed as the enlightened intellectual, devoted to
the wishes of the shah; and, Dr. 'Ali Amini came to the fore as
the enemy of corruption and of the ruling families. In addition
to candidates from a younger generation, a group of somnolent
elder statesmen, experienced in the game of musical chairs, waits
in the wings ready to serve the country *faute de mieux*.

The prime minister wields considerable power, and in recent
years each tenant of the office has had to make up his mind
whether to conduct business as usual or to strike out in an effort
to gather supreme authority into his hands. Each prime minister must tread delicately along the path of his relations with the
shah, and each searches for ways to build up a personal following within the Parliament, among officials, and in private circles.
Even the individual most dedicated to reforms finds that he must
make deals with opponents of reform lest he be out of office before he has implemented any part of his program.

Nearly every prime minister hopes to bring into being a political party that will be loyal to him: Ahmad Qavam created the
party of the Democrats of Iran in 1946 only to have it turn
against him; Dr. Eqbal placed his hope of survival in the Mel-

liyun Party; and as early as 1953, when the fever for high office was beginning to work in the veins of Dr. Amini, he planned to "rally into one political party supporting his government all the middle-of-the-road elements, including the right fringe of the leftists and the left fringe of the rightists."

The prime minister, named by the shah, selects cabinet members to head the ministries of the government: he may retain one or more of these posts and may name additional ministers of state. He then submits his cabinet and his program to the Parliament for a vote of confidence. Initially, this vote is always favorable, but soon the Parliament becomes increasingly critical of the cabinet. The cabinet draws up proposed legislation and the Majlis and the Senate refer the proposals to committees; thus the passage of legislation proceeds at a slow pace.

The prime minister may endeavor to persuade the Parliament to move more rapidly; this tactic is most effective when the shah lends his influence to the effort. Frequently he is successful in obtaining special powers—either from the Parliament itself, as in the case of Dr. Mossadeq, or from the shah, as in the case of Dr. Amini—which enable him to enact legislation by cabinet decree, pending later confirmation by the Parliament. These powers may be used with best effect in the intervals between the end of a term of the Parliament and the opening of the successor body.

The prime minister draws his cabinet from a limited circle of former ministers, government officials, members of the Parliament, and university professors. Although each cabinet contains a majority of individuals who previously held such posts, new figures do appear, notably men of middle age who were educated abroad and bring special training and capabilities to their posts. Ministers are frequently selected on the basis of their influence with important interest-groups of the country, such as teachers, merchants, and members of the Parliament.

Members of the cabinet supervise the activities of twelve ministries. Each ministry has its under-secretaries and directors-general who are career officials who stay in these posts for some years, and whose presence serves to promote continuity in the conduct of affairs.

The government employs some 325,000 persons. About 190,000

are directly employed as clerks and officials in the ministries, and most of them belong to the civil service. The balance is made up of the gendarmes and the police, under the Ministry of the Interior; schoolteachers; employees of government-owned banks and industrial plants; and employees of the Iranian State Railways and the National Oil Company of Iran. With a few notable exceptions, such as the Ministry of Foreign Affairs, which has less than 400 officials, and the Ministry of Justice, which has only about 1,300 judges, the government offices and agencies are notoriously overstaffed. The subject of an inflated bureaucracy has received the attention of a number of governments, but little headway has been made toward a practical solution.

Many of the ministerial employees are in menial posts, and in 1958, 29 per cent of all these employees were illiterate. Although salaries were inadequate in relation to the high cost of living, in this same year some 48 per cent of employees owned the houses in which they lived. Either these employees had other legal sources of income, or, as has been so insistently stated in Iran, used their posts to acquire illegal income. In other words, many of them engaged in corrupt practices.

The Iranians themselves do not deny that corruption is rampant in Iran, and they offer a number of explanations for this fact. Most frequently emphasized is the point that salaries are so inadequate that officials are compelled to find other sources of income. On the lower levels the common practice is to take sums for expediting the legitimate business of private individuals, and on the higher levels, of taking cuts on contracts between agencies of the government and local and foreign concerns.

As detailed elsewhere, the government has enacted legislation designed to supply the basis for prosecution of dishonest officials, and many have been brought to trial. Proponents of a pessimistic view hold that corruption within the government parallels that within private life and reflects a general decline in ethical conduct. Others state that the solution is to be found in removing the root cause of temptation by paying adequate salaries. Given budgetary limitations, substantial salary increases would be possible only if the size of the bureaucracy was drastically reduced. Several cabinets have tried to eliminate surplus employees, and a law calling for retirement at age sixty-five has been enforced, but the political power of the bureaucracy remains so strong that no real progress has been made.

The Parliament comprises the Senate, whose 60 members are elected for 6 years, and the Majlis, whose 200 deputies are elected for a four-year term. Senators must come from a number of specified categories, such as former cabinet ministers, former ambassadors, retired generals, ranking judges, former deputies in the Majlis, and ex-governors of provinces. Thirty are named by the shah, and thirty chosen in two-stage elections in which the more numerous electors first chosen make the final selection from among their own number. The Senate, housed in a very modern and extremely costly building, has equal legislative powers with the Majlis, with the exception that the Majlis alone makes decisions on financial matters. On account of the nature of its membership and the manner of its choosing, it is natural that the Senate should be more conservative in character than the Majlis and more responsive to the wishes of the shah. So recently established, it has not yet been able to exercise initiative in the legislative field or to obtain the position of prestige envisaged for it in the constitution.

Members of the Majlis are elected by universal male suffrage, with each body including a considerable number of individuals from the provincial branches of the so-called ruling families, as well as lawyers, merchants, journalists, intellectuals, and religious leaders. Many deputies keep their seats for several terms, and usually a majority of the members of a new Majlis will have served in the previous one. When the turnover is heavier, as in the more recent elections, many of the new deputies have close family relations with the individuals whom they displaced.

With the possible exception of the individuals elected, no one in Iran seems satisfied with the conduct of the elections. A variety of charges have been leveled against the conduct of elections: It is said that the imperial court, the provincial governors who represent the Ministry of the Interior, and the generals in command of provincial garrisons are all active in promoting the interests of selected candidates and that the electoral councils set up in each district to supervise elections actually arrange fraudulent returns. During the elections held in the summer of 1960 for the Twentieth Majlis, the press at Tehran published many telegrams and letters from unsuccessful candidates: some stated that they had been ordered by local authorities to leave the districts in which they were running, and others stated that the winning candidates had been chosen by the government before the balloting began.

The electoral law itself is very detailed and contains provisions designed to make fraudulent counting of the ballots impossible. The fact that so many electoral irregularities do occur reflects the general feeling in the country that laws are made to be broken by forces strong enough to disregard the possibility of prosecution. Elements representing varying political opinions may all argue that the elections should be free, but they may place different interpretations upon what is meant by "free elections." Thus, Dr. Mossadeq came to condemn the composition of a Majlis that he had earlier praised. In 1960, Dr. 'Ali Amini was an outspoken advocate of free elections, but in January, 1961, prior to his appointment as prime minister, he stated that the "Majlis is a consultative body, while the government directs affairs. The government should guide the Majlis, because initiative is always in the hands of the government: a representative government may well guide an unrepresentative Majlis." Once in office, he remarked that "at present, the Majlis is a luxury for which the Iranian people are not yet ready," and added, "Parliaments, good or bad, are an obstacle to reform."

Between 1945 and 1952, five separate proposals for the reform of the electoral system were put forward by cabinets or by groups of deputies. These proposals were not concerned alone with making electoral fraud more difficult, but also envisaged steps to insure a more responsible electorate and a more representative list of candidates. The specific suggestions included limiting the electorate to literates, limiting the number of candidates for each seat by requiring an advance deposit which would be forfeited by those receiving the smallest number of votes, and by holding country-wide elections on the same days instead of for a period of weeks, thus preventing candidates from running in several districts.

Once elected, the deputies of the Majlis assemble to examine their credentials, and this process offers an opportunity to reject

individuals whose backgrounds or political views are not acceptable to a majority of the members of the body.

As soon as a term of the Majlis gets under way, its members
tend to coalesce into factions. These factions cluster around a
powerful deputy or represent common interests or, less commonly, defend certain principles. In the period of the so-called
New Freedom, which followed the abdication of Reza Shah,
numerous political parties were organized from 1942 until 1946.
Some originated within the Majlis; some appeared outside of it
and sought to enroll deputies in their ranks; one—the Tudeh
Party—enjoyed Soviet protection; and two reflected the British
presence in Iran during the years of World War II. Each of these
parties had a program of sorts, but most of them failed to attract
significant public support. Indeed, deputies readily shifted allegiance from one party to another. Only the Iran Party and the
Tudeh Party survived the first flush of enthusiasm to become
permanent fixtures on the local scene.

In 1957 Muhammad Reza began, in his own words, "inten-
sively to promote the two-party system in Iran." He pointed
out that minor parties could exist as well, but his purpose was
to develop the two-party system common to the United States
and the United Kingdom in which the party receiving the larger
number of votes forms the government and the other acts as a
critical, yet loyal, opposition. He was aware of the local feeling
that these parties had been imposed from the top but was convinced that in time they would strike firm roots throughout the
country. Following his expressed wish, the Melliyun, or
National Party, and the Mardum, or People's Party, came into
existence.

Both parties started newspapers and began to build party organizations at Tehran and in the provinces, while many individuals were given not too gentle hints that they should join one or
the other party. Obviously, the Melliyun Party was to give
wholehearted support to the government of Dr. Eqbal, while the
Mardum Party was to strike off on a path of liberalism, in the
conviction that if liberalism was what the electorate desired it
would take over from the Melliyun in the next elections for the
Majlis. The Mardum Party favored the distribution of land to
the peasants, efforts to raise the living standards of farmers and

industrial workers, the development of social security programs, concentration upon public housing, equal rights for women in all fields, and the effective implementation of the law of universal education. In the area of foreign affairs, the party stood firmly behind the government.

The first test of the relative strength and the effectiveness of the two-party system came in August, 1960, with the elections for the Twentieth Majlis. Both parties ran into immediate difficulties, since many more of their important members were willing and eager to run for the Majlis than there were constituencies. The executive committees struggled to make decisions, and the results of their deliberations aroused much open critical comment from disappointed members. As the elections proceeded, it became rather apparent that some person or persons —probably the leaders of the two parties—had arrived at a formula to govern the results. After the ballots had been counted, two-thirds of the new deputies were members of the Melliyum Party and the balance, with the exception of a few independents, members of the Mardum Party. The new Majlis did display a different composition from that of previous bodies. Some 75 per cent of the deputies had never been elected previously, and many of them were members of the intellectual class of the country who had been drawn into politics only because either the Melliyun or the Mardum parties had urged them to become candidates. At the same time, those elected from both parties did not really hold sharply divergent views on the internal policies of the government, and many of them had close family ties that cut across party lines. While it could be said that the level of education and competence of the new body was higher than that of previous ones, the manner in which the elections were alleged to have been arranged had aroused a storm of protest which did not appear likely to die down.

At the end of August, 1960, Muhammad Reza made the following statement:

> As the Majlis should always be an honorable authority capable of fulfilling its duties and the recent incidents may have injured its position and prestige, and as the people of the country and the members of the parties want to be able to hold the members

of the Majlis in respect, it is advisable that the deputies should tender their collective resignation in order that there may be an opportunity for holding the elections in an impartial and neutral atmosphere throughout the country.

He went on to state that he would appoint a qualified board to revise the present election law and if this effort proved to be inadequate would ask for the enactment of a new and more comprehensive law.

Following the statement of the ruler, the deputies of both parties resigned: Asadullah Alam also resigned as head of the Mardum Party, and Dr. Manuchehr Eqbal resigned as prime minister and as head of the Melliyun Party. Both parties struggled to regroup under new leadership and in January, 1961, the second round of elections got under way. At Tehran there were student demonstrations protesting the conduct of the elections, although these reflected National Front hostility toward the regime rather than emphasis upon any specific charges.

Before the end of February, the first session of the Twentieth Majlis was held. The body contained only a few more members of the Melliyun Party than of the Mardum Party, and, in addition, there were nearly thirty deputies who had been elected as independents. However, almost before the Majlis had settled down to its duties, a riotous anti-government demonstration at Tehran in favor of higher pay for teachers led to the resignation of Prime Minister Jafar Sharif-Emami on May 5 and the appointment of Dr. Ali Amini to the post. On May 9, the Shah dissolved the Parliament, and within a week a huge, orderly meeting of supporters of the National Front called for immediate elections. As a result, the government announced that it would not permit the National Front to hold any more meetings or demonstrations. This prohibition continued throughout 1961 and 1962, with National Front leaders taken into custody each time there were rumors that demonstrations were planned. In this period it became increasingly apparent that the government had no intention of holding elections in the foreseeable future and that the experiment to promote and develop a two-party system had ended in failure.

In 1957, the Parliament passed a bill providing for the establishment of the National Iranian Security Organization, generally known in Iran as "Savak" from the abbreviation formed by the first letters of the words in its Persian name. Savak was assigned the mission of providing security protection for the ruler and members of the government; gathering material on subversive activities against the state; and carrying on counterespionage operations. With investigative powers somewhat comparable to those of the American secret service and the Federal Bureau of Investigation, its activity was to be within the framework of existing laws and regulations, and material on violations was to be turned over to the legal authorities of the government for prosecution. Within the structure of the government, Savak comes under the direction and control of the office of the prime minister, although its higher officials may also report directly to the ruler.

Named as the first head of Savak, General Timur Bakhtiar displayed great energy in developing its organizational structure and strength, and in so harassing the remnants of the Tudeh Party that it ceased to pose any threat to authority. However, there were complaints that Savak was exceeding its powers in maintaining censorship over the press, in harassing nationalist opponents of the regime, and in arresting and confining within its own headquarters individuals who were not subsequently turned over to the legal arm of the government. It was also believed to play a leading role in the effort to establish the idea that a community of interests existed between the Tudeh Party and the National Front. The charge was also made that it had escaped from the control of the prime minister's office and was leading the country in the direction of a secret police state. In March, 1961, General Bakhtiar resigned his post, and there was feeling at Tehran that the government intended to slow down the tempo of Savak's activity and exercise a more stringent control over its actions.

The armed forces of modern Iran were the creation of Reza Shah. By 1941, his conscripted army numbered some 127,000 men and was equipped with a modest number of tanks, heavy artillery, and mechanized transport. The air force had fewer than fifty planes, and the navy a few gunboats in the Persian Gulf. Then, the lightning attack of Soviet and British forces on

Iran in August, 1941, revealed that the Iranian units were not in an alert, defensive posture, and there was little effective resistance to the invaders. To many Iranians it seemed that the tremendous sums poured into the development of the armed forces had brought only negative results. However, Muhammad Reza was determined that, as a matter of national prestige and in vindication of the goal of his father, the army must be reconstituted, and as early as 1942, an American military mission began to instruct the supply and training sections of the reorganized forces.

In 1950, the armed forces of Iran began to receive assistance under the broad terms of the Mutual Defense Aid Program. Military hardware, in the form of tanks, artillery, arms and ammunition, and other types of equipment began to flow from the United States to Iran. Within Iran, a United States Military Mission (ARMISH) and the Military Assistance Advisory Group (MAAG) introduced their training teams, and, somewhat later, the United States Corps of Engineers began to assist in a military construction program which included the construction of barracks and other housing facilities and the building of airfields.

By 1961, the Iranian Army was believed to have a strength of between 125,000 and 200,000 men, with most published estimates favoring the higher figure. By this same year, the United States had contributed more than $550 million to the development of the armed forces of Iran, largely in the form of arms and equipment but also including budgetary aid for the construction of bases and other facilities. In that same year, nearly 40 per cent of the regular budget of the country was assigned to the armed forces, while the maintenance of the modern equipment and the military establishment loomed as an ever-mounting obligation.

By 1961, the strength of the Iranian Air Force approached 5,000 men, and it included some 120 jet planes of American manufacture. The pilots and the technical personnel of the air force had been trained in the United States, and three airfields in Iran had been developed to handle all the requirements of jet fighters. The defensive aspect of the Iranian Air Force was evident in its lack of offensive bombers.

Within these same recent years, the Iranian Navy, still a very junior member of the armed forces, has increased its limited facilities in the Persian Gulf and has undertaken to introduce vessels into the Caspian Sea, long a strictly controlled Russian preserve.

Adding up the presence of a force of gendarmes, numbering more than 20,000 men stationed in the rural areas, the special units of the frontier guards, and the police forces in the larger towns, the Iranian forces would appear to be more than adequate to maintain internal security against any local challenges to authority—with, of course, the essential condition that it remain loyal to the shah and his governments.

What size army do the Shah and the United States want Iran to have, and for what purpose? There appears to be no clear-cut answer. The ruler may feel that his armed forces should be more than a match for those of Iran's neighbors, including Iraq and Afghanistan, and he has consistently called on the United States to provide the latest-model jet planes in adequate numbers to provide an effective deterrent to an attack from the U.S.S.R. An early position of the United States was that substantial assistance would enable the Iranian armed forces to maintain internal order and to carry out the limited military objective of providing resistance to any Soviet aggression, and the program of military construction was oriented toward that goal rather than to that of strengthening the military posture of Iran against its neighbors.

The Iranian Army consists of some twelve divisions and several independent brigades, grouped into six army corps. Less than half the total forces are stationed in the north of the country, so that there is no heavy concentration in regions adjacent to the Soviet frontier. The bulk of the forces continue to be drawn from conscripts who serve for two years, with the exception of college graduates who spend only a year in the army, although there is a growing body of noncommissioned officers who stay on for a period of years. Although the Iranians are not noted for a pronounced martial spirit, the ranks are composed of hardy, obedient men whose lack of background and education is being met by special courses. The professional officers have shown a marked improvement over the recent years, since many of them have gone through the local military colleges and university and scores have received advanced technical and specialized training in the United States. Still, it remains an army without combat experience, and only the test of conflict will reveal its true mettle.

3. ORGANIZATIONS AND FORCES CHALLENGING AUTHORITY

The Communist Parties of Iran

Near the end of October, 1961, Dr. Reza Radmanesh had the opportunity of addressing the Twenty-second Congress of the Communist Party of the Soviet Union and spoke these words:

> The present rulers of Iran, headed by the Shah, who took over the country through a *coup d'état* against the legal government of Dr. Mossadeq, have turned our country into open territory for invasion and plunder by the imperialists. . . . The defeat of the usurper regime is now near, and the struggle of our masses during the past two years shows that we are now at the beginning of the rise of a great national liberation movement. . . . Our party . . . is more than ever gaining strength and strives to unite all the democratic and national forces in a united front of all the masses against imperialism and feudalism, in order to struggle in union for the overthrow of the usurper regime, the establishment of democratic freedoms, withdrawal from aggressive blocs, and the establishment of a national government.

His remarks echoed the current Soviet line of encouraging national, anti-imperialist movements in areas where local Communist parties were too weak to act effectively on their own. It represented a call for the return of Dr. Mossadeq to power in the expectation that given a parallel situation in Iran the Tudeh Party would not repeat the errors of 1953 and be more successful in exploiting such a national, anti-imperialist government.

By 1962, Dr. Radmanesh could point with pride to twenty-five years of Communist activity, but some of his associates, such as Reza Rusta, had been active in the field since 1922. The Tudeh Party remained alive in Iran and abroad.

Within Iran, the relatively few activists operated with considerable caution, and yet, from time to time, numbers were rounded up by Savak. They appeared to be concentrating upon collecting material to be used in broadcasts to Iran and in maintaining contact with the more extremist members of the National Front.

Abroad, the Communist apparatus of Iran was represented by two groups: first, the relics of the briefly autonomous state of Azerbaijan who were in residence at Baku and elsewhere in the Soviet Union, and, second, the members of the Central Committee of the Tudeh Party and their associates who drifted from its headquarters at Leipzig to the several countries of the Communist bloc. The first group may still contain hard-core members of the original Communist Party of Iran.

In 1962 the Central Committee of the Tudeh Party appeared to have four major functions: maintaining Party discipline, preparing propaganda material, conducting recruiting activities among the thousands of Iranian students in Europe, and keeping open channels of communication with Party members in Iran. Of these functions, only that of its propaganda work comes to public attention. The Party publishes *Mardum*, a four-page Persian-language monthly, in Europe and mails copies throughout Europe, to Iran, and to the United States. Its material is voiced in Persian and Azeri by Party members and announcers over Communist-controlled radio stations at East Berlin, Leipzig, Sofia, Moscow, and Peking—the peripatetic Reza Rusta has been heard from Peking. In addition, material communicated by Party members in Iran is used on the programs of the so-called National Voice of Iran, a clandestine station located in the vicinity of Baku, possibly at Bazuna. The Iranian Government has protested to the U.S.S.R. about this station, stating that its existence is in violation of treaties between the two countries. The programs are extremely vicious and malicious in character; they include savage attacks on the Shah, criticism of the Iranian Government and its leaders, and direct appeals to the people of Iran to overthrow the regime—this last theme represents a direct exploitation of the "national, anti-imperialist" line.

As instruments of Soviet policy in Iran, the local Communist parties have had their minor successes over the years but suffered major setbacks in 1921, 1929, 1946, 1953, and 1954. Their strength is now at its lowest ebb, and they have failed in the assigned objective of preparing for a Communist take-over of the country.

It has long been the aim of Russia to acquire all of Iran down to its warm-water ports. The testament of Peter the Great expressed the goal in these words, "And in the decadence of Persia, penetrate as far as the Persian Gulf"; while in 1941, Molotov stated to his German counterpart in Moscow, "The center of gravity of the aspirations of the Soviet Union is the area south of Batum and Baku in the general direction of the Persian Gulf." Numerous scholarly publications have traced the course of Soviet policy toward the Middle East and toward Iran in specific terms, while there are also comprehensive accounts of the attempt by the U.S.S.R., between 1918 and 1921, to establish a permanent foothold in the Caspian regions of Iran. It is not necessary to review that material, since present interest is concerned with a broader understanding of the origin and activities of the Communist parties of Iran.

The Communist Party of Iran, which held its first meeting at Enzeli (Pahlavi) in June, 1920, was the outgrowth of the Communist Edelat, or Justice, Party which had been founded in 1918 among the Iranians working in the oil fields at Baku. From its inception, it appears to have been headed by A. Sultanzadeh, for a time head of the Near Eastern Section of the Commissariat for Foreign Affairs of the U.S.S.R. In September of the same year he and Haidar Khan represented the Communist Party of Iran at the Congress of the Peoples of the East at Baku. The new party, aiming at the overthrow of the Shah, operated from the Caspian littoral of Iran, but the re-establishment of central authority in this region in 1921 by troops directed by Minister of War Reza Khan deprived it of a secure base, and it went underground in Azerbaijan and Khurasan. Sultanzadeh, a prolific writer, recounted its early successes and subsequent trials and indicated that its most effective members went to Tehran to support and direct the workers' unions that had been established in 1920.

This trade-union activity included the publication of newspapers at Tehran. Many of the individuals active at this time

were to reappear on the local scene many years later as leaders
of the Tudeh Party or of the Democratic Party of Azerbaijan,
and a few examples should be of interest. Jafar Kavian, who had
been active since 1918, was to emerge as minister of the people's
army of Azerbaijan in 1945. Jafar Pishevari, who put out the
paper *Haqiqat* at Tehran, became the prime minister of the
Azerbaijan regime. Reza Rusta had established peasant unions
in Gilan before being sent to Tehran; years later he headed
the Tudeh Party unions.

Members and Communist leaders of the Tehran unions celebrated May Day with public meetings until 1929, when Reza
Shah ordered the self-styled "freedom lovers" arrested. Those
named and a number of others remained in jail or in enforced
residence until the fall of 1941.

Other party members were rounded up throughout Iran between 1928 and 1931, and following the same pattern, emerged
from prison in 1941 to resume their interrupted careers. Some,
such as Bagher Emani, were also engaged in Soviet espionage
activities.

While those of its members engaged in trade-union activity
had consistently denied any Bolshevik ties, the Communist Party
of Iran was not as reluctant to disclose its plans and intentions.
In 1926, both the Party and the Young Communist League of
Iran urged the Soviet Union to intervene militarily in Khurasan
where a localized revolt had broken out. In 1927, the Communist parties of Turkey and Iran held a congress at Urmia (Re-
zaieh), in 1928 Sultanzadeh and Shareqi represented the Communist Party of Iran at the Sixth Congress of the Comintern, and
at the end of 1929, Sultanzadeh was still the head of the Party.

Then, in 1930, a series of articles by a Soviet defector, George
Agabekov, was published in Paris. At the final stage of his
career he had been resident general of the GPU in Iran from
1927 until 1929; his articles described in fascinating detail the
secrets of Soviet espionage and subversive activities in Iran and
included the names of many Iranian agents of the Soviet Union.
As an initial reaction to his revelations, some 350 minor Soviet
agents and activists were rounded up and in 1931 another 100 or
so arrested, including such an important figure as 'Abbas Mirza
Eskandari, a prince of the former Qajar dynasty.

The Majlis passed a comprehensive bill designed to remedy the fact that existing criminal legislation provided no penalties for individuals plotting to overthrow the government by force, and in 1932, thirty-two persons charged with espionage on behalf of a foreign power were brought to trial and all but five convicted. At this same time the Iranian Government expressed concern over the publication in Germany of pro-Soviet Persian-language newspapers. One, the *Setarehyi Sorkh,* or *Red Star,* the organ of the Communist Center of Iran, appeared at Leipzig, and another, *Paykar,* or *War,* published at Berlin, was succeeded by *Nezhat,* or *Insurrection.* In response to official protests, the German Government closed down these papers. The fact that thirty years later Leipzig and Berlin once again became centers of Communist activity directed against the government of Iran is not without interest.

The Communist Party of Iran was heard from again in 1932 in a long article published in *International Press Correspondence,* the organ of the Comintern. The article discussed the position of the Party with respect to Reza Khan [sic] and the dispute between the government of Iran and the Anglo-Iranian Oil Company, and propagated the slogans of the Party overthrow of the monarchy and establishment of a workers' and peasants' government in Iran. The Party continued to send Iranian Communists trained in Russia into the country. One of them was 'Abd es-Samad Kambakhsh, who was arrested in 1933 and released in 1941, just in time to become a founding member of the Tudeh Party. Ardashir Ovanessian was educated at the Young Communist School at Moscow, was sent back to Iran in 1933, and was arrested in 1934; after 1942 he was a member of the Central Committee of the Tudeh Party and later director-general of propaganda for the Azerbaijan regime.

After 1932, the Communist Party of Iran vanishes from the scene. The stern authority of Reza Shah had made ideological operations within Iran impossible; the center in Germany had been closed down; and the U.S.S.R. was, apparently, unprepared to permit the Party to operate openly on its territory. Since the disappearance of the Party took place so long ago, what relation has this fact to the contemporary scene in Iran? First, it brings up the question of what has become of the Communist

Party of Iran. Once such a party has been organized does the
Soviet Union ever permit it to be dissolved? What has happened
to Sultanzadeh? Was he later active in the Tudeh Party or in
the Democratic Party of Azerbaijan under a pseudonym, as
has been suggested by several students of Communist activity in
Iran? The personal opinion of this writer is that the Communist
Party exists, and that in appropriate circumstances it will emerge
to take over from the second team, the mixed bag of amateurs
and professional revolutionists who constitute the Tudeh Party
of Iran.

This second team, originally made up entirely of amateurs,
appeared on the Iranian scene about 1930. The members were
Marxists, but they were amateurs for they had not been trained
in the Soviet Union. These individuals grouped themselves
around Dr. Taqi Erani, who had gone to Germany for advanced
studies in 1922 and become deeply interested in Marxism. At
Berlin he came into contact with 'Ali Bozorg Alavi, Dr. Morteza Yazdi, and others. In 1930 he and his friends returned to
Iran, where he began to build up a personal following of students and professional men, and in 1933 he started publication
of a monthly intellectual magazine called *Dunya*, or *World*.

In May, 1937, Dr. Erani and fifty-two of his associates were
arrested; forty-nine of them were brought to trial in November,
1938. Forty-five were convicted of being members of a Communist party; receiving funds from a foreign power; and using
such funds for propaganda purposes. They were sentenced to
prison terms of up to fifteen years. They were welcomed to the
Tehran model prison by the real professionals and "the old
prisoners were grieved, but happy at the same time." These are
the words of Jafar Pishevari, who went on to say, "They were
all well educated, but they had not had our experience. Their
appearance gave us an opportunity to teach them. They learned
from us how to resist and endure, and we gave them moral support. Doctors and professors who were the intellectuals of Iran
acted like trained political warriors." Dr. Erani died in prison in
1940, but the others were released under the amnesty declared
by Muhammad Reza in September, 1941. Later on, a continuing
attempt was made to indicate that these individuals were patriotic

Iranians who had suffered because of their opposition to the dictatorship of Reza Shah.

On January 30, 1942, the Tudeh, or Masses, Party was created by the followers of Dr. Erani, with a small leavening of the professional Communists, who looked to three members of the Eskandari family, 'Abbas Mirza, Sulayman Mohsen, and Iraj, to add an air of respectability to the new party. Former prisoners Dr. Reza Radmanesh, Dr. Morteza Yazdi, Dr. Feridun Keshavarz, 'Ali Bozorg Alavi, and Dr. Muhammad Bahrami, the new party's Marxist theoretician, became members of the Central Committee of the Tudah Party of Iran.

The Tudeh Party of Iran avoided any mention of Communism, insisted that it had no ties with the Soviet Union, and stated that it was an antifascist party working for the defense of the constitution of Iran and for the independence of the country. In the first two years of its very active life, attention was concentrated upon organization and upon recruitment of members. Ardashir Ovanessian, a member of the Party's Central Committee, wrote a book entitled *Fundamentals of the Organization of a Party*, which explained in detail the Soviet concept of democratic centralism, or the control of the many by the few. He described the basic party unit of the *huzeh*, or cell, and explained the duties of the member of a cell and his relationship to the higher organisms of the Party.

Hundreds of Iranians seeking personal identification with an organization which had ready answers for their basic needs and aspirations joined the Party, taken in by the clever camouflage that concealed its Marxist goals. By 1944, the Tudeh Party had gathered most of the local trade-unions into its Central United Council of Trade Unions, headed by Reza Rusta, and in 1945, this body affiliated with the World Federation of Trade Unions.

Party support came primarily from the industrial workers of the country and from the intellectual class. Open direction was by the intellectual elite represented by the former associates of Dr. Erani, but the real power was wielded by the professional Communists who remained in the background and even, such as in the case of Pishevari, denied that they had any connections with the Tudeh Party. In 1944, eight of the Tudeh Party leaders were elected to the Majlis; and because of their discipline and singleness of purpose managed to come close to dominating debate in that body. Most of them were elected from the northern provinces of Azerbaijan, Mazanderan, Gilan, and Khurasan where Soviet troops were in occupation and where the Tudeh Party was more powerful and influential than the officials of the central government. In these early years, the Party began to develop front organizations but neglected the cultivation and recruitment of the peasants. Not until considerably later did it send agents to the villages to talk to the farmers, question them about their oppression by landlords, and begin to assemble the kind of derogatory material required for an all-out assault on the system of land tenure.

Until 1945, the Tudeh Party steadily grew in strength and influence, and the government seemed unable to counter what was finally recognized to be a serious threat to the political stability of the country. However, the clear indications that the international conflict would soon end with the defeat of Germany caused the Soviet Union to take steps to be certain that the withdrawal of its protection would not result in the repression of its adherents in Iran. What better way to associate this necessity with its positive goals than to establish a permanent foothold in the country?

On September 2, 1945, the Tudeh Party in the northwest was suddenly replaced by the Democratic Party of Azerbaijan although the leaders of the Party were not all in favor of this decision. Groups of armed members successfully attacked army garrisons and gendarmerie posts, while, in November, the commanders of Soviet forces refused to permit government reinforcements to move toward the areas in open revolt against the central authority.

All the Soviet instruments were now in place as the culmination of a carefully worked-out plan. About 1935, many thousands of Iranians long resident in the U.S.S.R. had been repatriated: hundreds had received training in the Soviet Union and had been told to await instructions. When the Soviet troops entered northern Iran in 1941, these individuals flocked to welcome them, and pointed out the influential individuals loyal to the Iranian Government who were then removed from the occupation zones.

After September, 1945, they formed the nucleus of the armed forces of the Democratic Party of Azerbaijan, as well as supplying a major part of the membership of the so-called legislative bodies of the autonomous regime.

Other persons emerged as leaders of the new regime. One element was made up of Iranian Communists who had fled to the U.S.S.R. to escape arrest during the reign of Reza Shah and had come back in 1941 in the uniforms of officers and men of the Soviet occupation forces. Typical of this element was Faraj Dehqan, who appeared in 1941 as a Soviet officer at Astara and in 1945 was the commander of forces of the Democratic Party of Azerbaijan in the Ahar District. Another element was composed of long-time Communists, most of whom had deliberately avoided identification with the Tudeh Party of Iran. In addition to individuals named earlier who were prominent in the Azerbaijan regime, such as Pishevari, Kavian, and Ovanessian, there were many others. Dr. Salamullah Javid, minister of the interior, had been a party to the attempt made in 1920 to separate Azerbaijan from Iran and had then fled to the U.S.S.R. Returning to Tabriz in 1929, he had been arrested for Communist activity and jailed until 1941. Muhammad Beeria, the barely literate minister of education, had received training in Russia and been sent to engage in trade-union activity at Tehran; he had been arrested in 1931.

In the hands of these individuals and their Russian advisers, the Azerbaijan regime had emerged as a totalitarian state. Its provincial National Assembly proclaimed the Autonomous Republic of Azerbaijan, approved a constitution, entrusted all authority to Pishevari and his associates, and then disbanded. On the southern fringes of Azerbaijan, Soviet officers brought the Kurdish Republic of Mahabad into being in December, 1945. In April, 1946, the "national governments" of these two areas concluded a treaty which stressed their fraternal relations and their determination to resist the central government.

The details of the activities of these regimes, their negotiations with the central government, and their relations with the Soviet Union are beyond the scope of this study. Both regimes faced increasing difficulties after the withdrawal of the Soviet occupation forces in May, 1946, and both collapsed when Iranian troops moved into the region in December of that year. At Tabriz many of the "democrats" were slaughtered by the populace, but others, including Pishevari, Beeria, Ovanessian, and Gholam Yahya Daneshiyan, commander of the forces of the regime, managed to escape and cross the frontier and make their way to Baku. There they joined the more than 200 younger democrats who had been sent to Baku earlier to study at the Air College and the Infantry College. Pishevari assured them that their training would be continued and that in due time Azerbaijan would be recovered. Although in late 1947 the Soviets disbanded the students' groups, the former leaders of the Azerbaijan regime have continued to reside in the vicinity of Baku, once more held in reserve.

The loss of Azerbaijan was a bitter blow to the Tudeh Party as well as to the U.S.S.R. itself. At the height of the apparent strength of these regimes the central government had adopted a conciliatory attitude, which included the appointment of three of the Tudeh Party leaders to cabinet posts. Dr. Feridun Keshavarz was Minister of Education, Dr. Morteza Yazdi, Minister of Health, and Iraj Eskandari was Minister of Commerce and Industry. By autumn, popular resentment had forced reorganization of the cabinet without these members, and after December the Party theoreticians met, as is customary in Communist parties, to discuss why the movement in Azerbaijan had failed, what errors the Party itself had committed, and what changes in the Party line seemed indicated. The fact was that the U.S.S.R. had pushed its local instruments and organizations too hard, misjudging the assumed receptivity of the people of Iran to "liberation" from its so-called reactionary regime.

While still engaged in the reorganization and regrouping of its forces, the Tudeh Party suffered a more serious blow by being outlawed in February, 1949, following an attempted assassination of the Shah. Most of the members of its central committee managed to flee abroad, including ten who escaped from detention at Tehran at the end of 1950. Early in 1950, a second echelon of Party members was engaged in the clandestine printing and distribution of leaflets attacking the government in terms similar to those employed by the Soviets at this time. In 1952, Reza Radmanesh discarded the fiction that the Party was a national, liberal one with no foreign ties when he informed the Nineteenth Congress of the Communist Party of the Soviet Union, "The Tudeh Party is the sole party of the workers of Iran; inspired by the ideology of Marxism and Lenin . . . [it] is based upon democracy and socialism, at the head of which are to be found the U.S.S.R. and Josef Stalin, our great standard bearer."

Suddenly, the rise of Dr. Mossadeq offered the Party a new lease on life. The xenophobic, anti-British nationalism of the Mossadeq regime was most welcome to the Soviet Union, which ordered the Tudeh Party to exploit the situation and direct part of its effort to discrediting the United States. Scrawled messages reading "Yankee Go Home" appeared on the walls of Tehran. Numerous front groups were quickly formed, including the Peace Partisans, Democratic Youth, National Society Against Colonialism, Democratic Women of Iran, Society Against Illiteracy, and Society to Defend the Rights of Villagers, and scores of newspapers were published by these ephemeral organizations. In addition, the Tudeh Party newspapers, *Mardum*, *Razm*, and *Zafar*, were clandestinely printed and circulated at Tehran, party cells sought fresh recruits, and arms were collected and stored.

The overt and covert publications sponsored by the Party attacked the Point Four program and all other manifestations of the American presence in Iran and condemned the foreign policy of the United States. Another task of the Party was to foster dissension among social groups within the country: attacks were made on the imperial court; the populace was encouraged to display hostility to the police and the army; and material critical of Islam appeared. In May, 1951, the Party massed 30,000 demonstrators in the square in front of the Majlis building.

Although the Tudeh Party was officially opposed to the Mossadeq Government, it directed its major effort to helping it stay in power. In so acting it followed a familiar Soviet tactic of encouraging a bourgeois nationalist movement, attempting in due course to form a common front with the movement, and planning to take over from that movement should the opportunity present itself. Thus, on July 21, 1952, the Party took part in a mass demonstration in favor of Dr. Mossadeq, and a year later celebrated the anniversary of the occasion with a huge rally at which speakers condemned the imperial court, asked that the Majlis be dissolved by popular referendum, demanded that American imperialism be expelled from Iran, insisted that Iranian oil should be sold to the Soviet Union, and called for a single front of anti-colonizing forces. It is interesting to note that the first two of the points coincided with views of the National Front, while the others were designed to draw the National Front away from the Western powers and toward the Soviet Union. The Party had been able to emerge into the open following a decision in March of that year by a Tehran court that members of the Tudeh Party were not liable to prosecution for activity against the constitutional monarchy and in favor of Communist doctrines: It is difficult to understand why the government of Dr. Mossadeq allowed this ruling to go unchallenged.

During the events of August 16-19, 1953, the Tudeh Party attempted to exploit a period of confusion and uncertainty to swing popular opinion in favor of a republic. Whether the second-level Party leaders who were in charge at Tehran believed that the Party was ready for such a test is not known; at any rate, they followed Soviet instructions. Groups of Party members went far beyond expressions hostile to the Shah which were uttered by members of the National Front: statues of the ruler and of his father were pulled down from their pedestals, showcases were smashed to remove pictures of the Shah, and inspired crowds were encouraged to surge through the streets shouting in favor of a republic. However, the effort failed. On the one hand, popular sentiment was not prepared to go all-out against the monarchy, and on the other, the Party could not put enough people in the streets to be able to resist counterattacks on the part of the National Front itself, and, later, of the armed forces.

For the second time, the Communists had been misled into believing their own propaganda. As in the case of Azerbaijan, the Iranians were not ready to discard familiar institutions, and they had not been unaware of the existence and motives of the hidden Soviet hand.

In September, 1954, the so-called Organization of Tudeh Officers came to light, and within a few days some 600 officers and noncommissioned officers of the Iranian armed forces were under arrest. As the interrogations proceeded, it was revealed that the atmosphere of the Mossadeq period had been most favorable to Tudeh Party activity within the armed forces, since the organization had grown in size from some 100 members to over 600 persons. Following military trials, a score of officers were executed and many others sentenced to long prison terms. Within a year, the government published a *Black Book* that described the Organization of Tudeh Officers. The text traced connections of the group with the U.S.S.R. and listed confessions of espionage activity, of attacks on the constitutional monarchy, and of training of Tudeh youth groups for street fighting and guerrilla warfare against the government. In addition, the organization was to assassinate Dr. Mossadeq after he had been successful in eliminating the monarchy from Iran and then stage an armed Communist take-over of the government.

The shock of these disclosures spurred the Parliament to pass a bill directed against organizations that promoted Communism, that attacked Islam and the constitutional monarchy, and that contained members of the Tudeh Party or other groups declared to be illegal. Over the years, a number of prominent Tudeh Party members had drifted away from it, including Nur ad-din Alamuti, an early secretary of the Central Committee, and Khalil Maliki. After 1955, many others had been pardoned by the Shah and released from prison, including Dr. Muhammad Bahrami, who stated that Iranian public opinion had condemned as traitors the leaders of the Tudeh Party living abroad.

While Communist activity in Iran sunk to an all-time low after 1954, the members of the Central Committee of the Tudeh Party ignored the realities of their position and Dr. Radmanesh informed the Bulgarian Communist Party that he brought greetings from the Iranian masses, at the head of whom was the Tudeh Party. However, the winds of chance favored Dr. Radmanesh and his associates. Following the July, 1958, revolt at Baghdad, the Communist Party of Iraq, long underground, was permitted to operate openly and the Qassem regime was on the best of terms with the U.S.S.R. In 1959, Dr. Radmanesh, Reza Rusta, Iraj Eskandari, Dr. Feridun Keshavarz and a number of other Iranian Communists arrived in Baghdad. One aspect of their mission was probably to put their experience in organizational activity and propaganda at the service of the Communist Party of Iraq, another was to take advantage of the fact that Iraq was the only country of the Middle East in which Communist activities were not illegal, and a third was to establish direct relations with remnants of the Tudeh Party in Khuzistan, immediately adjacent to southern Iraq. Couriers went from Baghdad not only to that area but also to Fars, Kurdistan, and Azerbaijan in Iran.

At the Sixth Congress of the Tudeh Party of Iran held in Leipzig in September, 1959, there was discussion whether the party should move its headquarters to a Middle East center of Communism at Baghdad. Steps were also taken to form a union with the Democratic Party of Azerbaijan, and Gholam Yahya Daneshiyan was welcomed as a new member of the Executive Committee of the Tudeh Party. However, in Iraq the Communists had overestimated their strength, and their criticism of the Qassem regime brought retaliatory action which limited their freedom of speech and action. As a result, Radmanesh and his little group were forced to move back to Leipzig and the Seventh Congress, held in the summer of 1960, seemed to have closed on a pessimistic note, according to the account supplied to the Communist press. One conclusion was that the retrogression of the deliverance movement in Iran would come to an end only gradually and that present conditions in Iran did not as yet denote the existence of a revolutionary situation. These words were not as vague as they sounded, and they did gloss over a new tactic. Soon the Party broadcasts began to recall with favor the days of Dr. Mossadeq and his government and culminated in the statement of Dr. Radmanesh quoted in the opening paragraph of this section. What seems to have happened is that Premier Khrushchev had decided to step up the propaganda campaign against the government and monarchy of Iran and had directed the Tudeh Party of Iran to concentrate on issues drawn from Party experience which might well find a receptive audience among the Iranian nationalists. Radio Peyk-i-Iran, located in Leipzig, took up this line as did the publication *Mardum*, when it encouraged Tudeh members in Iran to support the National

Front and stated that the people of the country would vote for Dr. Mossadeq in any free elections.

The Democratic Party of Azerbaijan, not heard of for some time until Daneshiyan joined the Executive Committee of the Tudeh Party, had renewed its activity in Iran; and in 1960, twenty-two individuals were convicted before a military court at Tabriz for having had relations with a foreign power on behalf of this Democratic Party and for plotting to destroy the constitutional regime. Finally, late in 1962, it was reported that Daneshiyan had been named as head of the Central Committee of the Tudeh Party—a change that seemed to place an activist in power.

In 1962, neither the Communist Party of Iran, the Tudeh Party of Iran, the Democratic Party of Azerbaijan, nor any combination of these Soviet instruments represented a serious menace to the political stability and integrity of Iran. Their role appeared to be that of watching and waiting for more favorable times. It is obvious that the U.S.S.R. must spend considerable sums to maintain these organizations within the Soviet Union and its satellite states. What is to be the future of these Communist parties of Iran? It seems reasonable to suppose that they will be kept alive on a stand-by basis pending direct Soviet intervention against the government of Iran. Under what circumstances might there be such intervention? Suggested answers to this query are to be found in other chapters of this book, but it may be assumed that the leaders of the U.S.S.R. have profited by the record of defeats in 1946 and 1953 and have taken a more sober view of the ability of their chosen instruments to win popular support for the overthrow of the constitutional monarchy.

The National Front

In August, 1953, many of the men who had been prominent in the National Front, either as the leaders of its constituent groups or as independents, were jailed. Some were tried and sentenced to short terms in jail, others tried and acquitted and still others released without trial. Gradually, they established contact and formed the National Resistance Movement, a clandestine, loosely knit organization which struggled to issue leaflets asserting its loyalty to Dr. Mossadeq and predicting the return of the nationalists to power. Initially, members of the Iran Party dominated the National Resistance Movement, but in 1955 when three Iran Party members of the Central Committee of the National Resistance Movement were arrested, another element took over its leadership. Its peak activity was reached during 1956 and 1957, when it issued a paper, *The Road of Mossadeq*.

In late September, 1957, a number of its most active members were arrested, probably as a reaction to the distribution of the paper and its pamphlets, and the effectiveness of the existing organization declined to such an extent that in 1958 the name of the National Resistance Movement was taken over by a group of younger men who were not veterans of the 1951–53 period. The new program included opposition to Communism and insistence on political freedoms and social reforms, and held the conviction that the shah should reign and not rule. These younger men were anxious for action, but they were unable to establish a common program with the Iran Party and other elements and lacked capabilities to act on their own. They did, however, compete with the Tudeh Party in spreading propaganda among the Iranian students abroad.

In 1959, nationalist activity slackened considerably, with most of the veterans of the movement engaged in their regular occupations. Then, on July 21, 1960, the National Front issued a statement concerning its reorganization for the purpose of contesting elections for the Twentieth Majlis.

This resurgent National Front was composed of the following elements: the Iran Party, the Pan-Iran Party; elements of the Third Force; the National Resistance Movement; and the small People of Iran Party. The politically minded religious figures, discredited by their earlier fanaticism and cynicism, were not included, nor was the Toilers' Party of Dr. Baghai.

The elections, which came to an end in August, 1960, returned no members or supporters of the National Front, but this organization had enjoyed access to the press and, together with a number of independents of status and influence, such as Dr. 'Ali Amini, had been successful in raising a storm of protest against the conduct of the elections.

Beginning in January, 1961, a second round of elections for the

Majlis was held. On January 20, the National Front announced that it would boycott the elections, and a little later some of its leaders took sanctuary in the Senate building to protest what they claimed was repetition of the controlled elections of the previous summer. Student demonstrations at Tehran supported the position of the National Front and some independents who had been active in the summer campaign also abstained. In February, the Twentieth Majlis was formally inaugurated with most of its members either associated with the Melliyun or the Mardum parties. It did include nearly twenty independents, and Allayar Saleh was elected from Kashan, thus giving the National Front an experienced public spokesman. Near the end of April, Saleh rose in the Majlis saying it was his sacred duty to voice the dissatisfaction of the people over the recent elections and to present specific charges against the acceptance of the credentials of election of one of the deputies.

During this period, the National Resistance Movement had decided to refuse to submit to the general direction of the National Front. In January, 1961, it issued its own lengthy program, and in May it was reorganized and appeared as the Freedom Movement of Iran. Prominently displayed was a reproduction of a handwritten note of encouragement signed by Dr. Mossadeq on May 15, while accompanying leaflets stated that the Freedom Movement of Iran stood for the establishment of honesty, justice, and freedom in Iran. It also advocated the return of Dr. Mossadeq to power; and to emphasize this stand it published material attacking such leaders of the National Front as Saleh and Dr. Karim Sanjabi, labeling them as tools of the Americans.

Early in May, massive demonstrations by striking teachers, supported by students and members of the National Front, resulted in the dismissal of the cabinet by the Shah and the selection of Dr. 'Ali Amini as the new prime minister. Generally regarded as more sympathetic to the nationalists than his immediate predecessors, Amini supported the decision of the ruler to dissolve the Twentieth Majlis but declined to predict when new elections would be held. A National Front rally scheduled for July 21 was preceded by the arrest and detention of many of its leaders and by the dispersal of the people who showed up at the meeting site. Subsequently, the Amini Government announced that no public meetings sponsored by the National Front would be permitted in the future.

However, in January, 1962, students at Tehran University, demonstrating in favor of early elections and for the return of Dr. Mossadeq, spilled out of the campus to stone police and passing cars. Troops cleared the university grounds with considerable brutality; there were student casualties, and scores of the demonstrators were arrested. The aftermath of the demonstration included the arrest and detention of National Front leaders concerned with student affairs. A feeling of bitterness existed on account of the alleged brutality, and a decision not to risk future forceful repression was taken.

Since the dissolution of the Twentieth Majlis, the National Front is believed to be engaged in strengthening its organizational structure against the time when new national elections will be held. The National Front is run by a Central Council, which may have up to fifty members. Members of the council may select additional members, and the body passes upon applications for affiliation with the National Front made by groups and individuals. An executive committee, headed by Allahyar Saleh, directs current activity and makes policy decisions. Special committees are concerned with such subjects as organization, publicity, and student membership. In preparation for the elections, the Central Council planned to set up provincial branches, each directed by a local council, which would have direct Central Council representation. Such local councils would screen candidates who wished to stand for the Majlis as representatives of the National Front. In 1962, some nine provincial branches were in operation.

No estimates of the membership of the National Front are available, and little is known about the general character of the rank-and-file adherents. There appears to be no unanimity of political policies and goals among the groups and independents within the organization, and, as could be expected, there is an uneasy state of tension between the moderate and the more extremist elements.

The moderates within the National Front are most effectively represented by the members of the Iran Party whose leaders dominate the Executive Committee. Following the downfall of Dr. Mossadeq, these leaders seem to have abandoned his policy of negative equilibrium in favor of a more realistic appraisal of Iran's role in the international scene. Thus, in 1957, the Iran Party issued a statement, indicating acceptance of the principles of the Eisenhower Doctrine; and it accepted the validity of the consortium agreement and did not challenge the allegiance of the regime to the Baghdad Pact. It seems possible that the party intended to recognize American interests in the area, and, through this recognition, attract American sympathy for the goals of the Iran Party—in other words, to attract American enlightened self-interest to liberal forces in Iran. The government of Iran reacted strongly to this declaration, and a bill to outlaw the Iran Party was drawn up. It was referred to a committee of the Majlis where it remained as a potential threat in case the party should again attempt to be the spokesman for Iranian public opinion on the subject of the country's foreign relations.

Directed by men of middle age, who have been associated with the party since its founding, the Iran Party has no strong appeal to the volatile student elements, and is felt by some other elements within the National Front to fail to display aggressive leadership in conducting overt demonstrations against the regime.

It is difficult to define the position of the Third Force within the National Front or even to be certain that it is formally affiliated with it. Khalil Maliki heads what he describes as the Socialist League of the National Front, and from time to time issues lengthy, verbose declarations in its behalf. These declarations have included such statements as: (1) Iran should make no commitments toward either of the two rival and hostile blocs; (2) a group of from three to five respected leaders be named with full powers to determine the policies and goals of the National Front; (3) that in Iran and other countries the most dangerous rivals of the Communists are the socialists. Maliki appears to have close relations with Dr. Baghai, as evidenced by the release of coordinated statements and pamphlets. A less conspicuous figure, Muhammad 'Ali Khonji, headed another faction of the Third Force, but in April, 1961, he announced the dissolution of the

Third Force itself and urged its followers to enroll in the National Front.

Another group within the National Front is the miniscule People of Iran Party headed by Muhammad Nakhshab, formerly an active member of the Iran Party.

The Freedom Movement of Iran appears to contain at least two factions: one allegedly of individuals holding pro-Communist views and the other with a religious orientation. Within the National Front, there is said to be some uneasiness over the motives of the activists within the Freedom Movement of Iran and some concern over the clandestine nature of the organization. These activists seem to believe that the present National Front leadership is too conservative and complacent; they are younger men who were not active in the regime of Dr. Mossadeq and are entirely uncritical of his tenure of office.

The spokesman for the important independent members of the National Front appears to be Gholam Husein Sadeqi, a professor in the Faculty of Letters at the University of Tehran who held two cabinet posts in the governments of Dr. Mossadeq. Other prominent independents include Dr. Shapur Bakhtiar, professor at Tehran University; Nasratullah Amini, Professor of Law at Tehran University, who was the mayor of Tehran under Dr. Mossadeq; and Dr. Said Fatemi, formerly Professor of Literature at Tehran University, who served on the staff of the paper *Bakhtar Emruz* under his uncle, Husein Fatemi, and who was jailed from 1953 until 1957. In general, these independents hold rather moderate views and are men who are well regarded.

In spite of divergent views within the National Front, there is general agreement upon certain basic issues. A declaration made by the Central Council after the abortive demonstration of July 21, 1961, emphasized a number of its objectives: freedom of the press and of assembly, at present denied by the government; security forces deprived of independent action and brought under civil authority; objection to slanderous branding of the liberals of the National Front as Communists by the regime; the intolerable economic situation; necessity of free elections; and granting to the Iranian people basic rights of freedom and of self-determination at present usurped.

The leaders of the National Front appear to hold similar views upon major internal issues and aspects of foreign relations. They seem to believe that the handling of the oil issue by Dr. Mossadeq was too drastic, having been detrimental to the larger national interests; and, therefore, not to be repeated when the National Front comes to power. Instead, they favor a deliberate renegotiation of existing contracts. They believe that the shah of Iran must reign and not rule; if he refuses to reign, the only alternative may be his abdication. At the same time, they are not convinced that Iran is ready for a republican form of government.

These leaders of the National Front would take Iran out of CENTO and move the country toward a position of neutrality. Neutrality looks economically attractive to the National Front, which favors accepting financial aid from both the United States and other Western powers and from the U.S.S.R. At the same time, the leaders are not at all certain that Iran should denounce the bilateral pact with the United States, and they appear to agree that Iran should continue its close ties with the West. There is apparent ambivalence in the attitude of these leaders toward the United States. On the one hand, there is a desire to attract the sympathetic interest of the Kennedy Administration in Iranian liberalism, based on a realization that the economic development of the country is dependent upon the continuance of American financial aid at current levels. On the other, there is a strong undercurrent of hostility toward the United States, which it accuses of having kept the present regime in power, thereby having helped to stifle freedom in Iran. Should the National Front be forced to take a firm position on its foreign policy, it is probable that anti-American, anti-Western hostility would come to the fore.

More extreme stands with regard to internal politics and foreign relations are taken by the student supporters of the National Front. Within Iran, the student committee of the National Front, believed to represent the views of the Iran Party, attempts to exert a restraining influence upon the students at Tehran University and in other schools and comes into conflict with the representatives of the Freedom Movement of Iran, who appeal to the more radically oriented students—those inclined to Communism who are prepared to take to the streets in defiance of authority.

The thousands of Iranian students abroad, including some 5,000 in the United States alone, have escaped from the restrictions against demonstrations and publications in force at home. There are associations of these students in France, Germany, England, and the United States, with most of them dominated by the more vocal supporters of the National Front, some of whom seek the advice and guidance of self-exiled former associates of Dr. Mossadeq. Couriers maintain contact with students in Iran and pertinent material is featured in the papers published by the students' associations. These papers are far more critical of the government of Iran and of the Shah himself than are the leaders of the National Front. In addition, they advocate a positive neutrality, which includes the withdrawal of Iran from its treaty commitments and agreements with the Western and regional powers and the acceptance of economic aid from the U.S.S.R.

It is impossible to determine what percentage of the Iranian students abroad hold views hostile to the government of the country, but it is certain that no voices are raised in praise of the ruler or the regime. In a single issue of one of these student papers one may find sentiments such as the following: "Dr. Mossadeq remains the living symbol of Persian honor and nationalism [and] he still has the backing of over 90 per cent of the Persian people. . . . In free elections over 90 per cent of the population would vote for Dr. Mossadeq and his supporters and candidates, [and] over 95 per cent of the Persian students are nationalist and pro-Mossadeq. Policies of the United States back . . . puppets like . . . the Shah of Iran."

These student associations abroad organize hostile demonstrations to greet members of the Iranian Government visiting European countries and the United States. The visit of Muhammad Shah Pahlavi to the United States in April, 1962, was marked by picket lines and the distribution of leaflets that featured the most intemperate language. According to this material, the Shah "has smeared his hands with many innocent people's blood," and in Iran "thousands of political prisoners are held in military barracks and concentration camps without trial." Facts in support of these allegations are not given.

Amidst the flow of rhetoric and invective, one may sense what these vocal students think they want are free elections that will bring back Dr. Mossadeq, the deposition of the ruler, and the establishment of a republic in Iran. Since these students were in their early teens in the Mossadeq period, they have never taken a critical look at the events of these years, and, quite unconsciously, view him as the *mahdi* who will set the wrongs of Iran aright. Students everywhere reflect the opinions of their elders who challenge established authority, and there are many of that generation who place their faith and their hope in the return of Dr. Mossadeq to power.

This continuing devotion to the popular image of Dr. Mossadeq poses serious problems to the leadership of the National Front. Are they to be the custodians of his authority pending his triumphal return? Dr. Mossadeq has asserted that he will never return to the political arena, but he welcomes the hero worship of a younger generation and as long as he lives no leader of the National Front would presume to take his place as the head of the movement. This situation inhibits its present leader, Allahyar Saleh, a man of integrity and long experience in government posts.

Political scientists and experienced politicians are in the minority in the National Front. The majority of members are men who would be active, public-spirited citizens in another kind of society, and they are in revolt against the traditional order of society in Iran because they deny its validity in the present day. They are neither frustrated malcontents nor socialist-minded dreamers. They are not opposed to the *status quo* because they are excluded from the benefits of the system; they oppose its continuance simply on principle. Their heroes are no longer the renowned rulers, poets, and philosophers of Iran, but Harold Laski, Bertrand Russell, and Muhammad Mossadeq; and the institutions admired are not those of age-old Islamic Iran but those of the social-welfare state.

Though repudiating the formalism, authoritarianism, and other social-behavior patterns of traditional Iranian society, they are still, in part, prisoners of these patterns, which shaped them, and remain suspended between two alien worlds—older Iran and an unknown future nation. Now in revolt against the social and political structure, their disorientation from family modes preceded their disorientation from established social patterns. Dr. Mossadeq restored the faith of a new generation in the personal virtues of integrity and nobility of spirit and his successor must also typify them, as well as possess family status, personal ability, and a charismatic appeal. The Iranians have not been prone to follow unknowns or self-made men, and it is for this reason that it seems unlikely that a real rabble-rouser could take over the leadership of the National Front.

Interestingly enough, many of the leading members of the National Front are either on the faculty of Tehran University, as earlier noted, or are trained engineers and successful businessmen. The engineers have been very successful in the construction industry and are now men of means if not of considerable wealth. Ahmad Zanganeh, a founding member of the Iran Party and head of the Plan Organization under Dr. Mossadeq, is a partner in the Nokar Construction Company. Engineer Kazem Hasibi, an early member of the Iran Party and a stalwart associate of Dr. Mossadeq, is in the construction business. Rahim Atai and Mehdi Bazargan of the Freedom Movement of Iran are in construction. Bazargan, who is a partner in three firms and a member of the engineering faculty of Tehran University, represents a link between the faculty and the engineering groups. The composition of these groups clearly reflects the fact that the leadership of the National Front is from the intellectual upper class, or upper middle class, rather than from the urban middle class itself, so frequently identified as the main strength of the National Front.

Some foreign observers tend to believe that in time the nationalist opposition will force the abdication of the Shah and bring into being a neutralist, republican Iran. As it is, the National Front is credited with having attracted the support of the most dynamic and progressive-minded element in Iran; starting from this premise, in a period in which the rising tide of emotional nationalism is sweeping away so many older regimes elsewhere, some observers make such a prediction with regard to Iran.

The government of Iran, having been unsuccessful in tentative attempts to effect a reconciliation with the moderate leaders of the National Front, believes that it is in the interest of internal stability to denigrate this organization. The line most commonly followed is to state that it is infiltrated, duped, and manipulated by the Tudeh Party, following Soviet instructions. The National Front vehemently denies this allegation, and its leaders stress the depth of their own anti-Communist convictions. They insist that there are no direct contacts between responsible elements in the National Front and the Tudeh Party but admit that Communist elements under the guise of ardent Mossadeqists are in contact with the students in efforts to draw them away from the present leadership. They repudiate the Tudeh Party and Soviet broadcasts which call for a united front of liberal elements and for an immediate nationalist revolution.

Although the National Front claims to believe that if elections for the Majlis were entirely free its members would win a majority of the seats, it has no comprehensive political program ready for implementation after victory and no clear vision of the future after these elections, beyond the expected installation of one of its leaders as prime minister.

The National Front leadership may well feel that it must push harder for early elections or lose followers to more radical elements. However, it is inhibited by the government both in the operation of its provincial organizations and in its ability to use the Iranian press to make its views known. It can continue to print and distribute leaflets, some of which will be confiscated, and some of the newspapers will continue to insert National Front announcements. It can attempt to publicize these restrictions by means of mass meetings which the government will suppress to the limit of its ability, or it can remain quiescent in the expectation that the actions of the government itself will create more and more National Front supporters. This choice must present a dilemma to National Front leadership and a rather vital one; for if the National Front seems unwilling to combat the government it may lose followers as well as the initiative to elements of the Tudeh Party or to the diverging Freedom Movement of Iran.

Let us suppose that "free" elections are held. Some National

Front leaders assert that they will win a majority and possibly as many as 80 per cent of the seats in the 200-member Majlis, although Dr. Sanjabi believes they would return only from thirty to forty deputies. "Free" elections have not been precisely defined by any Iranian within or without the government: They may be elections in which all agencies of the government abstain from any role in the nomination and election of deputies, or they may mean elections in which all the ballots cast are honestly counted. Under either of these suggested situations it seems doubtful whether the National Front would be as successful as its members believe.

The National Front candidates may be expected to be popular at Tehran, in a half dozen of the largest towns of the country, and in some other areas, but it seems probable that in many of the more remote electoral districts the influence of local families of long-established prestige, influence, and wealth would result in the return of many deputies who were not in sympathy with the National Front.

A Majlis that did contain a majority of National Front deputies would certainly result in a National Front government, a phenomenon unique to Iranian politics where no government since the adoption of the constitution in 1906 has represented a single political party or grouping. Faced with the diverse tendencies within the National Front itself, and the presence of an unsympathetic minority in the Majlis, such a government would have difficulty in functioning, particularly if it proposed a legislative program of a radical nature. On the other hand, a National Front minority could do much to hamper the operations of a more usual government, or, alternatively, could spur it toward a constructive program.

In summary, the National Front appeals to countless Iranians because it represents the emotionally based aspirations of a rapidly growing element of society which is not traditionally oriented. For example, the impartial administration of justice may be identified as the value most desired by most Iranians, and those attracted to the National Front feel that this goal and others of like nature will never be approached under traditional governments. These supporters probably have a very limited knowledge of the organization, factions, and internal problems of the National Front.

The existence of wide popular support for its ideals does not necessarily mean that the National Front is certain to come to power, nor are there grounds for believing that the National Front would be far more successful in governing and in retaining popular support than its predecessors. A dramatic rise to power by the National Front might actually threaten rather than enhance internal stability should this rise appear to constitute a mandate for drastic change of existing institutions. On the other hand, internal political stability could be enhanced if the regimes in power could accommodate themselves to National Front personalities and goals, or if National Front deputies were to support the constructive policies of another government and only attack its failures of response to popular aspirations. In other words, the role of the National Front in opposition is a potentially constructive one, while its role as a government might well exacerbate existing tensions and rivalries, resulting in the appearance of several competing political parties. Should a republic be established, this would usher in a period of pronounced instability. Perhaps the leaders of the National Front regard such developments as an inevitable result of the replacement of the traditional social and political order, but it seems possible that they have not closely examined the political reality of their potential role as a recognized element of government.

The Urban Middle Class

It is frequently said that the urban middle class of Iran holds the key to the future of Iran. Foreign commentators on the social scene (the Iranians themselves have given almost no attention to the subject) state: (1) that the revolution of rising aspirations centers in this class; (2) that it represents a monolithic backing for the National Front; (3) that its members are determined to share in the decision-making processes of the state; (4) that its rise to power offers the only hope for the establishment of genuine democracy in Iran. Not all these appraisals can be correct and they are in the category of personal opinions, since there is simply no reliable information on this class. There is no collected material on the incomes and occupations of its members, nor any research as to their basic desires and motivations. With equal facility an observer might suggest that this class is primarily concerned with achieving a more modern way of life, sufficiently replete with material benefits and leisure-time enjoyments.

The urban middle class is largely concentrated at Tehran, and the capital has doubled its population in a little more than a decade. This class has grown at an even more rapid rate. In 1958, some 560,000 persons were believed to be gainfully employed in the province of Tehran. This figure excludes farm laborers, domestic servants, home handicraft workers, and members of the police and the armed forces. The figure above and other statistics published in a *National Manpower Resources and Requirements Survey* by the Governmental Affairs Institute have been used in an effort to estimate the size of this middle class: it may be suggested that in the province, which has only two other towns of any size, there are some 200,000 employed individuals of this class. This suggested total includes government workers and those in private employ. Assuming that there are five persons in each of these middle-class families and that many wives and other older members of the families are included in the figure of the employed, the total approaches one-half of the population of the capital. This class is assumed to be entirely literate.

Although this estimated total seems very high, it appears to be supported by a detailed breakdown of the occupational statistics for the province. Some 34,000 men and women are engaged in professional, technical, and related occupations, including 14,000 teachers and 8,000 workers in the field of medicine and health. There are about 5,500 people in managerial and clerical positions, and some 117,500 engaged in retail and wholesale establishments and shops. In such occupations as mechanics and machinists, taxi owners and taxi drivers, electricians, construction workers, printers, food processers, and general services, it is here estimated—on an entirely arbitrary basis—that one out of every four has an income that places him within the lower middle class.

In the range of the average and upper middle class there is a definite shortage of trained personnel in the physical sciences, in medicine, in teaching, and in accounting, and a surplus of lawyers and younger people educated in the liberal arts. Some 50 per cent of those employed in the higher managerial, scientific, professional, and technical posts are graduates of the University of Tehran, while a much smaller percentage is represented by Iranian graduates of foreign universities.

Those members of the middle class who work for the government of Iran at Tehran are employed in offices of the various ministries, in state-owned banks and insurance companies, and in other institutions and industrial enterprises of the state. The levels of pay for government employees are considerably lower than those for private industry. Teachers, including college professors, are very poorly paid, and it is customary for the more talented or resourceful among them to take one or more additional jobs to augment the family income. Considerable social prestige is attached to the professor and the holder of a doctorate: most of the leaders of the National Front come from these groups and many active professors at the University of Tehran have been elected to the Majlis. The field of literature offers social prestige to the successful writers, but scant monetary rewards.

With some 80 per cent of the industrial enterprises in the province of Tehran privately owned, large numbers of the middle class are engaged in managing and staffing these plants and, even, in owning some of them. A traditional pattern of activity is followed by the many individuals engaged in sales positions and in food processing, but there has been a phenomenal development of the service trades within the last decade. Such trades include television, radio, electrical and automobile repairmen and mechanics, beauticians, restaurant operators, advertising and publicity specialists, owners of very elegant shops, real estate agents, dry cleaners, laundromat owners, and tourist bureaus.

In the service trades and in the field of small industrial plants there has been a rapid development of individual initiative and enterprise. At Tehran today, many hundreds of individuals seem to have no difficulty in collecting capital from their families and friends to start new businesses in which a considerable risk of failure or of marginal profits is involved. This new spirit is in great contrast to the traditional attitude of the bazaar, which sought for large profits in limited transactions.

Indicative of this new spirit of individual middle-class enterprise is the encompassing arc of small plants, most of them employing only a few persons, around the southern limits of Tehran. This growing group of entrepreneurs includes members of the wealthy elite as well as of the middle class. What is remarkable is that the individuals concerned have deliberately escaped from the traditional pattern of authoritarianism which discouraged the assumption of, or the acceptance of, personal responsibility.

These individuals are motivated, in contrast to earlier attitudes, by an intense desire to achieve wealth, a desire intensified by their conviction that they are living in a time of rapid change and uncertainty and security may be found only in material possessions. They feel that with money they will achieve status in society and thereby free themselves of its limitations and controls. While the members of the elite class have held similar views for a longer period of time their approach has been different, favoring speculation in commodities and in importing luxury items. Now, however, both the elite and the members of the middle class have invested heavily in real estate and housing construction at Tehran. Whereas the members of the elite attempt to pyramid their holdings, those of the middle class speculate in a more limited way. Typical of their activity is the construction of a house or an apartment building, which can be rented at present high figures until such time as the accumulated returns provide assurance that the owners can afford to move into their own properties. Several thousand such units are rented to members of the foreign colony of Tehran.

Within the past decade, areas of middle-class housing have sprung up in an arc around the earlier northern limits of the capital. Each year, more units are added to the eastern and western arms of the arc, while to the north construction creeps over formerly barren hills to approach the residential areas of Shemiran, five miles away and at a considerably higher altitude. The houses of the elite are more concentrated in the northern limits of the city, as well as in Shemiran.

A house with five rooms, suitable for middle-class occupancy, rents for about $75 a month and is provided with water and electricity. Telephones are not common. The families who can afford this kind of housing also pay income taxes. The first $700 of income is tax-exempt, between $700 and $950 the tax rate is 7 per cent, to $1,300 it is 12 per cent, and then in higher brackets attains 50 per cent. Brightly upholstered furniture of modern design is preferred, and each house will have a radio and probably a refrigerator and other appliances. The middle-class household will have at least one servant, even if only a teen-age boy or girl whose family has migrated to the capital from its farming village.

In the mornings and evenings, the avenues of the central shopping district are jammed with buses, taxis, and private cars. On these streets are about 1,000 buses, 12,000 taxis, and 8,000 cars. A decade earlier, the majority of the cars were of American manufacture. While the elite still prefers a Cadillac or other large American car, or a Mercedes-Benz, the upper-middle-class family will have a Volkswagen or a small French or British car. In fact, more than a third of the private cars are Volkswagens.

The pattern of leisure-time and holiday activity is a cosmopolitan one. Calls are made on relatives, and in the warmer months families dine out in open-air restaurants. The cinema is very popular; also the radio. Not only is Radio Tehran on the air, but the United States Armed Forces radio station at Tehran fills the ether with jazz and celebrity-studded recorded programs that are very well received. Throughout the spring and summer, the cars of the upper-middle-class families stream out of the city to points as much as forty miles away where there are pleasant river valleys offering cool shade and swimming. Picnic lunches are spread out on Persian carpets, the samovar bubbles with hot water for tea, and entertainment comes from musical instruments or a transistor radio. In the winter months many of these families go skiing in the vicinity of the capital.

Other than the upper-middle-class leaders of the National Front, the urban middle class at Tehran appears to have no organized groups to represent its interests, and no spokesmen of its own in the Majlis or other seats of authority. It is quite probable that many of its members are hostile to the entrenched elite, feeling that they could more effectively advance their own interests in its absence, but it is by no means certain that they are ready to defy authority for this reason, even under the guise of advocating social freedoms. A rally held by the National Front in May, 1961, attracted as many as 40,000 people, but no breakdown of participation by social groups and classes is available.

Within the urban middle class there is a sizable element made up of frustrated individuals who are inclined to political extremism, because they see no other solution for their personal problems. Many are educated youths who have not found positions worthy of what they consider to be their talents and capabilities: they feel their way is blocked by entrenched officials. Such individuals have broken from close family ties, and have turned to politics as a substitute for religious sentiments and ethical principles. They believe that the state is not meeting its obligations to them, yet they feel no obligations to the state. It has been suggested by Iranians that an improving economic situation will create jobs for the disgruntled and then hostility toward the regime will gradually disappear. This hopeful belief appears to be very largely wishful thinking.

Outside of Tehran, the urban middle class is most numerous at Isfahan and Abadan. Isfahan is an important point of National Front activity, while thriving Abadan contains ever-growing numbers of experienced technical and administrative personnel.

As a force that challenges authority, the urban middle class is having a measurable impact upon the economic scene and upon traditional occupations and ways of doing business. It does not appear to be a monolithic force concerned with obtaining drastic social and political reforms. Where it is vocal, it is heard through the National Front. In time it may move away from the National Front to follow less moderate spokesmen and agitators from its ranks. However, because of the unwillingness of Iranians to place their confidence in persons who lack established family connections and personal status, such a development seems unlikely. More likely would be a crystalizing of sentiment among the middle-class officers within the armed forces, a group in a better position to channel effective force behind a forceful leader.

Other Elements Opposed to Authority

The traditional elite is unwilling to give up any of its prerogatives. The thought that social and economic changes affecting its interests are inevitable, which would make it advisable to adapt to changing circumstances in order to preserve as much as possible of its position, apparently is given no consideration. Its firm position seems to be to exert all possible influence and pressure on the government to preserve the *status quo*. With respect to the Parliament, the elite believes that it should exercise control over the government. Since the system of arranged elections has always returned a majority of conservatives to the Senate and the Majlis, the elite opposes changes in the electoral law and insists that the government should meet its legal obligations with regard to elections. Naturally, this element opposes efforts by the government to implement laws and regulations harmful to its own interests, such as the land reform decree, stringent controls over imports, controls over banking transactions and speculation in commodities and the flow of capital abroad, and careful collection of income, property, and business taxes.

The reactionary members of the elite favor a return to the pattern of what may be called the conventional prime minister, that is, a head of state who does not advocate radical programs, nor press the Parliament for the enactment of social legislation. This element is most concerned over the possibility that leftist groups might rise to power, and appears to have faith in its ability to stage a preventive countercoup which would place the state under military control.

The reactionaries are well aware that the Shah regards the influence of some "two or three thousand people" as inimical to national progress, that he has described them as "pompous, overfed, and overprivileged," and that he has condemned "men of wealth who stoop so low as to accept bribes and gifts." In addition, he has stated that members of the Majlis and private groups have described him as a "Communist" and as a "revolutionary."

Nevertheless, the Shah and the traditional elite remain mutually dependent upon each other. The Shah must avoid arousing the active hostility of this element, since there are no groups further to the left which have the influence and the administrative, financial, and business competence to form an effective base of support for the regime. The Mardum Party may have been regarded by the ruler as a liberal, stabilizing counterforce, but it failed to meet the demand. On the other hand, the elite continues to regard the throne as the primary stabilizing institution and must refrain from attacking it directly or indirectly. Rather than weaken the position of the Shah, it seeks to moderate his actions and plans through its many contacts with him.

The rise of military regimes in Egypt, Iraq, Pakistan, Thailand, and elsewhere has not been without some impact upon ranking officers of the armed forces of Iran. In February, 1958, General Muhammad Vali Gharani, head of G-2, was arrested on charges of plotting against the government, and then thirty of his alleged associates, most of them civilians, were taken into custody. Only General Gharani was brought to trial: Convicted on charges of abusing his powers and of failing to carry out the orders of his superiors, he was dismissed from the army and sentenced to three years in prison. The press at Tehran were divided in speculating whether Gharani had plotted a military coup d'état or whether he had sought active support from foreign representatives at Tehran in a planned effort to have himself named as prime minister. It was alleged that he had already decided upon the members of his cabinet and that the name of Dr. 'Ali Amini was on this list.

Since 1958, there have been frequent rumors that individuals or groups of officers within the army, or retired from it, were plotting the forceful overthrow of the government. The departure of General Timur Bakhtiar for Europe in January, 1962, upon the order of the Shah, was believed to have resulted from a representation by the government to the ruler that Bakhtiar was plotting against it. Upon his arrival in Europe he said that there was the "possibility of grave upheaval unless the Amini government carries out reforms and calls genuinely free elections."

It is difficult to gain an understanding of the motives of these so-called military plotters. Some people believe that the National Front has placed loyal adherents within the armed forces as its only means of coming to power, by way of a military coup d'état. Another possibility is that, as in some of the countries where military men have taken over, officers within the army believe that the successive civilian governments are inefficient and ineffectual, and are incapable of implementing their announced programs. According to this view, a military government would move rapidly to carry out the plans and reforms already decided upon, and would not necessarily sponsor radical measures to change the social and political structures of the country. The final suggestion, already noted, is that elements within the army might stage a rightist coup d'état to forestall any move by the elements of the left to come to power.

4. Institutions and Programs Contributing to Stability and Progress

The First Government of Positive Nationalism

The sudden emergence of Dr. 'Ali Amini, a man of personal responsibility, as prime minister, indicated a complete break away from conventional prime ministers, and the character of the men he chose for his cabinet reflects a changed attitude about having complacent cabinets, so common to the Iranian scene. Although Dr. Amini did not remain in office long enough to match the post-World War II record of Dr. Manuchehr Eqbal —1,245 days—his tenure was of marked significance.

The selection by the Shah of an individual who he believed was capable of carrying out programs of reform and development more energetically than his predecessors, in spite of the fact that there was no personal friendship or real mutual trust between the two men, was a political innovation. It represented a retreat by the Shah from his role as ruler of the country and the cabinet, since he made it clear that he would give Amini a free hand in running the government. Prime ministers come and go in Iran; but despite the continual urging of the traditional elite for the replacement of Amini with a conventional type of prime minister, on the ground that Amini's policies were upsetting the established pattern of social stability, the Shah refused to intervene.

'Ali Amini, a son of Amin ad-dowleh and Fakhr ad-dowleh, was born to this Qajar family at Tehran in 1907. His father having died early, 'Ali and his brothers and sisters were brought up by their intelligent, forceful mother, of whom Reza Shah is said to have remarked, "Aside from myself there is only one real 'man' in Iran and that is Fakhr ad-dowleh."

As a young man, 'Ali Amini went to France to study at Grenoble and Paris and was awarded a doctorate in economics and jurisprudence. One result of his studies was a book entitled *L'Institution du monopole de commerce extérieur en Perse,* published in France in 1932.

In 1931, he returned to Tehran and entered the government service as a judge. In 1933, he went into the customs service, and by 1936, had risen to the post of director-general of the customs administration. By 1938, he was a director-general in the Ministry of Finance and, in 1940, was named under-secretary of that ministry and was also elected to the Majlis from Tehran. That same year, he served as deputy prime minister. Besides the similarity of their family background and education, he and Dr. Muhammad Mossadeq have in common their writing for publication and their entrance into the Majlis; and both have shown administrative competence.

After 1940, he served for several years as the member for Iran on an international commission for the control of narcotic drugs.

In the summer of 1946, Prime Minister Ahmad Qavam announced the formation of his personally sponsored party, the Democrats of Iran, and he named Amini as a member of the Central Committee of the party. Also, Qavam appointed him as secretary of a commission to draw up a Seven-Year Development Plan for the country.

In 1951, he returned to the political scene as minister of national economy in the cabinet of Dr. Muhammad Mossadeq but soon resigned from the post. From 1953 through 1954, he was minister of finance in the cabinet of General Fazlullah Zahedi, and was the principal Iranian architect of the agreement with the international oil consortium, which he signed in behalf of the government in September, 1954. One of the members of the foreign team described him as a "brilliant, capable, and tough negotiator." Immediately following the signing, he presented the agreement to the Parliament and defended its terms in the face of abusive remarks; both the Majlis and the Senate gave overwhelming approval to the agreement.

In 1955, he became minister of finance in the cabinet of Husein Ala, and was then moved to the post of minister of justice. In 1956, he was named ambassador to the United States. Completely devoting himself to the effort, within a few months he became fluent in English. Speaking frequently to groups in the United States, he represented the interests of Iran in an outstanding manner until he was recalled in the spring of 1958. According to one explanation, the recall was caused by the fact that his name had appeared on a list of individuals whom General Muhammad Vali Gharani intended to appoint to his cabinet, while according to another rumor it was because of a remark included in a speech delivered in Washington on the subject of "Oil and the Economic Development of the Middle East." Pointing out that there were oil-rich and oil-poor countries in the area, he remarked, "If the oil-producing countries of the Middle East combine . . . the proceeds of their oil income, in some sort of a common pool for development, that can surely contribute to the over-all development of the area . . . [since] some earn more than they can use."

For the next few years he moved between Paris and Geneva and his home at Tehran. In Iran he made determined efforts to establish personal relations with religious leaders, with liberal elements, and with the younger intellectuals of the country. His goal was clearly that of the premiership, but his chances were not rated as good. It was recognized that he was incorruptible and very competent and energetic, but he lacked a personal following, displayed no charismatic appeal, and had no sympathetic support from any of the Western powers.

In July, 1960, 'Ali Amini took the initiative in bringing together a group of independents to contest the elections at Tehran. He was much in public view at election rallies and his statements appeared in the newspapers during the period of weeks in which the elections were held. The votes cast at Tehran itself had not been counted prior to the suggestion of the Shah that those deputies already elected should resign, but Dr. Amini and his associates felt that they had been instrumental in exposing the abuses and were pleased by the ruler's decision.

When the second round of elections for the Twentieth Majlis was announced, Dr. Amini stated that he would not be a candidate, since his goal was primarily to test the freedom of the elections. He added that since there were no real political parties in the country he would work for the election of four independent candidates at Tehran.

When he was named prime minister on May 7, 1961, he named a cabinet that included two of the independent candidates to the Majlis and one former member of the Tudeh Party. He announced a seven-point program of reforms. The program included: distributing agricultural lands to the peasants; eliminating corruption within the government; reducing government expenditures; lowering prices of consumer goods; cutting down on imports with the aim of eliminating the unfavorable balance of trade; introducing efficient methods of tax collection; and improving methods of farming. None of these goals were new ones, but by immediately initiating an anti-corruption campaign he indicated his determination to implement the program.

At the end of his first year in office he was still advocating the same program, with the same cabinet ministers. Some thirty active and retired ranking officers of the army, high officials, and important business people had been jailed on preliminary charges of corruption, with a few already tried and convicted, and the program of land distribution was moving steadily ahead. His drastic austerity measures, which included sharp reductions in imports, strict controls over government expenditures, and stringent credit restrictions, had served to halt the heavy outflow of foreign exchange and to insure the solvency of the government. However, by bringing to an end a boom in real estate speculation and building, factory construction, and the import of automobiles, electrical appliances, and other luxury items, and by successfully slowing down the inflationary spiral, Amini and his government had made many enemies. These people included contractors, merchants, industrialists and entrepreneurs, importers, bankers, members of the traditional elite with investments in these fields, and members of the upper middle class. Many merchants had gone into bankruptcy, and some of the private banks were in critical condition.

To the torrent of complaints from those directly affected by the austerity measures, the Prime Minister pointed out that in order to preserve Iran the people must make sacrifices; that since the masses have nothing it is up to the wealthy to do so. He added that he had informed them that unless they cooperated there would be a revolution. Echoing earlier statements by the Shah, he remarked, "There are 2,000 egoistic people in Tehran who want everything in the country for themselves."

On the other side of the coin was the fact that the forced collapse of the boom in construction and other fields threw many industrial workers and laborers out of work and exacerbated the already serious problem of unemployment in Tehran and the other larger towns.

In his first year in office Dr. Amini made no apparent headway toward attracting a wide base of popular support. He had made no move to carry out his earlier plan of establishing a moderate political party representative of the right fringe of the left and the left fringe of the right. One of his original hopes, that of drawing moderate leaders of the National Front into his government, was frustrated by their reaction against his decision not to schedule elections. He had insisted that a further stabilization of the economic situation and a change in the electoral system were both necessary before the country could risk a return to possible parliamentary chaos. He had insisted that neither the National Front nor the conservatives banded together in the so-called Defenders of the Constitution would be permitted to hold demonstrations or to build up political organizations.

On the other hand, one step preparatory to the holding of "fair" elections was taken. This was accomplished by an imperial decree, which authorized the government of Dr. Amini, "until such time as the Majlis is convened, to legislate such laws as may be deemed necessary for the formation of village councils, and with regard to laws affecting urban councils and preliminary election committees, to review and carefully study the laws affecting them, and to modify them in the light of present-day requirements and circumstances." Although not so indicated in the decree, such actions as these could lead to the establishment of a party composed of members of the lower classes, those who will benefit most directly from the program of reforms and therefore might be prepared to support the government's candidates. It is to be noted that the minister of agriculture in the Amini cabinet suggested that the masses will not permit opponents of reform to enter the next Majlis.

The budget for the year 1341 (1962-63) should have been prepared and approved by the cabinet prior to March 21, 1962—(the first day of 1341). It was not. In the spring, preliminary estimates were discarded when it became apparent that the United States would not make a grant to bridge the gap between anticipated income and expenditures. As summer drew on, the press at Tehran reported that individual members of the cabinet were unwilling to slash the budgets of their ministries to the extent requested by Prime Minister Amini, and that officials of the Plan Organization viewed with alarm the prospect that it would receive a smaller share of the oil revenues than in previous years. However, just as other reports circulated to the effect that the details of a drastically curtailed budget were to be released, on July 18, Dr. Amini resigned. His initial statement emphasized that his action resulted from the inability to meet the budget deficit: This inability stemmed from the tardy economic assistance and the cutting-off of military assistance by the United States. According to his statement, Iran had received only $30 million in economic assistance and grants since he took office in May, 1961. In rebuttal, the State Department said that during these fourteen months the United States provided $67.3 million in economic grants and loans and had made committments for an additional $20 million for development loans.

In voluntarily relinquishing high office, Dr. Amini acted contrary to the pattern of his predecessors and recognized the fact of his own physical and mental exhaustion. Apparently, he had tried to carry the entire weight of responsibility while failing to assemble a cohesive cabinet, to bring together competent advisers, and to attract substantial public confidence and support. On the other hand, he had enjoyed the firm backing of the ruler and had never deviated from his original program. After his resignation, the Tehran press, again contrary to pattern, refrained from harsh criticism of his actions in office.

Thus, the first government of positive nationalism ended abruptly rather than simply withering away. In view of the suddenness of Amini's departure, it was quite natural for him to be succeeded by a more conventional prime minister. What is less predictable is whether the next step taken by the Shah will be to name another iconoclast to carry on the bloodless revolution of the social order—even to the extent of recalling Dr. Amini.

The Plan Organization

In 1937, the government of Iran set up a High Economic Council to plan the future economic development of the country. The initial impact of World War II upon Iran's economy and the ensuing occupation of the country by Allied forces served to prevent any progress in the field. However, by 1946, the mounting purchases of rials by the Allies for their needs within the country had so built up the gold holdings of the National Bank that prospects appeared much more favorable. In that year, a High Plan Committee was established and instructed to prepare a development plan for the country. After its preliminary studies, it concluded that local resources would be inadequate to finance the scope of the planned program and that the International Bank for Reconstruction and Development should be asked to finance part of the program. Since the IBRD granted loans for specific purposes rather than for general schemes, the firm of Morrison-Knudsen, Inc., was retained to prepare detailed project outlines for submission to the bank. Based on the firm's report, a revised draft plan was prepared. Following a suggestion from the IBRD, the draft plan was reviewed by Overseas Consultants, Incorporated, and the latter firm was employed to aid in administering the plan.

Early in 1949, the Majlis passed a law authorizing the Plan Organization—a new body set up to execute the plan—to carry out the First Seven-Year Plan. Overseas Consultants characterized the $650 million plan—later revised downward to $400 million—as "the largest industrial program in one country in history." Beginning in 1950, the Plan Organization was to have at its disposal all the revenue from the Anglo-Iranian Oil Company, then about $40 million a year. The first two years of operations were devoted to setting up the organizational structure of the Plan Organization and to reorganizing the state-owned industries, which had been turned over to it. Then, the nationalization of the oil industry and the resulting loss of oil royalties had a very damaging effect upon the program.

In 1954, Abol Hasan Ebtahaj, long the dynamic head of the National Bank of Iran and more recently with the International Monetary Fund at Washington, D.C., was named as managing director of the Plan Organization, and he gave immediate attention to completing selected projects and to planning for the future.

Early in 1956, the Second Seven-Year Development Law passed by the Majlis gave the Plan Organization authority and powers "for increasing production, developing exports [expanding] agriculture and industries, discovering and exploiting mines and natural resources, improving and completing means of communication, improving public health . . . and raising educational standards . . . and living conditions." Expenditures for the seven-year period were estimated at just over $1 billion: The allocations were broken down into 26 per cent for agricultural and engineering projects, 32.6 per cent for communications and transport, 15.1 per cent for mining and industry, and 26.3 per cent for social services.

The announced intention of the government and the Majlis was to channel all the oil revenues to the Plan Organization, but quite soon the figure was cut to 80 per cent and then to 60 per cent as successive cabinets were faced with the necessity of using a part of these revenues to help meet budgetary deficits. In March, 1958, the figure was cut to 60 per cent of oil revenues up to $188 million—all amounts in excess of this figure went to the Ministry of Finance. Finally, in 1959 a firm figure of $130 million annually from oil revenues was assigned to the Plan Organization. Naturally enough, the successive reduction in funds available from oil revenues posed serious problems to the Plan Organization.

According to the terms of the law, the Plan Organization was empowered to borrow from domestic and foreign banks and international agencies, obligating future oil revenues for the repayment of such loans. From 1956 through 1959, long-term loans from the IBRD, the Export-Import Bank, the Development Loan Fund, and other sources totaled $362.9 million.

The Plan Organization was authorized to carry out its projects by providing funds to the ministries and other agencies of the government, or, independently, by contracting with consulting engineers and private organizations. Several firms of foreign engineers and managerial consultants, employed in an advisory capacity by the Plan Organization, opened offices at Tehran, and, in 1957, a Harvard (University) Advisory Group arrived to work with the Economic Bureau of the Plan Organization. Also, in 1957, the Plan Organization concluded an agreement with the Development and Resources Corporation of New York for the integrated agricultural and industrial development of the province of Khuzistan. Finally, in the same year the government of the United States assumed the cost of providing the facilities of the Governmental Affairs Institute of Washington, D.C., to carry out manpower and management advisory services.

Contracts were let for a great number of projects, far too many to list. The major effort of the Plan Organization was concentrated upon the construction of heavy-duty, paved highways, upon the provision of potable water, electric light and power, and other facilities for more than 300 towns and villages, and upon the construction of tremendous dams capable of irrigating hundreds of thousands of acres and of supplying almost unlimited power for urban areas and for industrial expansion. To turn to specific undertakings, the Karej River Dam, 50 kilometers west of Tehran, was completed to its height of 180 meters in 1961. The Sefid River Dam, on the northern slope of the Elburz Range and some 103 meters high, was finished in 1962, and the Dez River Dam will be 203 meters high upon its completion in 1963.

The most ambitious project of the Second Plan was the one undertaken in Khuzistan by the Development and Resources Corporation, whose principal officers, David Lilienthal and Gordon Clapp, were former chairmen of the Tennessee Valley Authority. Their task was described by Muhammad Reza Shah as the "development of the fertile province of Khuzistan, the largest fertile valley in Iran . . . irrigated by the Karun River and its tributaries which flow into the Persian Gulf. . . . The project covers a series of dams and flood-control works, and the program is based on the coordinated exploitation of all the resources of the region by principles of cooperation between public and private groups and agencies, on the lines of the Tennessee Valley."

Emphasis was placed upon the fact that no other area of the entire Middle East offered such a comprehensive combination of petroleum reserves, vast, level agricultural lands, substantial hydroelectric and irrigation possibilities, ready access to sea and land transportation, and the existing nucleus of an industrial labor force. Unfavorable factors included a very scanty annual rainfall, which means that all crops must be irrigated, and an extremely hot climate during most of the year.

The Development and Resources Corporation set up the Khuzistan Development Service as its operating agency and, from the very beginning, undertook the training of managerial talent in anticipation of gradually turning over its direction to Iranian personnel. Within the general framework, the Khuzistan Water and Power Authority was established by law and allotted full powers to execute the numerous projects.

One of the major undertakings was the construction of the Dez River Dam, the seventh highest in the world, which will produce 520,000 kilowatts of power. In the Achaemenid and Sasanian periods and in the early Islamic centuries, the Khuzistan plain had been crisscrossed by a network of irrigation canals leading off from the Karun and its tributaries. These canals were filled only when the rivers were high, and so only a single crop could be irrigated and grown each year. In addition, devastating spring floods menaced the irrigation system. The Dez Dam was designed to put an end to the floods and to provide a constant level of water throughout the year to fill a new network of canals (utilizing some of the ancient ones), thus permitting at least two crops to be grown on some 360,000 acres. While the construction of the dam went forward, extensive experiments with fertilizers and with varieties of wheat were made on test farms, soil studies were conducted, and a public health survey of the region carried out.

Another major project included the planting of thousands of

acres of sugar cane and the construction of a sugar refinery which produced some 25,000 tons of refined sugar in 1962. Electric transmission lines linked the Dez Dam site with Ahwaz, Khorramshahr, and Abadan in order to provide abundant current for the industrial development of the region.

However, the path of the Plan Organization within the tangled morass of the established bureaucracy was far from smooth. By his many supporters, Ebtahaj was described as able, honest, blunt, hot-tempered, irascible, and uncompromising, while his opponents used much less complimentary adjectives. The Plan Organization had been envisaged as an island of administrative vision and competence within a sea of bureaucratic inertia, corruption, and incompetence, in the expectation that its example would have a salutary influence upon the operations of the ministries of the government. This hope was not fulfilled.

The ministries were jealous of the prerogatives of the Plan Organization and sought to implement projects of their own without reference to the over-all development plan. In addition, Ebtahaj was criticized in the Majlis and in other quarters for spending so much money on surveys and studies of proposed projects and for employing foreign advisers and firms. Also, he was criticized for allotting such a large percentage of the funds available to the Plan Organization for the construction of a few huge dams, instead of for application toward a large number of small-scale projects, which would be readily visible throughout the country and have an immediate impact upon local standards of living.

Ebtahaj was impatient, even abusive, toward his critics, saying that he would welcome constructive criticism but not biased, negative attacks. He stressed the belief that time was on the side of the Plan Organization and of the country as a whole, since as the people witnessed the direct benefits of the completed projects the political agitation against the regime would gradually fade away. For several years he enjoyed the unflagging support of Muhammad Reza Shah and then suddenly lost it for reasons that have never been explained. In February, 1959, the Majlis passed a government-sponsored bill, which transferred the direction of the Plan Organization to the office of the prime minister and gave him authority to appoint its director. Ebtahaj immediately resigned, to the accompaniment of sharp criticism of the government for eliminating Iran's most capable and honest public servant. That September, the government sponsored legal action to broaden control over the Plan Organization by the prime minister, but the Majlis restored the semi-autonomous powers of the Plan Organization.

In its own critique of the effectiveness of the Second Plan, the Bureau of Economic Affairs stated that, through a series of shock treatments, the economy of the country had been galvanized into action and the need for institutional and organizational changes made more apparent. In the field of agriculture, it stated, too much attention was given to building fixed capital assets without due consideration for future costs of operation and maintenance, although the groundwork was laid for an expanded seed-improvement program, for a fertilizer and pesticide program, and for extension services and rural cooperatives.

Within the period the production of construction materials, sugar, and textiles rose very significantly, and there was limited success in demonstrating to private investors the feasibility of new industrial and mining ventures. The completion of major highways brought down the cost of transport and aided in the integration of the domestic market, while the capacity of the Persian Gulf ports was substantially increased.

Within the period of the Second Plan, the Gross National Product rose at least 6 per cent a year. The development outlay rose from 12 per cent to 22 per cent of the GNP, and the industrial output increased 11 per cent annually. Although foreign loans and grants played an important role, some 75 per cent of the capital outlay was financed by domestic savings.

Less favorable factors had included a decline in the inflow of foreign capital, a sharp drop in foreign exchange reserves, an unprecedented rise in imports, and a general inflationary trend. These factors led, near the end of 1959, to the institution of a stabilization program designed to achieve balance-of-payments equilibrium and relative price stability through monetary and fiscal discipline. However, only after Dr. 'Ali Amini came in as prime minister was an all-out effort made to enforce this program.

The original draft of the Third Plan was the work of a sizable group of highly trained and very able young Iranian economists and specialists in other fields who had benefited from the presence of experienced foreign advisers and consultants. That this group had been assembled by Abol Hasan Ebtahaj remained a tribute to his vision. The text of the Third Plan, as drafted by this group, included a series of evaluations of existing institutions, and statements of policy objectives. It was permeated with frank, philosophical discussions of the problems faced by Iran in all fields—social as well as economic—and of the need for a long-term national effort toward their solution.

The Third Plan, as drafted, differed radically from the first two in that instead of being a series of individual projects of widely varying magnitude it represented a comprehensive scheme to integrate all normal and development expenditures and programs in order to raise the national income by at least 6 per cent a year. Secondary objectives included the creation of an optimum number of employment opportunities, a more equal distribution of income, and reforms—especially in agriculture—that would serve to encourage individual initiative.

The Third Plan began in September, 1962, and will run until March, 1968. The original draft envisaged a total development budget of $2.457 billion, including oil revenues of $1.84 billion (a figure that appears to approach 100 per cent of the total income from oil royalties during the period). This left a shortfall of some $1.6 billion and indicated a need for $200 million in foreign loans and grants during each year of the plan. Since it was quite apparent that no single agency, such as the government of the United States or the IBRD, would be willing to provide such sums, Plan Organization missions visited the United States and Europe in 1961 and 1962 to explain the Plan and to stimulate the creation of an international consortium of lenders whose members would assume appropriate percentages of the required foreign investment.

However, the original draft failed to materialize. A combination of various factors—severe budgetary problems, the lack of active political forces pushing for economic development, and the regime's concentration on the land-reform program—resulted in a re-evaluation of the entire concept. As approved by the cabinet in general terms on September 6, 1962—and in detailed form on October 31, 1962—expenditure funds were cut to $1.87 billion, of which only $530 million was to come from loans, foreign and domestic. Annual allotments from Iran's oil revenues to the Third Plan are to be stepped up from 55 per cent to 80 per cent. Drastic changes were made in the original draft: Projects drawn up by the Plan Organization are to be executed by the various ministries and carried out by Iranian firms rather than by foreign consultants and companies; the Managing Director of the Plan Organization is to be directly responsible to the Prime Minister; and the personnel of the Plan Organization is to be cut by one-third.

Expenditures for the Third Plan are allocated as follows: communications, 21.4 per cent; agriculture and irrigation, 21.5 per cent; power and fuel, 18.7 per cent; industry and mines, 13 per cent; education, 9.7 per cent; health, 7 per cent; manpower, 4.4 per cent; municipal development, 3.6 per cent; and statistics, 0.7 per cent.

As a result of the extensive changes in the Third Plan, many of its original drafters, men who had engaged in negotiations aimed at attracting an international consortium of lenders, resigned. Problems said to be inherent in the final form of the Third Plan include uncertainty as to whether promised shares of the oil revenues will be forthcoming; whether the loss of autonomy will hamper efforts of the Plan Organization to obtain foreign loans; the fact that it represents a series of projects rather than an integrated plan; and the probability that the decreased expenditures will be inadequate to foster a 6 per cent annual increase in the national income.

The Program of Land Reform

Within recent years, the concept that the transfer of ownership of land from landlords to sharecroppers is essential to the political stability and economic progress of underdeveloped countries has won many adherents, even in those countries where such distribution of land has not been undertaken in response to articulate demands from the peasants. Iran has not been immune to the friendly urging of the Western powers to facilitate such a program, although the initiative was taken by the ruler himself.

After his abdication in September, 1941, Reza Shah sent a letter to the prime minister stating that he was conveying all his property to his son and successor, Muhammad Reza Shah Pahlavi, in return for 10 grams of lump sugar, and he asked that the value and revenues of these properties be spent in accordance with the country's needs for works of charity, education, and the like. This property included deposits of 680 million rials in the Bank-i-Melli, vast landholdings, hotels and other buildings, and investments in local industries.

On September 21, 1941, the new ruler announced that this property would be given to the government and the people for agricultural progress, and for urban progress; for improving the life of the peasants and the laborers; for national industry; for the extension of education; and for the improvement of public health. At once, he made cash grants amounting to nearly 100 million rials for specific projects and relief programs. However, the question of what to do with the lands presented a special problem. His father had acquired vast properties through agents who purchased land at below its true value and also usurped holdings and then arranged forced transfers of some of this land against more productive areas in other parts of the country, and the records of all these transactions were complex, confusing, and often fragmentary.

In September, 1941, the new ruler ceded these lands to the state, and the members of the Majlis began lengthy discussions as to the most suitable and equitable means of returning them to their former private owners, if irregularities could be shown to have existed in such transfers. In June, 1942, the Majlis enacted a law that provided for such return and established special courts which were soon beset with hundreds of claims and counterclaims. Some progress was made: In 1947, the special courts were dissolved and in July, 1949, the Majlis passed a bill providing that all lands that had not been successfully reclaimed and all royal lands that had not been contested were to revert to the possession of the ruler and constitute a *vaqf* trust. The income of this trust was to be used by the Imperial Organization for Social Services for charitable purposes.

In January, 1951, Muhammad Reza announced that he would distribute all these lands among the sharecroppers then in occupancy. At that time these holdings were estimated to include more than 520 villages comprising 500,000 acres of cultivable land on which nearly 45,000 people were living. In 1952, the ruler provided capital for the establishment of the Bank of Development and Rural Cooperatives (Bank Omran) and turned over the task of land distribution to this organization. Representatives of the bank went to the villages and appraised the value of plots of adequate size to support a family. These appraisals were then reduced by 20 per cent and the plots sold to the sharecroppers on the basis of twenty-five annual installments.

The capital of the bank, together with the total sums received from all payments, was to be used in aiding the new owners to stand on their own feet and to improve the quality and quantity of their crops. It was recognized that many of them would need financial and technical assistance and that a system of agricultural cooperatives and of responsible village councils would be necessary adjuncts to the encouragement of private initiative. The bank extended interest-free loans to cooperatives and these, in turn, helped the peasants obtain seed grain and farming equipment. The bank also undertook the drilling of deep wells, constructed baths in many villages, built houses, established pools of tractors, and sent young farmers to West Germany and England for training in modern agricultural practices. In addition, its officials and employees had to assume the responsibility for resolving disputes among the new owners of land and to protect the interests of those least likely to stand on their own feet.

The program of land distribution came to an abrupt halt during the premiership of Dr. Mossadeq. Mossadeq sponsored the Farmer's Share Law in 1953, which provided that the income of landlords from the harvests was to be cut by a straight 20 per cent: 10 per cent was to be a deduction from the amount they received from the sharecroppers and 10 per cent a contribution to the financing of village councils, which would undertake local self-help programs. However, Mossadeq was opposed to the Shah's distribution of the royal properties. On one occasion, he stated that the government could not give similar opportunities to all peasants who wanted them, and on another, that it would upset the orderly relationship between other large landowners and their tenants. In fact, the Prime Minister was out to destroy this as well as all other royal prerogatives, and in May, 1953, instituted action designed to transfer title of these lands to the state.

After his removal the program of land distribution moved forward at a pace related to the ability of the Bank Omran to fulfill its mounting obligations. In 1957, it began to engage in commercial banking, and this venture was so profitable that additional funds were available to speed up the program. Finally, in April, 1962, the last of the royal lands passed to their new owners.

The Farmer's Share Law was replaced in 1956 by a new one entitled the Rural Community Bill, which fixed the amount to be collected from the landlords for the use of the village councils at 5 per cent of their net income. The responsibility for establishing and serving these village councils was given to the Community Development Institute of the Ministry of Interior. In 1956, the USOM (the Point Four Mission in Iran) extended financial support through contracts with the Near East Foundation—an American organization which had been active in agricultural demonstration programs in Iran for a decade—which functioned on behalf of the Community Development Institute. By 1957, some 17,000 village councils were established. These bodies undertook to build schools, make all-weather roads, construct baths, and improve existing irrigation systems. An auxiliary service, the Community Development Block Program, trained village-level workers (*dehyars*) to act as local leaders and institute sanitation measures, farm demonstrations, and livestock vaccination, and to encourage cooperative efforts. This program was carried out both in the areas where the lands of the ruler had been distributed and in other parts of the country.

Reza Shah had initiated the idea of transferring *khaliseh*, or state lands, by sale to private persons and by free distribution to the tribes who were to be settled. *Khaliseh* included all "dead" land, which encompassed uncultivated areas not registered, all forests not registered by private owners, and in addition all land to which the state had taken title. By custom, the cultivable land was rented by the state on terms unprofitable to the government, largely because of the deals made between tenants and officials of the state. Disposal of these lands was complicated because most of the lands had not been surveyed; some lacked water rights; and much of the total was simply undesirable land.

Relatively little of this land was disposed of under Reza Shah, and in 1946 the cabinet issued several decrees for the sale and distribution of *khaliseh*. In regions where the fields stood fallow for a year between crops, the new peasant proprietor was to receive fifteen acres. The Agricultural Bank was charged with the implementation of these decrees but, again, progress was slow. In 1955, the Majlis enacted a law relating to the sale of state lands, but it was not until 1958 that the program gained momentum, after strenuous efforts to complete the survey of large areas had been made. This time the pattern established for the sale of the ruler's lands was followed, with the Agricultural Bank collecting payments over a twenty-five-year period, aiding in the establishing of cooperatives, and financing the cultivators through these cooperatives. The eventual goal is to settle some 500,000 families on their own tracts of former *khaliseh*.

In 1958, Muhammad Reza began to speak sharply, in press conferences and speeches, about the large landowners who had refused to follow his example, even when he had spoken directly to them, and sell portions of their holdings to the tenants. He recalled that he had raised this question as early as 1942 and had been labeled a "revolutionary shah" by some of these same individuals. He said that he had decided to limit the size of individual landholdings and stated that the former owners would receive considerable sums which they could invest profitably in productive enterprises.

Once raised by the Shah, the issue could not be disposed of and was treated at length in the local press and became a subject of public discussion. In December, 1959, the government submitted to the Parliament a proposed "Law on the Limitation and Reform of Landed Property." Its text contained some thirty-five lengthy articles, supplemented by many remarks, and was as complicated as the issue itself was complex. Separate sections concerned limitations of holdings, the division of land, the appraisal of land, regulations concerning the sale and purchase of these lands, financial regulations, and technical assistance to and protection of the new proprietors. The size of the maximum individual holding of land used for dry farming was set at 1,480 acres, and of irrigated land at 780 acres. Land in excess of these figures was to be purchased by the government at its estimated value, with fifteen annual payments at 3 per cent interest, and could be purchased by the farmers of the same localities at the same price payable in fifteen annual installments at 4 per cent interest. The funds for buying these lands were to be provided in the annual budget and the receipts from sales were to go to the Agricultural Bank. In turn, the bank was to finance the operation of regional agricultural organizations.

There was sullen opposition to this bill in the Majlis and the Senate where the large landowners were strongly entrenched; and in lengthy debate some of its provisions were watered down prior to final passage by both houses in May, 1960. However, after its passage nothing seemed to happen, for the interests of the elite were sufficiently powerful to prevent action being initiated. It was not until the government of Dr. 'Ali Amini had come into office, with a cabinet containing Dr. Hasan Arsanjani as minister of agriculture, that the situation changed. Arsanjani was determined to push through land reform, and the cabinet prepared a law having conditions less favorable to the large landowner than the bill passed by the Parliament.

This law was signed by Muhammad Reza Shah on January 15, 1962, and in the absence of a Parliament had legal validity at once. However, it must be submitted to the next term of the Parliament for the approval of the Senate and the Majlis. According to its terms, a landowner may retain any single village of his holdings, or he may retain title to as many as six *dangs* in separate villages. (The ownership of a village is normally based upon six *dangs*, with the Persian word having the meaning of a sixth part of a piece of real estate.) Within forty days after the effective date of the law, all landowners with holdings in excess of the limit were required to select the property they wished to retain. All the excess holdings are to be purchased by the government through its Land Reform Organization at figures equal to ten times their present annual incomes, with payments made to the former owners in ten annual installments. Privately owned orchards, tea plantations, and forests are exempt from the provisions of the law, as are lands farmed by mechanized equipment.

The villages acquired by the Land Reform Organization are to be sold to the peasants of the same villages or those in the vicinity at prices 10 per cent above those paid by the government, with the differential being used to develop irrigation facilities and other agricultural improvements. The new owners pay for their land in fifteen annual installments to the Agricultural Bank.

Dr. Arsanjani took immediate action, sending teams of surveyors, tax officials, and agriculturalists to the district of Maragha in Azerbaijan, which had been chosen for the pilot project. On March 13, 1962, the Shah himself arrived at Maragha and distributed deeds of title to 520 families in seven villages of the district. The teams then on the scene were to extend their efforts throughout the province of Azerbaijan before moving on to other areas. In the following months, the distribution of land began in several other areas, including the Caspian littoral, where Dr. 'Ali Amini and other major landowners had complied with the law by registering their excess holdings.

In November, the Minister of Agriculture was able to say that by the first anniversary of the inception of the program, some 11,000 villages will have been distributed. According to the regulations issued by the Ministry, all new landowners had to join the local cooperatives and pay membership fees. Local cooperatives were grouped into regional ones, with the regional cooperative unions serving as purchasing centers for the farm produce, and as wholesalers of seed grain, chemical fertilizers, farming equipment, and staples. Capital obtained from the regional unions and the Agricultural Bank was to be used to establish a Central Bank of Cooperatives; according to Dr. Arsanjani, this bank was destined to become the most important one in Iran. Undertaking a wide range of activities, such as wholesaling textiles to the regional unions at sums far below the retail market price, it was anticipated that the bank would eliminate many private wholesalers and middlemen.

Resistance to the land-distribution program was sporadic, and, lacking press outlets, limited to private complaints. Disturbances occurred in areas where the former landlords tried to maintain ownership of the water supply, as distinct from ownership of land, and where peasants in individual villages retained by landlords attempted to evade their obligations. Those most immediately affected were numerous families who had lived on the income derived from owning one-sixth share, or a much smaller portion, of the village. Real tests of the program were in the offing, involving cases of landlords who refused to register their excess holdings and sought to challenge the legality of the program.

Good will and speedy action alone will be inadequate to carry through this huge program. Dr. Arsanjani has estimated that the cost of acquiring all the lands eligible for distribution (about 25,000 villages) will be the equivalent of $950 million. The costs of acquiring these lands are astronomical; those of the district of Maragha alone are valued at 6 billion rials ($80 million). The budget for the year 1341 (1962–63) included two billion rials for the purchase of privately owned lands, and the Third Seven-Year Plan includes a total of 10.4 billion rials for land reform. These figures would indicate that the government has allotted less than $55 million annually for purchasing land, for instituting the agricultural cooperatives on which so much importance is placed, and for meeting the financial and technical needs of the new proprietors. Then, too, the faster the distribution of land takes place the more pressing and numerous will be the problems. For example, in a region in which thousands of farmers are thrown on their own, aided only by newly organized cooperatives, it seems probable that agricultural production will fall rather than rise. Finally, the Shah himself stated in 1960 that if all the agricultural land in the country were divided among the farmers, each farmer would receive only two acres while he requires twelve acres to support his family. Although this statement may have been made to indicate the need for expanding the amount of land under cultivation and irrigation in the country, it does seem to suggest that many potential proprietors whose hopes have been so heightened by the enthusiasm of the government itself will be disappointed, even disgruntled, in the end.

However, the government of Iran appears to be very optimistic about the success of the program. Dr. Arsanjani, the chief spokesman on the subject, who continued as minister of agriculture in the Alam cabinet, stated that the abolition of the landlord-tenant system has been, for sixty years, the ardent desire of all liberals and reformists in Iran, and now that "feudalism is being abolished, the middle class grows, and a democracy of the bourgeoisie will be established." Dr. Arsanjani seemed well aware of the political implications of the program. The National Front charged that the program is at once a sham and illegal, since the enacting legislation had not been approved by a Parliament. Dr. Arsanjani stated that no future Parliament will discard or modify the law because the individuals who would wish to preserve the special privileges of the landlord class will be kept out of the Majlis by the people. It seems clear that the government looks forward to political support from the newly enlightened masses rather than from the traditional elite.

5. External Forces Operating on the Iranian Scene

The United States and the Other Western Powers

The American presence in Iran had long been felt in the devoted efforts of missionaries conducting schools and operating hospitals, in the work of archaeologists, in the activities of financial advisers W. Morgan Shuster and Dr. Arthur C. Millspaugh, and in the interest of American oil companies in obtaining concessions in the country. Occasionally, the United States made diplomatic protests against active British and Russian interference in Iran's affairs.

Suddenly, late in 1941, another kind of American presence appeared. Service troops of the Persian Gulf Command streamed into the gulf ports to operate an Allied supply route from these ports to the U.S.S.R. These troops, which totaled 30,000 men, came into contact with the 40,000 Persian employees of the command, and with countless other Iranians at Tehran and in other towns. Their presence made real the image gained through motion pictures of America as a land of material progress and prosperity.

Then, at the end of November, 1943, Franklin D. Roosevelt, Winston S. Churchill, and Josef Stalin met in the Tehran Conference. At its conclusion, President Roosevelt outlined to an associate a tentative policy toward Iran which might set a pattern for postwar American efforts to develop and stabilize backward areas. Specifically, the objective was to make Iran sufficiently strong and healthy to discourage foreign intervention, while promoting American interest in sharing in Iran's commerce and resources. In raising the American Legation to the rank of an embassy and in intimating that the American missions to the Iranian Army and gendarmerie would remain for some time, the United States gave a clear indication that it was moving against the established British position in the country. To many Persians this indication was very welcome. Although the American Government refrained from intervening in favor of the Millspaugh mission in the period of local criticism, which led to the departure of Dr. Millspaugh and his staff in 1945, the embassy at Tehran expanded rapidly and was charged with executing a policy along the lines of President Roosevelt's goal. In 1949, Muhammad Reza Shah made his first state visit to the United States, seeking to turn moral commitments to help Iran into substantial financial assistance. Disappointed in his expectations, he later blamed the rise of negative nationalism upon American indifference to the country's urgent needs.

However, the United States was not indifferent, and in October, 1950, it concluded with Iran the first Point Four agreement to be reached with any country. In 1951, an International Cooperation Administration mission was in Iran with a modest budget of $1.6 million. Almost before it had laid out a program, Iran's oil income ceased, and in order to help stave off internal financial collapse the allotment for fiscal 1952 mushroomed to more than $23 million. In addition, some $22 million was allocated for 1953. These impressive sums failed to persuade the government of Dr. Mossadeq to take a more "reasonable" position on a settlement of the oil issue. At the end of June, 1953, President Eisenhower replied to a letter from Dr. Mossadeq that had called his attention to the existence of a dangerous situation in Iran, by stating that failing Iran's resolution of the oil issue the "United States is not presently in a position to extend more aid to Iran or to purchase Iranian oil."

The overthrow of the Mossadeq regime resulted in an immediate increase in aid, so that the total for fiscal 1954 amounted to $84 million. By the end of fiscal 1957, the United States had extended some $322.7 million in grants, loans, and technical assistance. The total amount of direct ICA aid exceeded that granted to any other country during this same period. However, nearly $200 million of this total went to budgetary support and to so-called development assistance. The absence of Iranian oil from world markets caused a flow of funds to Iran, and the prospect of its reappearance stimulated a still greater flow. In other words, American funds were spent to keep the U.S.S.R. out of an unstable Iran and to restore the flow of its oil to the Western world.

In 1956, the International Operations Subcommittee of the Committee on Government Operations of the House of Representatives was critical of the ICA program on the grounds that it had been merely an *ad hoc* method of keeping the Iranian economy afloat during the years of dispute and uncertainty following the nationalization of the oil industry. In reply, ICA insisted that the program had contributed to the maintenance of Iran's independence, that the numerous Point Four projects had resulted in substantial internal economic progress, and that the program had established a sound base for long-range economic and social developments.

None of the parties to this dispute—the Department of State sided with ICA—brought out the point that the expenditures to restore the financial stability of Iran after the fall of Dr. Mossadeq were made without obtaining any *quid pro quo*, although some Americans and many Iranians felt that the occasion was propitious for the United States to insist to the regime that it undertake political and social reforms, which would serve to encourage public participation in the government and to enhance political stability.

Aside from extraordinary expenditures for budgetary support and for development programs, the United States Operations Mission in Iran, the local arm of ICA, and later, USAID, has moved steadily along consistent guide lines in the area of technical assistance. Emphasis has been upon close cooperation between the mission and agencies of the government of Iran. Aspects of this cooperation include the joint planning of projects and the participation of the Iranian agencies in their funding.

The mission operates in the fields of agriculture, public health, education, community development, labor, industry, audiovisual aids, engineering and construction, and public administration, from its headquarters at Tehran and a number of regional offices. These are staffed by American and Iranian personnel with an average strength of 400 people. An earlier interest in contributing to the construction costs of irrigation and power facilities, new industries, and potable water systems gave way to increased concentration upon rural community development, health services, and training and teaching programs, including on-the-job training in the United States of mature Iranians. A particularly successful example of efforts in these fields is the continuing program of malaria control, which has all but eliminated that debilitating illness throughout Iran.

Still more recently, emphasis has shifted toward supporting specific requirements of the Plan Organization. Officials of the Plan Organization have repeatedly stressed that national planning goals could not be attained with the present inadequate administrative machinery, the absence of adequate managerial talent, lack of proper statistical information, and lack of advanced training of many types of technicians and specialists; and ICA and AID have helped meet the costs of the services of American firms and individual consultants in these vital fields.

In May, 1950, Iran adhered to the United States Mutual Defense Assistance Agreement. This agreement provided for the establishment of a Military Assistance Advisory Group to Iran (MAAG); and members of this group were on the scene when American military equipment began to arrive in 1951. As suggested in earlier pages, Iran, in the person of the Shah, and American officials continue to discuss questions relating to the size, equipment, and purpose of the armed forces and to the location of a major defense line across Iran.

The armed forces of his country are a major interest and concern of the ruler. First of all—according to his view—these forces must be so large and well equipped that they serve to enhance the national image of a powerful Iran. Then, they must be strong enough to be able to hold off a possible Soviet attack until the arrival of the forces of the United States and other allies, and they must be more than the equal of those of potentially hostile neighbors. With respect to equipment, Iran urgently needs more of the latest-model jet planes and other modern weapons. Stressing the point that neighboring Turkey has received far larger amounts of financial assistance and of military equipment than Iran, the Shah would like to have the United States underwrite a larger share of the cost of the defense of

Iran, thus enabling the country to devote all of its oil revenues to economic development.

Apparently, American officials began with a concept of the Iranian Army as a modernized police force capable of maintaining internal tranquility. Then, after the creation of the Baghdad Pact, it was considered to represent a link in the long line of global defense against Soviet aggression. The location of bases designed and constructed under MAAG direction clearly indicates that the United States has not been concerned with strengthening Iran's military posture vis-à-vis its neighbors. With regard to planes and weapons, the American view would appear to be that such equipment should be provided in direct relationship to the ability of the Iranians to operate it and to maintain it. Finally, American officials have suggested that the armed forces of the country are too large and represent too great a drain upon the financial resources of Iran.

By the end of fiscal 1961, Iran had received from the United States some $1.3 billion, recorded under the general headings of a Mutual Security Program and a Non-Mutual Security Program, for economic aid, military assistance, and other grants and loans. About 15 per cent of this total was represented by loans provided by the Export-Import Bank and the Development Loan Fund and by loans for the purchase of American surplus property in Iran.

In the years 1958–61, the annual amounts of economic aid declined steadily, and this trend appears likely to continue. President Kennedy's message to Congress in March, 1962, on the foreign-aid program contained guidelines which will certainly be reflected in future American aid to Iran. These include: (1) a drop in military assistance expenditures; (2) the urging of countries receiving such aid to employ military forces in civil action programs; (3) special attention to the self-help and self-reform programs of recipient countries; (4) the replacement of grants and "soft" loans repayable in local currencies by loans repayable in dollars. To select a specific aspect of this program as it would relate to Iran: it would seem to forecast the end of American grants to meet budgetary deficits.

In 1962, there were some 3,000 Americans resident at Tehran and elsewhere in the country. The largest contingents were those of the American Embassy, AID, and the missions to the Iranian armed forces and the gendarmerie, while there were smaller numbers of businessmen and of the staff members of philanthropic foundations and organizations. Locally, apart from the American school, the American presence was visible in its occupation of some of the more modern houses of Tehran and its suburbs, in the chauffeur-driven American cars on the streets, and in the service clubs of the military missions. A clear-cut gulf separated this community from its surroundings and from the Iranian community, except for its limited social intercourse with the social elite, the intellectual group, the ranking officers, and working associates.

More than seventy-five American business firms maintain offices at Tehran. The rapid rise to this number in a very few years reflects both the activities of the Plan Organization in the fields of construction and industry and the previously mentioned effort by the Iranian Government to attract foreign investment in productive enterprises. In 1955, the Parliament passed a bill entitled "For Attracting and Protecting Foreign Capital." Its several clauses provide for the repatriation of capital investments in the same currency or form in which the investments are made, for the withdrawal of annual profits in such currencies, and for equitable compensation in the event of the nationalization of such foreign-financed enterprises. In 1957, the United States guaranteed private American investments against losses resulting from failures by the Iranian Government to abide by all the terms of the law. The initial reaction by American companies was slow in appearing, but investments now are on the increase and are apparent, for example, in the opening of an automobile assembly plant and of a tire factory, and in the inauguration of the Industrial and Mining Development Bank.

While United States policy toward the country has been based upon the desirability of an independent Iran, strong and prosperous and allied with the non-Communist world, there have been various judgments on the effectiveness of this policy and suggestions as to methods by which it might be more effectively implemented. The Iranian regime feels that the position of the country as a bastion against the U.S.S.R. entitles it to greater American economic assistance. Comparing the levels of this assistance with that extended to certain nonaligned nations, such as India, officials complain that the United States gives better treatment to neutrals than to its true friends. From time to time, members of the government suggest that Iran should accept assistance from any country that offers aid without strings, while members of the Majlis have complained that the bogey of Communism is the only reason for American concern with the future of Iran. Upon occasion, the United States is charged with being only lukewarm in its support of the present regime. Thus, in January, 1960, the Department of State flatly denied that "the United States is considering a change in policy toward Iran, which would supposedly entail encouraging opposition elements as a result of allegedly growing dissatisfaction with the present government and its policies." On the other hand, the National Front contends that the more than a billion dollars spent on Iran by the United States was dissipated by the regime, which it claims is incapable of constructive action. However, its leaders do not suggest that such aid would no longer be required should they come to power. Less moderate elements of the National Front cling to the belief that the United States was instrumental in the removal of Dr. Mossadeq and that it will continue to support its puppet, the Shah, at any cost.

Within the United States there appear to be divergent official and private views on alternative courses for the execution of American policy toward Iran. One view holds that it is fallacious to believe that the rapid economic development of the country will result in a decline in present political tensions and feels that continuing aid should be made contingent upon the *quid pro quo* of even more rapid social and administrative reforms. Parallel to this view is the one that the Shah should be forcefully persuaded to reign rather than to rule—that only this course can serve to stave off violent political upheaval—and that the regime should be encouraged to draw moderate opposition elements into political and administrative posts. Still another suggested approach is that the United States should openly encourage the moderate political opposition to the regime, as a measure of insurance against the alternatives of the rise of demagogic leadership or growing Communist influence. All such views imply interference in the internal affairs of Iran, but they are based upon the feeling that the very existence of an important program of economic and military aid is a form of interference and should be exploited in a positive, constructive manner.

Such friends and allies of the United States as the United Kingdom, West Germany, France, and Italy follow its general lead in supporting the constitutional monarchy and in participating in the industrial and economic development of the country. Beset by many problems and financial pressures after World War II, the United Kingdom was not too reluctant to see the United States move into its former role as the opponent of Soviet designs against Iran, although it continued to make every effort to protect and to expand its markets there. An active partner in CENTO, the United Kingdom extends some economic assistance through this organization, while regretting its inability to contribute directly to the financing of the Third Plan.

Prior to World War II, Germany was the leader in Iran's foreign trade and in participation in its industrial growth. Since 1950 West Germany has moved rapidly and effectively to recover first place among Iran's trading partners, to re-establish German business enterprises in Iran, and to give a sympathetic response to the proposal that it join an international consortium to support the Third Plan. While the commercial and other relations of France with Iran have not recovered their pre-World War II level, those of Italy have grown, as indicated, in part, by the establishment of a joint Irano-Italian oil company to exploit three areas of the country.

Finally, moving into the area of friendly non-Western powers, Iran maintains relations with Nationalist China and has never recognized the People's Republic of China. It has important commercial relations with Japan, a country which may join the international consortium to support the Third Plan.

The U.S.S.R.

To employ familiar Soviet terminology, "it is a well-known fact" that the U.S.S.R. has as a major policy objective the complete dominance of Iran. Its alternative strategic goals include the persuasion of the existing regime to adopt a foreign policy of neutrality and nonalignment with the free world, the establishment of a Soviet-controlled bridgehead in Iran, and the replacement of the regime and the monarchy itself by a "popular" government, which will be open to subversive penetration and direction and eventual replacement by the Tudeh Party of Iran.

Soviet efforts throughout the twentieth century toward these goals, some of which have been described in earlier sections, ended in failure because of the effective resistance offered by the successive governments of Iran. Upon several occasions the Soviet Union overestimated the capabilities of its tools within Iran and underestimated the determination of the country as a whole to oppose any and all attempts at foreign domination.

The occasion of the failure of the Tudeh Party to take over Tehran in the critical days of August, 1953, may have led the U.S.S.R. to make a more objective appraisal of its capabilities. At any rate, since 1954 the U.S.S.R. has been alternately "soft" and "hard" toward the governments of Iran, offering the carrot for relatively brief periods and then laying on with the stick month after month. Although in that year there were Soviet attacks against the "enslaving character" of the international consortium agreement, the two countries did reach agreements on the delineation of their common frontier and upon financial matters.

The adherence of Iran to the Baghdad Pact in February, 1955, brought on a series of Soviet notes of protest and the opening of a Soviet propaganda campaign against Iran and the other signatories of the Pact. With respect to Iran, this campaign stressed three themes: The Pact was an expression of intentions hostile to the U.S.S.R.; Iran had nothing to fear from the U.S.S.R. and was flanked by other friendly neighbors so that such an agreement was unnecessary; American aid to Iran would have disastrous effects on its economy and make the country a vassal of the United States. In later months emphasis shifted to the strong desire for neutrality among the Iranians; and the assertion was made that the regime needed foreign military assistance in order to put down dissatisfaction within the country. Within Iran some of these themes, notably the desire for neutrality and the opposition to American economic penetration, appeared in newspapers at Tehran that had not been previously identified with the Tudeh Party or the Soviet Union.

However, the general tone was one of an appeal to self-interest on the part of the Iranians, and threats of reprisals were seldom voiced. In June, 1956, Muhammad Reza and Queen Soraya made a state visit to the Soviet Union. Just prior to their departure, Marshal Bulganin summarized the results of the visit in a friendly and conciliatory speech, although it did contain a reference to military groups as a new and disguised form of the old colonial policy which had damaged the vital interests of the peoples of the Near and Middle East. Direct light on the conversations of the Shah with Khrushchev and his associates may be found in the Shah's autobiography. Explaining the reason for the adherence of Iran to the Baghdad Pact, Muhammad Reza reviewed the history of Russian aggression against Iran in 1908, 1920, 1941, and 1945–46, and stressed his country's need to establish effective measures against possible future aggression. Khrushchev admitted that Russia had made mistakes in the past with regard to its policies toward Iran but protested against the aggressive and militaristic implications of the Baghdad Pact. He added that Iran might be forced by its stronger partners to make its territory available for an attack on the U.S.S.R. In reply, the Shah promised that Iran would never tolerate such action.

It seems reasonable to assume that the U.S.S.R. has not been seriously concerned over the development of the Baghdad Pact and CENTO, its successor, as such. However, its related minimum objective continued to be the agreement on Iran's part to refuse to permit foreign military bases and missile installations on its soil.

The "soft" Soviet attitude toward Iran continued throughout 1957 and into 1958. In 1957, the two countries concluded several important agreements: a treaty relating to the security of the common frontier, an agreement on the question of transit rights, and an accord relative to the exploitation of the irrigation and hydroelectric potentials of two rivers along the common frontier. To a group of Iranian journalists in Moscow, Marshal Bulganin said that "the attitude of the Soviet government in the question of [Iranian] Azerbaijan was regrettable," and in so doing underlined the repudiation of the Stalinist attitude toward Iran. However, whether because Soviet statements are not always completely coordinated, or because Soviet leaders believe that threats should be delivered at appropriate intervals, in September, 1957, Marshal Vershinin stated that "to bombard military centers in Western Europe, Turkey, Iran, and other countries, we will not [even] need to use long-range rockets."

Near the end of November, 1957, Nikolai Pegov, Soviet ambassador to Iran, returned from leave to Tehran. In an unprecedented arrangement, he was permitted to speak over Radio Tehran: he paid a glowing tribute to Irano-Soviet friendship and stressed the desire of the Soviet Union for peace and security in the Middle East. From this time until the end of the year Radio Moscow, in its Persian-language broadcasts, praised Reza Shah, the founder of modern Iran, and his son for his efforts to make the country prosperous, and, in particular, for his initiative in concluding an agreement with an Irano-Italian oil company which would return 75 per cent of the profits to Iran. Soviet offers of technical and economic assistance were made to Iran, and Russian technicians came into the country to complete the erection of grain-storage silos in several towns.

In March, 1958, Premier Khrushchev spoke at Moscow and included statements about Soviet relations with the countries of the Middle East. He said:

Another of our neighbors in the south is Iran. During the stay of the Shah of Iran in the U.S.S.R. we had many useful conversations with him. Frontier questions in dispute for hundreds of years have now been settled to mutual satisfaction. Today we are negotiating with Iran on some economic questions: the building of dams, irrigation, the utilization of frontier rivers in the interest of both countries. . . . We have told the government of Iran that the Soviet Union did not have, and does not have, any unfriendly intentions with regard to Iran. We think that the Iranian Government has become convinced of this.

In April, Iran and the U.S.S.R. reached an agreement on the items and quantities of goods which were to flow between the two countries, and in July, Ambassador Pegov stated that he was still awaiting the Iranian reply to Soviet offers of technical and economic assistance and of cultural collaboration. He added that the Soviet Union had offered to supply equipment for the

exploitation of the oil resources of Iran, to send in oil technicians, and to train Iranians in oil technology in the Soviet Union;
he pointed out that this generous offer would permit Iran to receive 100 per cent of the revenues obtained from the exploitation
of its own resources. By November a Soviet spokesman at
Tehran began to express dissatisfaction over the fact that the
government of Iran had failed to request assistance from the
U.S.S.R., and, suddenly, in the same month the U.S.S.R. moved
toward a "hard" line on Iran.

On November 10, 1958, Khrushchev stated that Iran was being increasingly drawn into the aggressive NATO bloc and
that the threat had arisen of its territory being turned into an
American military stronghold. He added that this was a dangerous road for the Iranian Government and for the Shah of Iran
and asked, "How, under these circumstances, should one regard
the actions designed to turn Iran into an American springboard,
in particular through the conclusion of a new military treaty
with the United States? . . . We shall regard it as an act hostile
to our country [and] if it does take such a step, it means that it
will be committing an aggressive act against the U.S.S.R."

Khrushchev had been stirred up by reports that the United
States, although it had declined to join the Baghdad Pact, was
offering to conclude bilateral agreements with Iran, Turkey,
and Pakistan. At the end of December the U.S.S.R. delivered a
long *aide-memoire* to Iran, which employed the sharpest terms
in warning the latter country against concluding any new military agreement that would permit a third country to send forces
into Iran. Separately, the Soviets made their countermove by
suggesting their willingness to conclude a long-term non-aggres-
sion pact and to provide tremendous economic aid to Iran. The
Iranian Government was not above stalling for time in an effort
to determine what could be gained by playing off the U.S.S.R.
and the United States, since it felt that the draft terms of the
proposed bilateral pact left something to be desired and its armed
forces were not receiving adequate military equipment from the
United States.

In January, 1959, a Soviet mission came to Tehran to negotiate a nonaggression treaty, and although it dropped the initial
demand that Iran quit the Baghdad Pact it did insist that it refrain

from concluding a bilateral agreement with the United States. The Iranian negotiators, instructed by the Shah, refused to abandon the concept of the bilateral pact and found the suggested terms of the nonaggression treaty unacceptable; and after two weeks they broke off the talks. Early in March the bilateral agreement was signed: It contained provisions for the American defense of Iran in case of Communist aggression.

Furious at the treatment of its mission and the conclusion of the agreement with the United States, the U.S.S.R. recalled Pegov to Moscow and initiated a series of notes to Iran condemning its "anti-Soviet policy." Radio Moscow put out inflammatory material attacking the Shah and the government; the station near Baku, which called itself the National Voice of Iran, went to extreme lengths to supplement the official broadcasts; and the Soviet press stated that the bilateral agreement contained a secret supplement permitting the United States to station its forces in the Persian Gulf area of Iran and to construct missile bases in the north of the country. In addition, alleged flights of Soviet planes took place over northern Iran. The propaganda war against Iran waxed hotter and hotter until by the middle of August the Soviet leaders seemed to have felt that the pressure had become so intolerable that the Iranian Government would have to respond favorably to fresh Soviet proposals. On August 21, Radio Moscow broadcast a long commentary on the subject of Irano-Soviet relations: It included a summary of the earlier Soviet proposals concerning a treaty of nonaggression with Iran and outlined the nature of the Soviet offers of economic aid. Also, it pointed out that the offers of aid to Iran paralleled in substance those currently in force with Afghanistan, which program of aid was cited as a good example of friendly, peaceful coexistence between a great socialist country and a small, neutral monarchy.

In September the Soviet stations suddenly ceased their hostile broadcasts and Pegov returned to Tehran to meet with the Shah and the foreign minister of Iran. While parallel talks were going on in Moscow between the Iranian ambassador and Soviet officials, at the end of November the U.S.S.R. addressed a special message to the Iranian Parliament on the subjects of the international political situation and the aims of Soviet foreign policy.

Neither party gave out any information regarding the talks: Later it was revealed that the Shah and Khrushchev had been in personal correspondence and that the Shah had reiterated his personal guarantee that no foreign power would be permitted to establish medium- or long-range ballistic missile bases in Iran.

In the spring of 1960, the U.S.S.R. renewed its extremely hostile propaganda war against Iran and maintained this effort at the same intensity throughout 1961 and 1962. While the press and radio attacks have failed to force Iran to yield to Soviet pressures, there are no indications that the U.S.S.R. plans to undertake more direct and provocative measures. Iran has taken the precaution of denouncing the articles of the Irano-Soviet Treaty of 1921, which authorized the entry of Soviet forces into Iran in case its government was unable to put down the activities of elements aiming at the restoration of the Czarist regime in Russia.

Perhaps the U.S.S.R. is awaiting a suitable opportunity to switch to a "soft" line toward Iran. Such an opportunity would occur if the National Front came to power, since its leaders are committed to an independent foreign policy for Iran and to giving consideration to the acceptance of Soviet economic aid. In addition, the U.S.S.R. may believe that the difficulties inherent in financing Iran's Third Plan will make the government more responsive to offers of Soviet aid. Preliminary indications of a tentative switch to a "soft" line appeared in the fall of 1962, when the Soviet Union officially recognized assurances that the missile bases would not be permitted in Iran.

Certainly the U.S.S.R. will continue to push the thesis that the United States is in Iran in order to pursue the old colonialist policy of taking an underdeveloped nation's raw materials and sending in unwanted processed goods; it will neglect to reveal, however, that the Soviet Union continues to import Persian rice, cotton, and wool and to send textiles and manufactured items to Iran.

Meanwhile, the U.S.S.R. will continue its efforts to detach Iran, Turkey, and Pakistan from CENTO and from their bilateral agreements with the United States. It will continue to use its own facilities, those of its satellites, and those of the Tudeh Party and other subversive agencies to call for a revolutionary uprising against the government of Iran. The guidance for this latter line comes from a speech made by Premier Khrushchev in May, 1960, in which he referred to the fact that the bilateral agreement provided American assistance to Iran in case of indirect aggression. He went on to say, "By 'indirect aggression' is meant an attempt by the oppressed people to rise in struggle for its liberation from its oppressors. In this way the United States has assumed the shameful role of the gendarme—it has committed itself to come to the rescue of a regime against which the anger of the people is rising."

Iran in the Middle East

Although the term Middle East dates back only to World War II and has never been precisely defined, Iran's relations with the other Muslim countries of this general region have been long-standing, and, traditionally, not too cordial. Its closest approach to its neighbors came in the Saadabad Pact of 1937, which brought Iran into treaty relations with Turkey, Iraq, and Afghanistan and which is, theoretically, still in force.

Membership in the Baghdad Pact served to promote warmer ties among Iran, Iraq, Turkey, and Pakistan, and later, in CENTO, again with Turkey and Pakistan. None of the three members seem very satisfied with the organization and strength of CENTO, and Iran consistently urges the United States to join the United Kingdom and become a full partner in the alliance.

In 1958, Muhammad Reza Shah and the then premiers of Turkey and Pakistan were interested in the concept of an "Aryan" confederation, which would bring together the so-called Northern Tier countries, including Afghanistan. The Afghan Government was cool to the proposal and denounced alliances that had a military basis, but the desire for such a union, possibly without Afghanistan, remains dormant. Indeed, in the summer of 1962, General Ayub Khan, President of Pakistan, spoke of the value of such a confederation. In fact, the increasing emphasis within CENTO upon regional development, such as a railway and highway joining Pakistan with Turkey and improved telecommunications, points up the value of closer economic ties. In addition, there have been efforts to establish regional ties based upon the common denominator of Islam.

Although Iran has not engaged in hostilities with Afghanistan since the middle of the nineteenth century, there has been no great cordiality between these neighbors in spite of the common heritage of the Persian language and culture and the Muslim religion. For a number of years there has been a running dispute over the amount of water from the Helmand River, rising in the mountains of central Afghanistan, which is permitted to reach southeastern Iran across the frontier. More recently, Iran has been alarmed over the swing of Afghanistan toward the Soviet orbit, including the equipment of its army with Russian tanks, artillery, and late-model jet planes, and the construction by Soviet technicians of military airfields in Afghanistan. Members of the Iranian Government, including the Shah himself, are concerned over the possibility that the U.S.S.R. may move directly into Afghanistan or stir up the Afghans against the Iranians, and, in either event, threaten Iran's eastern flank. However, in 1962, at the suggestion of the United States, the Iranian Government concluded an agreement with Afghanistan to provide transit facilities at reasonable rates for the movement of Iranian petroleum products and of goods landed at Persian Gulf ports to Afghanistan. This action was intended to reduce the reliance of the Afghans upon the Soviets for oil and for the transit of the bulk of its trade through the U.S.S.R.

Relations with the Arab states are normally lukewarm: The Shah himself has stated that the Iranians just do not like Arabs. Iran has never been able to conclude a clear agreement with Iraq over navigation rights in the Shatt al-Arab, the confluence of the Tigris and Euphrates rivers at the head of the Persian Gulf. A 1937 treaty between the two countries governing the delimitation of their common frontiers failed to state whether the boundary along the Shatt al-Arab was the *thalweg* or was the high-water line on the Iranian shore, and Iraq continued to control the piloting of vessels to the oil port of Abadan and the commercial port of Khorramshahr. Relations worsened in 1958, after Qassem came to power in Iraq. Baghdad radio broadcast propaganda hostile to Iran and began to refer to the Persian Gulf as the Arabian Gulf, while the government itself was thought to be stirring up the Kurdish tribes in and adjacent to northwestern Iran. In 1961, the dispute over navigation rights in the

Shatt al-Arab resulted in a cessation of the movement of oil tankers to Abadan for a period of several weeks, but then Qassem's troubles with the Communist Party in Iraq and with opposition from the Kurds in his own country caused him to adopt a friendlier attitude toward Iran.

In the last decade Iran has labored to strengthen its position in the Persian Gulf, motivated in part by irredential ambitions, in part to counter the penetration of the U.A.R. into the area, and in part by the desire to control the oil resources. In 1959, the Parliament passed a bill extending the sovereignty of Iran twelve miles from its Persian Gulf and Caspian Sea coasts, and to the same distance around all its islands in the Persian Gulf. Since that date, drilling for oil has gone forward in these territorial waters of the Persian Gulf.

In 1958, a new political department of the Ministry of Foreign Affairs was set up to handle relations with Saudi Arabia and the shaykhdoms of the Persian Gulf. Following that action, invitations to visit Teheran were extended to the *shaykhs* of Kuwait, Qatar, Sharja, Debai, Ajman, and Ras al-Khaimah. All accepted, were royally treated, and were reminded of the ancient ties of their areas with Iran and of the necessity of resisting penetration by the U.A.R.

Of paramount interest to the nationalists of Iran is what is described as the urgent need to re-establish Iran's sovereignty over the Bahrein Islands of the Persian Gulf. In 1820, Iran lost control over the Bahrein Islands, which came first under the protection of British India and then of Great Britain proper. Diplomatic moves toward their recovery began in the 1930's, and in 1957 the islands were designated as the fourteenth province of the empire of Iran. The fact that the Shaykh of Bahrein derives important revenues from the exploitation of the oil reserves is not without interest to Iran. Diplomatic notes have failed to persuade the United Kingdom to recognize the claim of Iran, and Saudi Arabia is firmly opposed to the claim. However, the possibility of dispatching an expeditionary force to recover the islands—a plan favored in the period of Dr. Mossadeq—now seems remote.

The U.A.R. joined Iraq in renaming the Persian Gulf as the Arabian Gulf. In 1960, Egypt broke off diplomatic relations with

Iran, as a belated reaction to the fact that Iran had extended *de facto* recognition to Israel in 1950, and initiated radio broadcasts attacking the government of Iran that were eagerly quoted by the propaganda organs of the Soviet Union. Israel is a purchaser of Iranian oil and has taken the initiative in developing commercial and military contacts and relations with Iran, stressing the mutual advantages to be gained from cooperation in the face of the hostile attitudes of the Arab states.

V.

Challenges of the Future

Possible Development in the Monarchy, the Government, and Politics; the Attitudes of Society, Economic Prospects, and Foreign Relations

At present, Iran is embarking on a social revolution initiated and directed by the Shah himself—the culminating effort at royal leadership of the country. Measures reflecting this revolution were enthusiastically approved in a popular referendum held on January 26, 1963. The voters approved of the Land Reform law, of a decree-law nationalizing the country's forests, of a decree providing for the sale of state-owned factories to supply financial backing for the implementation of land reform, of a decree providing that workers shall share up to 20 per cent of the net profits of factories and industrial establishments, of a decree amending the election law, and of a decree establishing a nation-wide Literacy Corps.

Some of these measures, and other plans such as enabling the cooperative structure to engage in the manufacture and sale of staple items of village need and consumption appear to strike at the prestige and financial position of the landowners, religious leaders, industrialists, and merchants. Cumulatively, they may weaken or even destroy the graded social structure of Iran and thus put an end to the uneasy alliance between the monarchy and the social elite that has long been a major factor of internal stability.

A parallel may be drawn between some of the actions sponsored by the Shah and those of Dr. Mossadeq, such as the by-passing of the Parliament and reliance upon a popular referendum, and the emotional appeals for mass support against enemies of Iran. However, the enemies are now internal rather than external ones, and the program is constructive, not negative. Questions for the future are numerous: When and under what arrangements or controls should elections be held and constitutional government restored? How long will the aroused masses willingly follow the charismatic image of the Shah? What new forces or political parties will fill the vacuums in the social order resulting from the elimination of the traditional elite? How can the growing, cumbersome structure of the agricultural cooperatives be financed and administered? How effectively will the transfer of unprofitable state-owned industries to private hands be effected? And how can the profit-sharing scheme for industry be made to function? It can be said that the ruler is endeavoring to create a public consensus for his vision of the country's future, and the people themselves must decide whether or not they share this vision.

The Shah, the high officials of the government, and the managerial and planning elite of the Plan Organization place great faith in the culminative effects of the Third Plan as providing the take-off for self-sustaining economic growth—said to be the most desirable achievement of underdeveloped and under-industrialized nations. The capability of reaching this so-called take-off point is dependent upon the more effective functioning of the agencies of the government, and the fact that the Plan Organization has lost its power to exercise measures of control over the design and details of the annual budgets and over the expenditure of funds derived from foreign loans is a depressing indicator. The Third Plan must find acceptance as the national aim of the country; it must be so presented and publicized as to capture the imagination of various interest groups, including opposition elements. It should be noted that neither the First nor the Second Plan was able to arouse such national interest and faith. It must also be noted that the long delay in determining the final form of the Third Plan worked against the interests of the nation for two reasons: first, through indications that all the funds envisaged in the project outlines would not be provided by the government; and, second, through making it impossible for officials of the Plan Organization to present a final projection of requirements to an international consortium of lenders prior to the opening date of the Third Plan.

Areas of the local financial and economic picture present specific difficulties. In the years ahead the necessity of making payments both of interest and on the principal amounts of a long series of foreign loans will constitute an increasing burden on the national budget. This burden will complicate the problem of attempting to bring these budgets, which have risen nearly 20 per cent annually in recent years, into balance, avoiding the usual deficits. Members of the Plan Organization base their calculations regarding sums available for development expenditures on the assumption that budget increases will be held down to less than 5 per cent annually during the term of the Third Plan and that the cost of maintaining the military establishment, also rising at 20 per cent per annum, will be held at a constant level throughout the period.

Since it appears rather unlikely that the United States will continue to provide funds to meet budgetary deficits or to extend military assistance above current levels, the austerity program currently in effect must be prolonged. Within this program, major areas of control on spending will continue to be represented by drastically reducing the quantity of imports, in order to cut down the highly unfavorable balance of trade with its resulting drain on foreign exchange holdings, and by curtailing the credits available to unsupervised private enterprise.

These measures of control have already had an unfavorable impact upon the remarkable and unexpected upsurge of private investment in industry which began in 1954. A typical illustration of this upsurge was the flood of applications against a loan fund of $50 million established by the government in 1957. This fund—a windfall resulting from the revaluation of the fiscal cover of the currency—was to provide up to 50 per cent of the capital required for private industrial ventures, and it was exhausted within two years. Although half the total went to finance large textile plants and sugar refineries, the balance was obtained by 239 firms engaged in some 53 different industries.

In 1955, the liberalization of restrictions placed on private banks, including a reduction in the proportion of their deposits that had to be placed in the National Bank of Iran and authorization to deal in foreign exchange, resulted in the establishment of a substantial number of private banks between 1957 and 1959. Several reflected local capital and management, but others were mixed banks in which up to 49 per cent of the shares were held by banks and investment concerns in Switzerland, Japan, Holland, the United Kingdom, and other countries. Possibly there were too many banks competing for the privilege of making loans to local entrepreneurs, contractors, and merchants. At any rate, in 1962 some were in serious difficulties as a result of the impact of the austerity program of the government imposed upon importers and upon firms engaged in the construction field. By this same time, the National Bank of Iran had been reconstituted into a Central Bank (with powers to regulate the money supply) and a Commercial Bank, and it would seem that the day of the small, private banks was passing in Iran.

As has been suggested, the continuation of the austerity program will be strongly resented by private investors and segments of the middle class that have profited by the previous lack of strict controls and the mounting inflationary trend. These elements, primarily devoted to the accumulation of wealth, are apt to be unenthusiastic about the Third Plan, since it sharply defines the fields in which private investment in industry will be encouraged. In addition, former landlords will be faced with the problem of what to do with the payments received from the sale of their lands.

The original outline of the Third Plan included a hard look at the problem of unemployment in Iran. It indicated that the overabundance of unskilled labor will continue, even grow, throughout the period and that urban unemployment will become more acute. Since 1950, the regime has exercised paternalistic controls over the many labor unions of the country and has managed to keep the country free from major strikes in any field. However, should the regime take serious steps, recommended by the Plan Organization, to weed out the surplus workers in industry, and should the labor force begin to feel that the distribution of agricultural lands to the villagers was not balanced by a comprehensive program to improve its own situation, the workers might well become restive and less responsive to supervision.

The production of oil and natural gas and internal consumption of these resources should increase by a very considerable extent. In 1957, the National Oil Company of Iran divided the entire country into twenty-seven petroleum districts and opened these districts to bidding by foreign companies. Successful bidders were to form joint companies with the NIOC, and three such companies have been established. They are SIRIP, with the participation of an Italian concern, Societa Agip Mineraria; IRCAN, with the Sapphire Petroleum Limited of Canada; and, IPAC, with the Pan American International Oil Company. The last-mentioned firm paid a cash bonus of $25 million upon the acceptance of its bid.

The foreign partners in these joint companies must put up all the capital required to locate and bring in producing wells in their areas and then the NIOC repays half the total cost of these investments. NIOC receives one-half the value of the petroleum products extracted, minus the annual costs of production, and the Iranian Government collects income tax on the net profits of the foreign partners on a sliding scale up to a maximum of 50 per cent. By 1962, both SIRIF and IPAC had brought in producing wells.

The activities of the NIOC are financed by its receipt of 20 per cent of the revenues from the international consortium, and it is empowered to conduct independent operations. As an example, it has successfully developed a field of natural gas and light petroleum at Sarajeh, less than 75 miles south of Tehran.

The expansion of the network of pipelines for the export of crude and refined oil and for the internal distribution of petroleum products is moving ahead at a rapid rate. In 1960, a pipeline some 100 miles long was completed from a producing field to the island of Kharg in the Persian Gulf, with 25 miles of this length under water, and a tanker terminal came into operation on the island. To augment the existing tanker terminals at Abadan and Ma'shur, another terminal is to be constructed at Khor Musa, just to the west of Ma'shur. These new terminals not only provide deeper water for the largest tankers, but decrease the reliance upon facilities in the Shatt al-Arab where there has been friction with Iraq.

Several years ago, a 10-inch petroleum products pipeline was run from the southwestern fields to Tehran, with a branch line to Isfahan, and at present extensions are being constructed from Tehran to Resht on the Caspian littoral and to the east in the direction of distant Meshed. In the near future a second, larger line will be built from the fields to Tehran. At the end of 1961, the first natural gas pipeline was completed from a southern field to Shiraz, a distance of 155 miles. It supplies the primary material for the country's first fertilizer plant and fuel for local industry. Another natural-gas line will run from the Sarajeh field to Tehran. If the resources of the Sarajeh field prove adequate, an agreement reached between Iran and Turkey in 1958 for the construction of a crude-oil pipeline from Iran to a Turkish port on the Mediterranean Sea will be implemented.

There would appear to be three probable developments in the petroleum industry. The production of natural gas will rise more sharply than that of crude oil; the financial resources of NIOC will come under severe strain as the result of its independent operations and its obligations to the foreign partners in the joint companies; and expanding production by the joint companies at rates more favorable to Iran will increase the pressures on the international consortium for an upward revision of the royalty rates now in effect.

From 1950 through 1958, agricultural production increased about 3.3 per cent annually. The Third Plan envisages an annual increase of 4.1 per cent, associating this figure with an anticipated population growth of 2.5 per cent annually. However, as the gross national income rises in this period, so will the per capita consumption of food, and the planners expect certain items to be in short supply and these and other items to rise in price. Even with these reservations to the optimistic estimates of increased production, the immediate future of agriculture would seem to be somewhat more uncertain. Occasional seasons of drought have had disastrous effects upon crop production, and in 1962 the government was faced with the necessity of importing several hundred thousand tons of wheat. Not until the vast areas irrigated by the newly completed dams have been brought into production and a network of feeder roads constructed into the less accessible areas will the total supply of food crops and animal products be adequate for the growing population.

If much more attention has been given to probable developments in the areas of economics and finance than to those of politics and society, it is certainly because forecasts based upon statistics are less risky than those concerned with the reactions of governments and individuals to their changing environment.

In the field of foreign relations any predictions must stem from the assumption that the present type of regime remains in power. Then, it may be suggested that relations with the United States will continue to be close, but somewhat less cordial on the Iranian side because of American efforts to shift full responsibility for the financial problems of the country to the government of Iran. No marked improvement in relations with the U.S.S.R. can be expected, unless larger policy considerations in other areas of the world should induce the Soviet Union to swing to a "soft" attitude toward Iran. Relations with the countries of the Middle East are more likely to improve than to deteriorate. However, a prime danger point in the region remains the Kurdish areas, with the ever-threatening possibility that the U.S.S.R. may move to extend the present conflict between the Kurds and the government of Iraq onto a larger scene through its encouragement of an autonomous Kurdistan.

Bibliography

Advice to the Plan Organization of Iran, 1956–1961. Washington, D.C.: Governmental Affairs Institute, 1961.

AFSCHAHR, DR. (MAHMOUD). *La Politique Européenne en Perse.* Berlin: M. Nay, 1921.

AGABEKOV, GEORGES. *Ogpu, the Russian Secret Terror.* Translated by HENRY W. BUNN. New York: Bretano's, 1931.

AL-AFGHANI JAMAL AL-DIN. *Réfutation des Matérialistes.* Paris: P. Geuthner, 1942.

AZADI, M. "Iran Today," *International Affairs* (Moscow), December, 1960.

BAHAR, MALEK AL-SHO'ARA. *Tarikh-e mokhtasar-e ahzabe siyasi (A Short History of Political Parties).* Tehran, 1942–47.

BANANI, AMIN. *The Modernization of Iran, 1921–1924.* Stanford, Calif.: Stanford University Press, 1961.

BAYNE, E. A. "Crisis of Confidence in Iran," *Foreign Affairs,* XXIX, No. 4 (July, 1951).

———. *Persian Horizons: A Survey of Contemporary Social, Economic, and Political Trends in Iran.* Part III: "The Managing Director." New York: American Universities Field Staff, 1960.

The Black Book Concerning the Organization of Tudeh Officers (in Persian). Tehran, 1328 (1949).

BROWNE, EDWARD G. *The Persian Revolution of 1905–1909.* London: Cambridge University Press, 1910.

———. *The Press and Poetry of Modern Persia.* London: Cambridge University Press, 1914.

CAMPBELL, JOHN C. *Defense of the Middle East: Problems of American Policy* (rev. ed.). New York: Harper and Brothers, 1960.

CAREY, J. P. C. and A. D. "Oil and Economic Development in Iran," *Political Science Quarterly,* LXXV, No. 1 (March, 1960).

COTTAM, RICHARD. "Image and Reality in Iran," *Land Reborn,* XII, No. 1 (May, 1961).

Education. Third Plan Frame. Tehran: Division of Economic Affairs, Plan Organization, 1961.

EHTESHAMI, ABOL HASAN. *Political Actors* (in Persian). Tehran, 1328 (1949).

Electricity. Third Plan Frame. Tehran: Division of Economic Affairs, Plan Organization, 1961.

ELWELL-SUTTON, L. P. *Persian Oil. A Study in Power Politics.* London, 1955.

———. "Political Parties in Iran: 1941–1948," *Middle East Journal,* III, No. 1 (1949).

ESKANDARI, I. "Histoire du Parti Toudeh," *Moyen-Orient* (Paris), No. 5

(November, 1949) through No. 18–19 (January, 1951). This series of articles had not been completed when the magazine suspended publication.

ESKANDARI, KHU'INI M. *The Pahlavi Age* (in Persian). Tehran, 1335 (1956).

ESSAD-BEY, MOHAMMED (LEO NOUSSIMBAUM). *Reza Schah. Feldherr, Kaiser, Reformator.* Vienna: Dr. R. Passer, 1936.

"Exchange of Messages between the Shahanshah and Mr. Khrushchev," *Echo Reports* (Tehran), No. 23 (August 23, 1960).

FARMANFARMAIAN, KHADADAD. "Oil Industry and Native Enterprise in Iran," *Middle Eastern Affairs,* VIII (1957).

FATEMI, N. S. *Oil Diplomacy: Powderkeg in Iran.* New York: Whittier Books, 1954.

FILMER, HENRY (JAMES RIVES CHILDS). *The Pageant of Persia: A Record of Travel by Motor in Persia with an Account of Its Ancient and Modern Ways.* Indianapolis and New York: The Bobbs-Merrill Company, 1936.

Foreign Trade Statistics of Iran, 1939 (21 March 1960–20 March 1961). Tehran: Ministry of Commerce, Department General of Statistics and Researches, n.d.

FORD, ALAN W. *The Anglo-Iranian Oil Dispute of 1951–1952: A Study of the Role of Law in the Relations of States.* Berkeley, Calif.: University of California Press, 1954.

GABLE, RICHARD W. "Culture and Administration in Iran," *Middle East Journal,* XIII, No. 4 (1959).

GASTIL, RAYMOND D. "Middle Class Impediments to Iranian Modernization," *Public Opinion Quarterly* (Fall, 1958).

HAAS, WILLIAM S. "Persian Psychology," in *Iran.* New York: Columbia University Press, 1946.

High-Level Manpower Development in Iran. Tehran: Governmental Affairs Institute, May, 1960.

Implementation of Iran's Land Reform Program, March 12, 1962. Tehran: n.p., n.d.

Iran. Washington, D.C.: The Military Assistance Institute, Department of Defense, 1959.

Iran Almanac and Book of Facts for 1961. Tehran: The Echo of Iran, 1961.

"Iran-American Negotiations Regarding Military Issues and Military Aid," *Echo Reports,* No. 29 (August 16, 1960).

"Iran, How Americans Help Her," *International Affairs* (September, 1961).

Iran Plans for the Future. A Summary of Activities [of] the Plan Organization of Iran. Tehran, 1958.

"Iranian Air Force," *Echo Reports,* No. 6 (February 18, 1960).

ISHAQUE, M. *Modern Persian Poetry.* Calcutta: n.p., 1943.

KHRUSHCHEV, NIKITA S. *For Victory in Peaceful Competition with Capitalism.* New York: E. P. Dutton Co., 1960.

LAMBTON, ANN K. S. "Impact of the West on Iran," *International Affairs* (London), XXXIII (January, 1957).

———. *Islamic Society in Persia.* London, 1954.

———. *Landlord and Peasant in Persia: A Study of Land Tenure and*

Land Revenue Administration. London and New York: Oxford University Press, 1953.

LENCZOWSKI, GEORGE. "The Communist Movement in Iran," *Middle East Journal,* I, No. 1 (1947).

——. *Russia and the West in Iran, 1918–1948.* Ithaca, N.Y.: Cornell University Press, 1949.

MAKKI, HUSEIN. *The Fall of the Qajar Dynasty and the Formation of the Pahlavi Dynasty.* Vol. III: *History of Twenty Years of Persia* (in Persian). Tehran, Majlis Press, 1323–25 (1944–46).

——. *Dr. Mossadeq and His Historic Speeches in the Fifteenth and Sixteenth Parliaments* (in Persian). Tehran, 1324 (1945).

——. *Kitab-i siyah (The Black Book: The Story of Iran's Oil).* Tehran, 1329 (1950).

Manpower. Third Plan Frame. Tehran: Division of Economic Affairs, Plan Organization, 1961.

MARGOLD, STELLA. "The Streets of Teheran," *The Reporter,* IX, No. 8 (November 10, 1953).

MELZIG, HERBERT. *Resa Schah, der Aufstieg Irans und die Grossmächte.* Stuttgart: Union Deutsche Verlagsgesellschaft, 1936.

MILLSPAUGH, ARTHUR C. *The American Task in Persia.* London and New York: The Century Co., 1925.

——. *Americans in Persia.* Washington, D.C.: The Brookings Institution, 1946.

MOBAYEN, GHOLAM RÉZA. *Les élections en Iran de 1906 a nos jours.* Neuchâtel, 1960.

MOHAMMED REZA SHAH PAHLAVI. *Mission for My Country.* London: Hutchinson, 1960.

"Mosaddeq's Role in the Events of 1951–3 in Persia [according to Soviet sources]," *Central Asian Review,* IX, No. 3 (1961).

MOTTER, T. H. VAIL. *The Persian Corridor and Aid to Russia.* Washington, D.C.: Office of the Chief of Military History, Department of the Army, 1952.

NAKHAI, M. *L'Évolution Politique de l'Iran.* Brussels: Editions J. Felix, 1938.

NARAGHI, EHSAN. "Les classes moyennes en Iran," *Cahiers International de Sociologie,* XXII (1957).

National Manpower Resources and Requirements Survey, Iran, 1958. Tehran: Government Affairs Institute, July, 1958.

Outline of The Third Plan (1341–1346). Tehran: Division of Economic Affairs, Plan Organization, 1960.

Pahlavi Foundation serving the People of Iran. A Synopsis of the activities of the Pahlavi Foundation and the Pahlavi Estates Administration— 1950–61. Tehran, 1961.

"Persia," *Central Asian Review,* VIII, No. 1 (1960). Soviet writings on Iran up to the early part of 1959.

"Persia and Afghanistan: A Contrast in Foreign Aid," *Central Asian Re-*

view, XI, No. 1 (1961). Summary of an article by A. Z. Arabadzhyan entitled "The Foreign Policy and Economic Development of Persia and Afghanistan," in *Problemy Vostokovedeniya*, No. 3 (1960).

PESIAN, N. *It Was Dead, It Returned* (in Persian). Tehran, 1328 (1949).

The Plan Organization of Iran: Historical Review, September 25, 1955– March 20, 1958. Tehran, 1958.

RAMAZANI, R. K. "Modernization and Social Research in Iran," *American Behavioral Scientist*, V, No. 6 (1962).

"Reformer in Shako," *Time*, LXXVI, No. 11 (September 12, 1960).

"Return of Ambassador Pegov to Tehran," *Echo Reports*, Nos. 31 and 32 (September, 1959).

Review of the Second Seven Year Plan Program of Iran. Tehran: Division of Economic Affairs, Plan Organization, 1960.

ROOSEVELT, ARCHIE, JR. "The Kurdish Republic of Mahabad," *Middle East Journal*, I, No. 3 (July, 1947).

SHADMAN, FAKHR AD-DIN. *The Mastering of European Civilization* (in Persian). Tehran, 1327 (1948).

SHAHID, JA'FAR. *The Pahlavi Line* (in Persian). Tehran, 1328 (1949).

SHEEAN, VINCENT. *The New Persia.* London and New York: The Century Co., 1927.

SHIFTEH, N. *Representatives of the Nation* (in Persian). Tehran, 1327 (1948).

SHUSTER, W. MORGAN. *The Strangling of Persia: Story of the European Diplomacy and Oriental Intrigue that Resulted in the Denationalization of Twelve Million Mohammedans. A Personal Narrative.* New York: The Century Co., 1912.

SIASSI, ALI AKBAR. *La Perse au contact de l'Occident: Etude historique et sociale.* Paris: E. Leroux, 1931.

SPECTOR, IVAR. *The Soviet Union and the Muslim World, 1917–1956.* Seattle: University of Washington Press, 1956.

STARKE, G. "Iran and 'Global Strategy,' " *New Times* (Moscow), No. 52 (December, 1958).

Statistics. Third Plan Frame. Tehran: Division of Economic Affairs, Plan Organization, 1961.

SYKES, PERCY. *A History of Persia.* 2 vols. London: Macmillan and Co., 1958.

TAQIZADEH, SAYYID HASAN. "[Lectures on the] History of the Revolution of Iran" (in Persian), *Yaghma*, XIV.

"Text [in English] of the Land Reform Law of January 15, 1962," in *State Visit of Their Imperial Majesties, Mohammad Reza Shah Pahlavi Shahanshah of Iran and Queen Farah to the United States of America, April 1962.* Washington, D.C.: Imperial Embassy of Iran, 1962.

Third Five-Year Development Plan Law. Approved by the Council of Ministers in the session dated Shahrivar 15, 1341 (September 6, 1962).

Transport and Communications. Third Plan Frame. Tehran: Division of Economic Affairs, Plan Organization, 1961.

"U.S. Military Mission in Iran and Iranian National Interests," *International Affairs*, July, 1961.

United States Aid Operations in Iran. First Report by the Committee on Government Operations. Washington, D.C.: Government Printing Office, 1957.

United States Aid Operations in Iran. Hearings before a Subcommittee of the Committee on Government Operations. Washington, D.C.: Government Printing Office, 1956.

WARNE, WILLIAM E. *Mission for Peace: Point 4 in Iran.* Indianapolis and New York: The Bobbs-Merrill Company, 1956.

WESTWOOD, ANDREW F. "Elections and Politics in Iran," *Middle East Journal*, XV, No. 2 (1961).

WILBER, DONALD N. *Iran Past and Present.* Princeton, N.J.: Princeton University Press, 1958. Chapter III.

YOUNG, T. CUYLER. "Iran in Continuing Crisis," *Foreign Affairs*, XL (January, 1962).

———. "The Interaction of Islamic and Western Thought in Iran," in *Near Eastern Culture and Society.* Princeton, 1951.

ZVYAGIN, Y. "Iran: the Urge for Neutrality," *New Times*, No. 24 (June, 1961).

Index

Abadan, refinery at, 17; port, 210
'Abbas Shah, 27, 30, 52
Abdur Reza, 105, 106
Afghanistan, 200, 202, 203
Agabekov, Georges, 136
Agency for International Development, *see* Point Four
Agricultural Bank, 184, 185, 186
agriculture, 9, 211
Ahmad Reza, 105
Ahmah Shah, 66, 69, 70, 71
Ala Husein, 89, 169
Alam, Asadullah, 116, 121, 129
Alamuti, Nur ad-din, 145
Alavi, Ali Bozorg, 138, 139
'Ali Reza, 105
American aid, 131, 172, 192
American presence in Iran, 108-9, 188-95
Amini, Dr. 'Ali, 148, 149, 167-73; named prime minister, 119-20, 170; resigns, 121, 172; image of, 122; views on elections, 126; views on Majlis, 126, 166; career, 168-70; negotiates consortium agreement, 168; in the United States, 169; contests elections, 169-70; reform program of, 170-71; drive against corruption, 170; criticizes United States aid, 170; stabilization program of, 178
Amini family, 47, 168
Amini, Nasratullah, 152
Anglo-Persian (Iranian) Oil Company, 17, 18, 78-80, 87, 88, 91, 94, 95, 102, 173
Anglo-Soviet occupation of Iran, 80, 106
Aqa Muhammad, 13, 28
arbab, 45
arbabi, 45-46
Arcasids, 23
armed forces of Iran, *see* Iran
Arsanjani, Dr. Hasan, 185, 186, 187, 188
Aryan confederation, 202
Aryan movement into Iran, 21
Atai, Rahim, 156

Autonomous Republic of Azerbaijan, 141
Ataturk, 74
ayatullah, 33
Ayub Khan, 202
Azerbaijan, recovery of, 110

Bab, the (Mirza Ali Muhammad), 34, 61
Baghai, Dr. Muzaffar, 93, 97, 148, 151
Baghdad Pact, 151, 196, 197, 199, 202
Baha'is, 7, 34
Baha'ism, 61
Bahrami, Dr. Muhammad, 139, 145
Bahrein Islands, 204
Bakhtiar, Dr. Shapur, 152
Bakhtiar, General Timur, 130, 166
Bakhtiari, 11
Baku, 134, 135, 142
Baluchi, 11
Bank of Development and Rural Co-operatives (Bank Omran), 182, 183
Bank-i-Melli Iran, 72, 208, 209
bast, 63, 87
Bazargan, Mehdi, 156
Beeria, Muhammad, 141, 142
Benes, Dr. Eduard, 79
Bolshevik Revolution, 66-67
Bulganin, Marshal, 197
Buvayid dynasty, 25, 32

capitulary rights, 61, 72
Central Treaty Organization (CENTO), 153, 195, 197, 201, 202
Central Bank of Cooperatives, 186
Central United Council of Trade Unions, 139
Christianity in Iran, 24
Christians, Nestorians, 7, 24, 25
Churchill, Winston S., 188
Communist Center of Iran, 137
Communist Party of Bulgaria, 145
Communist Party of Iran, 135-38, 147
Communist Party of Iraq, 145
Communist Party of the Soviet Union, 133, 143